Threats of Pain and Ruin

Designed by Richard Bentley (1753)

Threats of Pain and Ruin

Theodore Dalrymple

Published by New English Review Press
a subsidiary of World Encounter Institute
PO Box 158397
Nashville, Tennessee 37215
&
27 Old Gloucester Street
London, England, WC1N 3AX

Cover Art and Design by Kendra Mallock

ISBN: 978-0-9916521-1-2

First Edition

NEW ENGLISH REVIEW PRESS
newenglishreview.org

The applause of listening senates to command,
The threats of pain and ruin to despise,
To scatter plenty o'er a smiling land,
And read their history in a nation's eyes,

Their lot forbade: nor circumscribed alone
Their growing virtues, but their crimes confined;
Forbade to wade through slaughter to a throne,
And shut the gates of mercy on mankind...

— *Thomas Gray*

Contents

Introduction

What is written without pain, said Doctor Johnson, is rarely read with pleasure. Rarely perhaps, but not, I hope, never: for the little essays in this book were written, I must confess, without much angst. In part this was because, in writing them, I had no thesis to prove, no axe to grind, except that the world is both infinitely interesting and amusing, and provides us with an inexhaustible source of material for philosophical reflection.

Here by philosophy I do not mean either a pre-formed lens though which everything has to be examined, or a lens to be manufactured from the material examined and then used to look at everything else in the world. Few of us are what in philosophy are called system-builders, and in practice we are rarely worried that our attitude to the phenomena that come under our purview lead us to opinions that are not strictly congruent with one another. Sometimes we use utilitarian arguments, and sometimes we do not. But if no one were allowed to utter anything that was inconsistent with what he had uttered at other times in his life, we should all be silent—or the most terrible bores. Monomania may be the beginning of many things, but not of wisdom, and certainly not of amusing things to say.

This, however, should not prevent us from taking disparate things in the world and reflecting upon them in a way that can only be called philosophical. Many of the subjects treated of in this book were found by serendipity or came to me in flashes—it would be immodest to call them of inspiration—of previously unsuspected connection and interest. I can only hope that they entertain the reader as they have enter-

11

tained me. At least they will do no harm, in compliance with the first principle of medical ethics.

I am grateful to Rebecca Bynum, not only for her editorial help and skill, but for having allowed me to write about whatever I pleased in the *New English Review*, irrespective of its topicality or lack thereof. In a world in which the press of current business and current obsessions is a little like the *peine forte et dure* applied to journalists such as I, it is an enormous privilege to be able to write elliptically, to come at things from strange angles. For there is no other way to:

> Tell all the truth but tell it slant,
> Success in circuit lies,
> Too bright for our infirm delight
> The truth's superb surprise;
>
> As lightning to the children eased
> With explanation kind,
> The truth must dazzle gradually
> Or every man be blind.

1
Oh Calcutta!

A difficult lesson to learn and to accept, emotionally if not intellectually, is that there is rarely gain in society entirely without loss. That is surely one of the reasons why nostalgia is so common a response to the passage of time: it is not only lost youth that is regretted, but a lost world, at least in some or other of its aspects.

Nostalgia is generally derided as at best a useless, and at worst a harmful emotion or mood. It is useless when it leads to nothing except indulgence in itself; the nostalgic person is suspected of a kind of auto-intoxication. But nostalgia is harmful when it is made a guide to policy. The person who tries to recover the past in practice fails to understand one of the preconditions of the nostalgia which makes him want to do so, namely the irrecoverability of that very past.

On the other hand, nostalgia helps to counteract the Icarus view of life, which is that life is nothing but ascent nearer and nearer to the sun of perfection. The awareness that in some respect or other life was once better than it is now is a recognition, implicit at least, that a precondition of the possibility of improvement is the possibility of deterioration. There is no law written into the constitution of the universe that guarantees overall improvement, steady or sudden as the case may be; and that is why prudence is so great a political virtue.

Like any other virtue, prudence can be carried to excess, until it becomes the enemy of bravery, determination and daring; and even the most nostalgic among us do not wish for a return to the old days with regard, say, to medical treatment. What we really want is the pleasure of gain without the pain of loss. It is surely the role of prudence to mini-mise the latter while not discouraging the former.

There can hardly be a city in the world where improvement is more evident than Calcutta. When first I visited, forty years ago, it was still the city of dreadful night (Kipling's story of that name referred to Lahore, but with how much more justice might it have been Calcutta!). In those days, what Kipling wrote seemed just as true a description of contemporary Calcutta:

> The mat-weaver's hut under the lee of the Hindu temple
> was full of men who lay like sheeted corpses...

The difference between those who slept by the side of the roads and those who were dead seemed not so very great. It was said that fifty thousand people made their home each night in Howrah station. When your taxi stopped in traffic, beggars with leprosy would push their hid-eously disfigured limbs in at the open windows to solicit alms. One of the most unpleasant sensations one could ever experience, all the worse because one felt guilty for feeling it, was that of a beggar woman in the street, a baby in one arm, clawing or pawing lightly at one's side with her other arm as one walked along, her voice uttering a supplication whose tone one also felt bad for finding melodramatic and not wholly truthful. This irritation, perhaps, was born of an awareness that one could not wave the terrible poverty away with a wand, that the money spent on an idle visit (little enough as it was by my present standards) would have been better spent on relieving the poverty of at least a handful of people.

Needless to say, there was far more to Calcutta than its poverty. Among other things, it was by far the most literary city in India. There was as much energy as despair, and the Bengalis prided themselves on their artistic refinement and creativity, and relative indifference to the grosser aspects of economic existence.

Forty years, and several visits later, the city is transformed. The lepers are gone, the beggars are few. Perhaps a first-time visitor would be struck by the poverty, but not absolutely horrified by it. The middle class has expanded enormously. Many of the cars are new. At night there are bright lights advertising the consumer goods that are available ev-erywhere else in the world but a few years ago were unheard of in India. There are riverside marinas under construction and you can tell that, unlike many now in the west, people think that tomorrow will be bet-ter—that is to say, richer—than today. The age of the shopping mall has well and truly come to Calcutta for substantial numbers of people, who can at long last afford what they do not need—a form of religious humbug or legerdemain that has always seemed to me rather unattractive.

I should rejoice at all this, of course, and in general I do, even if I have not looked sufficiently into the question of the remaining poverty and whether the worst of it has merely been ruthlessly pushed out of sight. The recrudescence of the Maoist Naxalite movement in India is a symptom that not everyone is content with the way things are going, and it is not difficult to find Indian commentators who regard the Indian economic miracle as a disaster, social and ecological. But no very poor society ever became rich in an instant, and it is probably unreasonable to expect that any should do so; India is no exception to this stony rule. Even if the progress has been uneven, therefore, there is no reason to deny that it has taken place.

But not every change is to be welcomed. A Bengali friend of mine, a doctor now practising abroad, said that he noticed a coarsening of the worldview his fellow-countrymen and an intense hunger for money that was not pleasant for him to behold. The refinement of people, still in many respects superior to that of westerners, was declining in favour of grossness and vulgarity. Fast food was making inroads into the local diet not because it was inherently better, cheaper or even more convenient for the middle classes (very far indeed from that, for they still had servants, including cooks), but because they thought it was modern and western: in other words, they lacked the proper discrimination to reject what was worthless.

Certainly the consumer goods on offer in the malls are often inferior to home-grown counterparts in point of elegance and beauty; the malls themselves are like any others, offering designer brands at high prices with inescapable rock music thrown in free of charge. It seems odd to criticise a public space in India for being blandly antiseptic and anonymous when outside people are inclined to drag up phlegm from somewhere near their ankles and spit it to the ground, but bland antisepsis and anonymity do not inspire affection. It is as if modernity dissolves critical faculties and involves throwing babies out with bathwater.

The street on which I stay with friends when I am in Calcutta, the Ballygunge Circular Road, has been renamed, in a delayed fit of nationalist re-naming, the Pramatesh Barua Sarani. Pramatesh Barua was the founder of the Bengali film industry, and it so happened that my friend's flat overlooked Pramatesh Barua's house, a grand and elegant two-storey Hindu-Palladian stucco villa in a state of charming decrepitude.

I used to enjoy looking into the house from the balcony of my friend's flat. There were no curtains, and I watched the inhabitants padding about the dimly-lit and crumbling, but grand and beautiful, marble-floored rooms. They lived in a kind of luxurious penury.

Then, overnight, the current owner had the house of Pramatesh Barua, after whom the whole street had been renamed, demolished: by morning it was gone. I suspect that he had let the house fall into such disrepair so that it might be the more swiftly reduced to rubble. This was quite illegal, for the city council had placed a preservation order on the building; but the owner will almost certainly not suffer any consequences. The land on which Barua's house was built was simply too valuable for the house to be preserved: in its place, a totally non-descript and charmless block will be built at great profit to the owner and those he has presumably bribed.

Perhaps it seems a trifle precious to mourn the loss of a mere building in a city still as rich in suffering as Calcutta. Not one in a hundred thousand of its inhabitants, perhaps, would care very deeply about it one way or the other; generations to come would not even know that Pramatesh Barua's house had existed or what it was like. More people would live in relative comfort in the block that the businessman would build on the land than could ever have lived in Pramatesh Barua's house. The thrusting kind of entrepreneur who behaved like this was precisely the type of unsentimental entrepreneur upon whom India's present and future prosperity depended. All things considered, he did more good than harm.

None of these arguments lessened my regret, however. But the melancholy was as nothing compared with that which I felt on visiting the synagogues of Calcutta.

There was once a thriving community of Baghdadi and Armenian Jews in Calcutta, numbering several thousand. My friend's elder brother lived in a building with two Jewish families during his early childhood, and remembers when he was very young being asked to turn on the lights in their flats when dusk fell

There are three synagogues in Calcutta, but one of them, the oldest, on Synagogue Street, is in such disrepair that it is said to be too dangerous to enter and is now closed. Nearly within sight of a Greek Orthodox church, an Anglican church and a mosque is the grandest of the three, the Mogen David synagogue, built much in the style of Calcuttan Anglican churches. On the nearest lamp-post was an intriguing advertisement for the Telenet Ultrasonic Pestrepeller: 'Repel rat, mice, lizard, snake, fly, bird, bat, animals, etc.' It was the etcetera that intrigued me.

The third synagogue is the Beth El, opposite what was once the Jewish school in Pollock Street, which had 800 pupils.

Both the Mogen David and the Beth El synagogues are very grand, capable of seating congregations of several hundred, and indicative of a once very prosperous community. The benches and chairs are beautifully-made and proportioned. There are pictures of the patriarchs of the powerful, wealthy and philanthropic Elias and Ezra families on the walls, who once dressed in Turkish costume and then adopted western costume. There are plaques commemorating their donations and in one case their sacrifice: killed over France in 1944, fighting in the RAF.

The synagogues have been declared historic monuments by the Indian government, and that is what they now are. The last cyclostyled notice posted on the notice-board of the Beth El synagogue, about a meeting of the committee, was dated May 21, 1989. No services are ever held there now, the community having dwindled to about six or eight people, mostly in their eighties, only one of whom is fit enough to come to the synagogues to light a candle on Friday evenings. Soon the Jewish community of Calcutta, more than two hundred years old, will be completely extinct.

The great majority of the community emigrated, not because of persecution, for India has never persecuted its Jews, but because of greater opportunity elsewhere. For them, the opening up of the Indian economy came too late; the community was by then too small to survive.

Both the Mogen David and Beth El synagogues were looked after by two elderly Moslem retainers. One of them showed us the women's ritual bath and other features of Beth El with something akin to pride, not wanting to let us go until we had seen everything. I imagine he would have heard of the antipathy of Muslims for Jews with surprise, for he had worked in the synagogue since the days when there was still a large congregation.

Progress there has been, self-evidently so, but not in everything.

2
Dictatorship: The Wave of the Future?

N o one ever deserved a grisly death more than the late Colonel Muammar Gaddafi, but this is only a proof—if such a proof were needed—that justice is far from the only human desideratum. Gaddafi was responsible for untold misery, its amount limited only by the relative insignificance and impotence of the country in which he seized power; but when I first saw the photograph of him taken, lying bloodied but conscious, by a French photographer (a photograph that is surely destined for such immortality as the world can confer), I felt for him what I did not think I could ever feel for him—compassion. The fact is that no one should die as he died, or be killed as he was killed.

Other dictators have met grisly ends, of course. Mussolini was strung up, Ceausescu shot and Saddam Hussein hanged, all unceremoniously and without dignity. It is possible, even, that Gaddafi's death was not absolutely the worst suffered by a tyrant in the last hundred years. President Guillaume Sam was dragged out of the French Embassy in Port-au-Prince, in which he had taken refuge, by an enraged mob, impaled on railings, cut into pieces and his parts exhibited in the city. President Sam was no guardian angel of the rule of law: he had just had 169 political prisoners summarily executed, but this should not prevent us from accepting as a basic moral principle that impaling and cutting up people is wrong.

The President of Liberia, Samuel Kanyon Doe, was captured by the militia of the self-styled Brigadier-General Field Marshal Prince Yormie Johnson, who had him trussed up naked like a chicken and his ears cut off, his death by blood loss recorded on a video that became for a time Liberia's greatest cultural export. Doe also was no pacifist: I visited the church in Monrovia, St Peter's, in which he is alleged, during the last days of his presidency, to have taken part personally in the mass murder of six hundred people who had taken refuge there. The dried blood, with the silhouettes of the bodies of the massacred, was still on the floor of the church and the mounds of the graves still raw in the churchyard. Even if he did not take part personally in the massacre, he knew of it and approved it.

Nevertheless, when I saw the video of him being tortured to death (not retribution for his wickedness but the numbers of his bank accounts was the object in view), I felt what I had fondly, but no doubt mistakenly, thought was natural human sympathy for him. Appalling as he undoubtedly was, his screams of agony were not such as should be deliberately extorted from any man; and what was almost as horrible, and ultimately more chilling, was the calm self-righteousness of the man who ordered the brutality. Nothing dissolves salutary moral barriers more completely than sadism in the name of an alleged higher purpose. (Johnson supposedly sought the bank account numbers to recover the money for the people of Liberia, not for himself.)

Of course, some might say that such feelings are easy enough to indulge in for someone who has not lived under any of these dictators. To have existed for forty years, or your entire life, under someone like Gaddafi might be more than enough to overwhelm you inhibitions against vengeful cruelty. Passion has, if not its rights exactly, at least its excuses; and when I recall how misled I had been into thinking, after having spent only two weeks in Romania under the Ceausescus, that it was right that they were summarily shot, a certain reticence on my part in condemning the passions of others is in order. Of course, the Romanian revolution was more of a palace coup than it at first appeared; but in any case, the charges against the Ceausescus, such as genocide, were ridiculous and trumped up, despicable as the pair may have been. No one should be shot like stray dogs in a courtyard, as they were shot; and I became ashamed of my initial enthusiasm for their demise.

But what is the correct way to deal with fallen dictators? This is a delicate question. To put them on trial has its inconveniences and dangers, since one of the qualifications for the post of tyrant is a long and detailed memory; and since no tyranny is ever so personal that the tyrant does not need accomplices, usually many of them, if his trial is not of the merely kangaroo variety *à la* Ceausescu, it is clear that the ex-tyrant in the dock can spill the beans about a lot of people, many of whom will have benefited from his overthrow or even have been the leaders of it. Those about whom the beans have been thus spilt will in turn be able to spill beans, until the whole society is torn apart by an orgy of accusation and counter-accusation. Much better, then, say some, just to execute the fallen tyrant, pretend that he had acted entirely alone, and repress memories until they fade in any case.

When Gaddafi was maltreated to death by a crowd, it was said that, no matter how revolting the scene, it was a good lesson to other dictators, most notably Assad of Syria. But the lessons that people draw from events are not like the ineluctable conclusions of a syllogism; the conclusion that Assad should flee his country does not follow from the fact that the longer he stays the worse his eventual fate. Lessons in human conduct are usually ambiguous. Assad might just as well have learned from Gaddafi's horrible fate that it is best to go down fighting, and if necessary take whole populations down with him, as that he should take the next flight to Estoril (the Portuguese resort where deposed crowned heads used to live out their enforced retirement, and potter the rest of their lives away). After all, flight does not ensure the safety of ex-dictators: Maximiliano Hernández Martínez, the ex-strongman of El Salvador, who believed he could train his eyes to stare at the sun and that it was worse to kill an ant than a man because an ant had an eternal soul, was stabbed to death by his chauffeur years after his downfall and exile in Honduras. Anastasio Somoza was blown up in his car in Paraguay after his movements had been watched for six months. Not many dictators find a refuge as completely safe and well-guarded as Mengistu of Ethiopia has found in Mugabe's Zimbabwe. Uneasy, then, sleeps the head that has once exercised dictatorial power.

When General Pinochet was arrested in London (he had not realised that Albion, always perfidious, was now perfidious even though not in its own interests?), was he being punished for having been a brutal dictator, or for having peacefully relinquished power? From the point of view of the average Guardian-reading person, obviously the former; but from the point of view of the average dictator, the latter. Fidel Castro's class or professional solidarity with dictators overcame his political differences with the General; and it was surely somewhat ironical that Erich Honecker, the fallen leader of the German Democratic Republic, should have chosen Chile as his country of exile while Pinochet was still commander-in-chief of the army there. Dictators must stick together.

Some dictators slip away quietly, and not a few re-invent themselves as democratic candidates in presidential elections, by no means always unsuccessfully. Often people begin to feel nostalgia for the days when they made the trains run on time, the streets were swept and there was little crime. Carlos Ibañez of Chile and Getulio Vargas of Brazil come to mind who were elected democratically after having ruled despotically. The thirst for order is at least as great as the thirst for freedom.

My contact with ex-dictators and their henchmen has been slight. I once had the idea of going round the world and interviewing the more bizarre dictators in exile (at the time, ex-dictators were both more numerous and more colourful than they are now, deposed tyrants such as Ben Ali of Tunisia seeming rather dull and ordinary by comparison), to find out what had made them tick, but I could persuade no one that the project was of sufficient interest—compared, say, with the extra-marital affairs of starlets—for him to advance me any money.

Still, I was able in one country, Guatemala, to visit a few ex-dictators and their henchmen. The reason was that they were all in the telephone directory, not in the yellow pages under the rubric of *Dictators* (*ex*) or *Dictators* (*former*), but listed in the ordinary residential pages. More surprising was that when I called, they answered the phone themselves and invited me round for a chat. Most surprising of all, perhaps, was that when I took them up on the offer, I found that there was no security procedures to be gone through, unlike say the Chicago to Atlanta, or the Bristol to Aberdeen, flights, not even so much as a check of my identity. When I rang the door, either the ex-dictator or his maid answered and ushered me straight in, with no thought that I might be an assassin or a suicide bomber. This was all very odd, because some of them had been compared to Hitler. No search of my person was ever made.

Now if I were to try to interview a supposedly democratic ex-politician of my own country, say Mr Blair, I doubt that I should approach within a hundred miles of him without voluminous and intrusive checks, and access would probably be granted only on condition that I mortgaged my house to pay for it.

What is the moral of this contrast, if there is one? Perhaps it is merely that, in a world in which even Dutch and Swedish politicians face assassination, times have changed in the direction of the self-preserving paranoia of politicians. In any case, it would be wrong to make too much of the contrast, even if sometimes I am inclined to have night thoughts about the relative freedoms to be enjoyed under British parliamentary democracy and Latin American military dictatorship, not always to the advantage of the former. This, of course, is to forget the sheer scale of the brutality of the latter.

There is, perhaps, no perfect solution to the problem of what to do with a fallen despot. To allow him to live in peaceful, and usually very prosperous, retirement seems unjust to the victims of his despotism, and is likely to embitter them. He will seem to them almost to have been rewarded for his deeds, for a prosperous retirement is the wish of many, rarely fulfilled. To treat him as a scapegoat, as if he alone were responsible for his despotism and he had no accomplices, is to create an abscess of hypocrisy and historical untruth that sooner or later will have to be opened, or will burst spontaneously. To punish not only the despot but all who co-operated with or benefited from his rule is to risk endless social conflict and violent reaction.

It might be thought that this a problem of an age that is now past; that after the Arab Spring, we are entering an age of universal democracy. I think this is the case no more than it was ever the case that history was at an end. Astonishing though it may seem, there were rumours in Europe of a possible coup in Greece as a solution to the impasse there. When disorder becomes great enough, men (as Goethe said) long for the man on the white horse, for we love order at least as much as we love liberty, for the former is a precondition of the exercise of the latter, and of much else besides. Europe, the Yugoslavia *de nos jours*, is becoming ungovernable, thanks to its governors. Another age of the man on the white horse might be dawning.

3

My Problem of Evil

As someone who has spent much of his life investigating the darker sides of human existence, either as a tourist of civil wars, or as a doctor working among criminals and misfits, I have a weakness for books with the word 'evil' in their title. I am still trying to understand, or at least make sense of, what I have witnessed, seen and heard, and have failed to do so to my own satisfaction. And so when I gave a talk recently in a bookshop for which my reward consisted of any book I wanted from the shelves, I chose *The Myth of Evil* by Phillip Cole, instead of the most expensive volume I could find.

Dr Cole is a philosopher who argues for the uselessness, indeed the harmfulness (I almost said the evil), of the concept of evil. And I confess that, though I have sometimes had a strong sense of being in the presence of evil, I have had some slight difficulty with the meaning of the concept myself. What exactly does it mean? Can we, ought we, or must we, do without it, philosophically, ethically, psychologically and sociologically?

Cole argues that the concept is redundant both as a description and as an explanation of human conduct. In fact, he says, its main use or function, when stripped of its unsustainable pretensions to describe or explain anything, is to frighten populations into acquiescence to the extension of power over them by ruling elites whose legitimacy might otherwise be called into question. For it is not common values or characteristics that unite political entities such as states in the modern world, he says, but common enemies, who are either wholly imaginary or whose power and malevolence are much exaggerated.

Indeed, he continues, the concept of evil is responsible for much harm (again, I almost said evil) in the world. The reason for this is clear. When we say of someone that he is evil, we are saying that he is a being of a quite distinct category from ourselves, such that normal ethical limits and restraints do not apply in the way that we must deal with him. For evil is the ultimate – well, evil, and must be destroyed by any means possible. Without the concept of evil, then, we would be much less likely to treat people evilly.

Is there any way that we can infallibly distinguish between what (or who) is evil, and what (or who) is merely bad? Or is evil just the extreme end of a moral spectrum? This would not entail that evil did not exist, just as the fact that, in any human population, there is a continuum of heights does not mean that there are no tall men. The fact that there is a continuum of haemoglobin concentrations in human blood does not mean that no one is anaemic. But it does mean that we should have to give up the search for the defining characteristic of evil as a positive force in the world, as if it were something wholly distinct and *sui generis*.

The acts that we are prepared to describe as evil must be morally reprehensible in themselves, do practical harm to others, be done from choice and with malevolence, and usually be characteristic of the agent rather than impulsive or exceptional to his character. All these conditions are dimensional rather than categorical; we still have not found the essence of evil, if there be one, that distinguishes it from the bad, the very bad, and the very, very bad.

And yet moral categorisation is not wholly dimensional. We do not say of a serial killer who kills twenty victims that he is twice as bad, morally, as one who kills 'only' ten. While on my peregrinations through civil wars I saw terrible things on a scale incomparably greater than anything I saw in medical practice, and yet I saw things in medical practice that caused the word evil to reverberate in my mind. To give only one example: a man was so jealous of his successive girlfriends that, in order to ensure that they attracted no one else, he threw acid in the face of the first and ammonia in the face of the second, maiming them for life. If anything could be called evil, this surely could, and should, be.

But what is the use of the word 'evil' here, beyond severe moral condemnation? Does it help to explain anything? Dr Cole tells us that it rather inhibits attempts at understanding than contributes to it.

We use the word 'evil', says Dr Cole, to fill in the inevitable gap (or black hole) in our understanding of deeds that seem to us to be quite outside the normal human repertoire. This is because any set of explanatory factors that we may use to account for such deeds never accounts for them totally. Thus, when we find that a certain form of bad behaviour is much more common among people of a certain background or with certain formative experiences, there nevertheless remain many people who are from the same background or have had the same formative experiences who do not behave in like fashion. So there is a gap; and the gap remains however we refine or multiply the factors that we use to explain the behaviour.

Evil rushes in where psychology (or sociology) fails to tread. But, says Dr Cole, evil itself fails to explain anything.

He uses as an example the notorious and brutal murder of the two year-old James Bulger by two ten year-old children, John Venables and Robert Thomson. Both of the culprits came from highly disturbed and indeed sordid backgrounds, in which there was a lot of violence, emotional instability, excessive drinking, etc. The statistical connection between such a background and violent criminal behaviour is clear; but what the two boys did was nevertheless exceptional (murder by children, even from the worst circumstances is very rare).

The press called them monsters, and demanded that they should be locked away for the rest of their lives. But if they were monsters by birth, not only did this seem to reduce their moral culpability (for monsters by birth have no choice but to be monstrous), something must have accounted for their monstrosity: genetics, birth injuries, chemicals in their environment and so forth.

To invoke Satan, as many still do, is merely to postpone the problem: for why does Satan wish to corrupt humanity? He is a rebel against God, of course, but why, given his angelic constitution, did he rebel? If he was differently constituted from the other angels, that is to say was created distinct from them, he is not to blame for his rebellion, or not wholly to blame. Was he misled in turn by an ur-Satan, who tempted him to deviate from the path of God? We are faced here by the prospect of an infinite regress, in which we never reach the origin of evil.

In his discussion of the emblematic case of the murder of James Bulger, Dr Cole sometimes confuses things. He is highly critical (as many others have been) of the trial of the two boys accused of the murder according to the procedure that would normally have been used for adults, which he thought was traumatic for them and failed to recognise that they were still children and therefore not fully formed from the point of view of their character.

The confusion is twofold. First, a trial is not a therapeutic manoeuvre designed to do the accused some good. It has quite other purposes. The fact that a solemn trial was inevitably traumatic for the children was not, in itself, sufficient reason to avoid one. Second, although the children were not fully-formed as human beings, they were nonetheless moral agents. They lied to the police, and tried to throw the blame on each other, in quite cunning and sophisticated ways, indicating that they knew that they had done wrong and had something to hide. They knew perfectly well that stealing a child and smashing it to death with rocks was wrong.

But on the larger point on this case, Dr Cole is surely right: to have dismissed them as irredeemably evil, or possessed by evil, would have been mistaken and cruel, as is proved by the fact that the children subsequently turned out well, much better in fact than they would have done had they never committed the murder, for they received intense and humane attention thereafter. As the writer of a book on the case, Blake Morrison, put it (I quote from memory), 'It was a pity they had to murder James Bulger to get an education.' I don't think I have read a more succinct and damning indictment of a society and its educational system than that, and no doubt it does not apply only to Liverpool, England. (The fact that the children turned out well suggests also that the trauma of the trial was not as great as supposed by its critics, or may actually have done the children some good. Not every experience we don't like or want is bad for us.) [1]

Now Dr Cole extends the lessons of this case to all human evil, if I may call it such for lack of a better word, whatsoever. Venables and Thompson were redeemable precisely because those who looked after them thought they were redeemable and did not consider them as evil by essence; by extension, everyone else who commits evil is redeemable, though perhaps with more difficulty.

I am not sure this holds. Venables and Thomson were redeemable relatively easily because they were so young when they committed their crime. They were carefully abstracted from the kind of social environment in which they would have been encouraged to commit further violence. Rather unusually for someone who is a hard-liner on the ques-

---

[1] One of the boys did not in fact turn out well. He is back in prison, and has apparently committed a number of crimes, including of a sexual nature. This raises the possibility that he was congenitally predetermined to commit such acts, or the influence of his childhood experiences was simply too strong to be overcome. At no point will we be able to say, 'Ah, now we understand.'

tion of crime, I found myself in agreement with the lenient party in this case, who argued that they should be set free, with supervision, at the age of 21.

But the case is not a typical one. Most murderers, torturers, rapists and so forth are not 10 years old, but adults. And what Dr Cole, who is of a very different political stripe from me, does not appreciate is that his naturalistic account of evil (to the effect that what is called evil requires no special understanding beyond that we apply to all other human traits and conduct) does not lead to conclusions that he would easily find acceptable.

If the connection between evil acts and the life experiences of those who commit them is so strong and intimate that it is morally exculpatory, in other words that those who act evilly can do no other, and if as a matter of empirical fact there is no procedure that can reliably reform them, then the case, in the name of public safety, for ferociously long and incapacitating prison sentences, until time has done its work, is made. In other words, the connection between exculpation and penal leniency is a psychological one in the minds of penal liberals, not a logical one dictated by evidence and argument. The more circumstances 'determine' criminal behaviour, the more firmly ought criminal behaviour be repressed.

Only if we accept that there is something deeply mysterious about human freedom—that men are free, despite our inability satisfactorily to explain exactly what we mean by it—can we dare to hope that neither ferocity nor prolonged incarceration will always be necessary for people to change.

But sometimes they will be necessary. That is why we shall always have to exercise judgement, and can lay down no hard and fast rules as if life could be lived out of a book of recipes.

As for the naturalistic theory of evil, it raises the hope, or rather the mirage, of a society so perfect that no one will have to be good (to use T S Eliot's formulation). And that mirage has been responsible for as much evil as the concept of evil itself.

I confess that the problem is too difficult for me to solve. I am not philosopher enough—and neither, it seems to me, are most philosophers. I own myself defeated, but I shall go on using the word just like everyone else, as if its signification and implications were perfectly obvious.

4

The Art of Destruction

When I was about nine or ten years old my father had a bonfire of Victorian paintings. Like many a person who was inclined by nature to hoard, he sometimes had fits of clearing things out to make space, presumably for something else to accumulate. The paintings shared a loft for several years with crates of tinned fruit that he had bought during the Korean War, in the fear that the conflict would spread and rationing re-introduced. He kept the fruit and got rid of the paintings.

This rather strange choice was, I suspect, connected to his communist leanings. He believed that use value was a higher value, both ethically and in reality, than mere market value, and tinned fruit was to him obviously more useful than paintings. When he died, I discovered that he had assiduously thrown away everything he possessed of resale value—first editions of Gibbon and Pope, for example—and accumulated such prosaic items as pins and paper clips, carefully sorted by size and placed in old tobacco tins. He also left a supply of carbon-copy paper that would have been sufficient to last a lifetime even if the word-processor and electronic printer had not already been invented. In fact, use value was for him something almost mystical, quite divorced from any actual use to which the thing allegedly possessing it might be put, for example by me.

I remember it still: the gilded frames and pastoral scenes going up in flames. Only one picture was saved from the general conflagration and I have it on my wall, now worth, in nominal terms, at least 20,000 times what my father gave for it at Sotheby's during the War (the Second World War, that is). Even at the age of nine or ten I knew that burning paintings was the wrong thing to do, and I asked my father not to go ahead. The wrongness, as I conceived it, had nothing to do with economics or fear for my inheritance, of which I had absolutely no conception at the time, although I would not be quite frank if I did not admit that I now slightly regret the frivolous disappearance in acrid smoke of hundreds of thousands of dollars. Be that as it may, I suggested to my father that if he didn't like the paintings any more he should give them away rather than burn them. But my father, who was a brilliantly gifted but strangely flawed man, knew best, and he lit the fire. A nine or ten year old boy was wiser than a fifty year old man.

I was reminded of this strange scene of iconoclasm in my childhood by an article I read about Antonio Manfredi, a Neapolitan artist who decided to open a public museum of contemporary art in his home city. Unfortunately, the museum attracted so few visitors that it soon became financially unviable. Manfredi wrote to every possible provider of funds that he could think of, from local businessmen to the municipality, from the Italian state to the European Union, but without success. In the end, exasperated by what he saw as an almost universal philistine indifference to culture, he set fire to twenty of the art works in his museum (with the permission of the artists who created them) and made a video of himself sitting in front of the pile of ashes. This video, lasting an hour, is now considered a work of contemporary art in itself. Furthermore, two hundred artists in Europe have burnt one of their own works in solidarity with Manfredi.

This is surely a most extraordinary story, and it reflects very ill, though perhaps accurately, on Manfredi, contemporary artists and contemporary art, at least of a certain kind.

Let us suppose for a moment that you possessed works of art of minor artists of the past, of the stature, say, of David Teniers or Nicolas Lancret, and that, for some reason, you wanted to show them to the public in a museum of your own founding. You open the museum but very few people are prepared to pay the admission fee, so that the museum becomes impossible financially for you to sustain (you are not a rich man or woman). Appeals for public or private funds to keep the museum open are fruitless: would it occur to you, even for a fraction of a second, to burn your pictures in protest, even though they are by artists very far from of the first rank of their own time? The question answers itself—unless, of course, you are of the ilk of my father.

In other words, the action of Manfredi and the artists who expressed their sympathy with him by burning their own works was in effect an acknowledgment that those who failed to provide Manfredi with funds were actually quite correct in their judgment not to do so: for why subsidise an institution whose contents are so worthless that they can be burnt without any apparent awareness that to burn works of art is an utterly barbaric thing to do? When the Taliban blew up the Buddhist statues in Afghanistan, we felt anger that an invaluable artistic and cultural heritage had been destroyed, and for the vilest of reasons; when Manfredi burnt the contents of his own museum, all that we (or at any rate I) felt, in a rather resigned way, was that he was making an irrefutably eloquent comment upon what now passes in some quarters for art. The Rijksmuseum in Amsterdam has been closed for many years, for a renovation that is apparently costing more than the museum cost to build in the first place, to the great disgrace of the Dutch state and nation; but no one in his right mind would suggest that a Vermeer or two should be destroyed in protest against this bureaucratic insult to one of the greatest artistic traditions and inheritances in the world. What would we think of the Director of the Rijksmuseum if, frustrated at the slowness of the renovation of his institution, he slashed the canvas of The Night Watch and scraped its paint off? Again, I do not think this enquiry requires my answer.

The question naturally arises as to how it has come about that so rich an artistic tradition as the European should have reached the point when contemporary works, presumably chosen for their special excellence by comparison with others, can be burnt without the slightest regret on anyone's part, without anyone feeling that the world has thereby been deprived of anything of aesthetic, intellectual or spiritual value. Even the artists who made these works of art seem to feel that the world would not be not impoverished in any way by the incineration of their handiwork. This being the case, neither Manfredi nor the artists have any reason to complain of the philistinism of the times, unless they are prepared to turn the complaint equally upon themselves, which is doubtful.

The loss of taste and judgment is not confined to Naples, of course. One startling example is the tower erected in London to celebrate and commemorate the Olympic Games. Built at a cost of $5 million to the design of Anish Kapoor, the famous Anglo-Indian sculptor, it seems to have been specifically erected with the intention of giving vandalism a good name, in so far as a vandal, if he were to destroy it utterly, would have added slightly to the beauty of the world. Indeed, so hideous, lumpen, inelegant and meaningless is this construction that it reverses the roles of the aesthete and the iconoclast: the latter is he who made it and thereby polluted so many visual fields, the former is he who destroys it utterly.

The collective loss of artistic taste and powers of discrimination is an interesting sociological phenomenon. I first noticed it in India and Africa. Peasants who seemed to have an instinctive sense of form and colour while they lived in their natural surroundings lost it within days or weeks after moving to a town or city. Suddenly their taste turned to kitsch; and those who shortly before had lived in simple or humble dwellings of elegant shape and restrained and tasteful decoration now lived in shacks where the only decoration was garish and cheap in the aesthetic sense of the word. I do not know why this should be so: I cannot say whether, for example, their previous seemingly instinctive good taste was merely lack of opportunity to express or act upon bad taste, or whether their good taste was something more positive than that. Perhaps their previous good taste was disciplined or constrained by a tradition which, so long as they remained peasants, they were unable for reasons of social pressure to depart. But this begs the question: for why should an aesthetically pleasing tradition, rather than an unpleasing one, have emerged in the first place, if no one had ever possessed good taste? You will hardly see an inelegant hut in the whole of Africa. I am not suggesting that peasants are better off where they are, and that moving to industrialised or semi-industrialised society causes a deterioration in the quality of their lives (if this were so, the voluntary migration or drift of peasants to towns, which has happened almost everywhere, would be inexplicable); I am referring only to matters of taste which, while very important, are obviously not all-important in life.

In Western Europe, for reasons that I do not claim to understand, it has become almost impossible for anyone to construct an aesthetically decent house, let alone public building: this, be it remembered, in a continent with an unrivalled aesthetic tradition in architecture going back, with one or two interruptions, two millennia and a half. Why this sudden collapse? If our descendents should ever recover their sense of taste, in what contempt and detestation they will hold us (from the aesthetic point of view)! Not content with being unable to build anything of which future generations might grow fond, we have also destroyed much of our heritage. I defy anyone to look down the rue de Rennes in Paris, for example, in the direction of the Tour Montparnasse, and not to ask 'Where is al-Qaeda when you need it?'

I asked an architectural historian why we could not build an aesthetically decent house in Europe any more, and he gave an answer that at least confirmed my premise, whose veracity I had expected him to deny. No, he issued no denial; rather he answered with a single word, industrialisation. We construct houses almost in the way that we construct cars, he said; for ineluctable economic reasons we mass produce them, by means of pre-formed or ready-made units of construction.

I felt at once that his answer was neither wholly wrong nor wholly right. The fact is also that those with immense fortunes are no more capable of having a beautiful house built, whose beauty will endure for centuries, than are the poorest inhabitants of quarters where half the population is unemployed. There is something more wrong than the means, methods and materials of construction.

There is a word that haunts our architects and gives them nightmares: pastiche. They cannot simply reproduce patterns of the past, for two reasons.

First, when they try to do so the results almost always look wrong, perhaps because it is not sufficient merely to follow a pattern or design from the past in order to reproduce the buildings of that past, it would be necessary to build in the same way, using the same materials, and (this is where the architectural historian is right) it is simply out of the question to do so.

Second, architects, as supposedly original artists, would find it a wound to their vanity simply to follow the patterns of the past. To do so would turn them into mere technicians, and that is not what they went into architecture to be. At the same time, they do not have the ability to innovate with beauty.

But there is a deeper problem yet: aesthetics simply do not matter to most Europeans, at least not the aesthetics of the public space. They no longer notice the ugliness by which they are surrounded, at least not consciously (the fact that graffiti-daubers in countries such as France and Britain confine themselves largely to ugly surfaces suggests that subconscious aesthetic judgment still exists, even among the underclass). We live in an age of the convenience of the moment, including or especially financial, when no sacrifice for the sake of aesthetics is deemed to be worth making. We do not build *sub specie aeternitatis*, because we do not believe in eternity of any kind, spiritual, artistic or cultural.

Thus the ugliness of modern Europe is not the same as the ugliness of the past, a manifestation of poverty. It is the ugliness of a society in which people believe in nothing but their standard of living, as measured by their personal convenience and consumption. It is the ugliness of civilisational exhaustion.

5

The Bruised Heel Healed

There is a baby in the world that seems never to get beyond its
ninth month. It has been following me for at least forty years,
but it makes its appearance only when I board a long-distance aircraft,
when it is to be found in the row immediately behind or in front of me,
and proceeds to scream unconsolably for what seems like an age from
the moment of takeoff. All manner of paranoid thoughts then come into
my mind: for example that the airline has designedly, though for reasons that I cannot fathom even in my paranoid moments, disturbed my
peace and prevented me from reading by seating the baby there, very
close to me. In any case, why does that wretched creature never grow
up? For if there is one sound in the whole world that cannot be ignored
or screened out by attention to something else it is that of a baby crying
on an aircraft.

And now I am being followed by snakes, scorpions and giant spiders. They seem increasingly to be everywhere I go. For example, only a
few months ago I had occasion to spend time in the city of Nottingham,
a dreadful place but interesting in its way, as most dreadful places are;
and not more than a couple of hundred yards from my lodgings was
a reptile pet shop. Such shops, I have noticed, are far commoner than
they used to be; the keeping of reptiles as pets, though declining slightly
with the economic crisis, the price of frozen rats and other reptile nour-
ishment having risen as incomes have stagnated at best, is a noticeable
cultural trend. What does it mean?

Snakes, to say nothing of scorpions and spiders, never respond to or recognise their owners; the relationship, if it can be called such, is entirely in one direction, from man to creature. Feelings are not and can never be returned. The creatures are objects, not subjects. Cold blood is for cold hearts, or at least for hearts that have had bad experiences with warmth. If that is so, then there are more such hearts about than there used to be, or at least more of them that express themselves in this rather peculiar way, the keeping of snakes, scorpions and spiders.

Those who patronise reptile pet shops are usually dressed and adorned in a conventionally unconventional way: tattooed, pierced and beleathered. (Leather clothes are to man what scales are to reptiles. It is no coincidence that the NKVD and Gestapo liked leather coats.)

But why snakes, scorpions and spiders? After all, there are plenty of other creatures in the world that are cold-blooded and (more or less) automata. The reason, I suspect, is these favoured creatures are antinomian by implication or connotation, and the keeping of them a reversal of the Biblical curse that there shall be 'enmity between thee and the woman, and between thy seed and her seed': most people are scared of them and hold them in abomination, to be both repellent and dangerous. Those who keep them, therefore, mark themselves out as people who reject the conventions and standards of bourgeois society—as if bourgeois society really existed anywhere any more other than in tiny enclaves such as Switzerland and Liechtenstein. As generals are said to fight the last war, so the unconventional reject only the conventions that are already dead and destroyed.

Returning to France some time after my sojourn in Nottingham, I was surprised to see appear in the nearby village or small town of St Paul le Jeune notices advertising a performance with live reptiles, to be held one evening in the village hall or *Salle des fêtes*. So even in France I am followed by a rising tide of reptiles. (We have wild reptiles near our house in the form of lizards, some of them bright green and eight inches long, slow worms and even snakes, but I am not speaking of these. These reptiles are unavoidable; I speak only of what one might call voluntary reptiles.) A friend and I decided to attend the performance.

The *Salle des fêtes* turned out not to be a very festive place in atmosphere, but rather the kind of dismal utilitarian space that one might have expected municipal bureaucrats with limited funds to have planned. And my friend and I were, in fact, the only adults to have turned out without small children in their wake. In all, the audience was about fifty or sixty, with three or four children to every adult.

The performance was conducted by two travelling Germans, Dieter and Uschi, the former to handle the animals, the latter to provide the commentary in good, but not native, French.

Dieter was, to judge by his appearance, an aging biker. He wore jeans, highish-heeled boots (necessary for the performance, as I shall relate), and a strongly patterned shirt. He had the long, uncultivated beard of bikers; I should guess he was in his mid-sixties, but I might be wrong; certainly he had the look of a man who had knocked about the world a bit.

Uschi was considerably younger, but still not in the first flush of youth; she was tall, lithe and slender, but with the thinness that spoke of cigarettes rather than natural metabolism or dietary self-control. She wore very tight jeans, a cut-away shirt, and long boots with snakeskin bands and long leather tassels. She wore her hair nearly to her waist. She stood to one side with a microphone in her hand while Dieter displayed the animals.

Before the performance began, as the audience trickled in (I thought that *le tout* St Paul le Jeune would be there, but I was wrong), heavy metal guitar music, not unskilfully played, was relayed over a ste-reo system: this was Dieter's music, and the audience was invited to buy a CD of it. Parked not far away from the *Salle des fêtes* was the large white camper van in which Dieter and Uschi lived and worked and took their being.

Dieter came into the hall and stood behind a small and battered white metal table. Behind him were ranged boxes of various sizes con-taining his creatures. I could not help but notice that the end of one of Dieter's middle fingers was missing, and of course I jumped to the most obvious conclusion about the fate of the missing portions.

Dieter started with the giant scorpions, taken out of a Tupperware-like box. The audience gasped. With swift and practised movements, Dieter provoked the vile creatures into activity, and then brought them close to the audience for their inspection.

Next came the giant spider. I was at this point strongly reminded of a film I once saw high on the Bolivian altiplano, in the Teatro munici-pal of Uyuni, called *The Invasion of the Giant Spiders*, in which the eggs of vast spiders fell to earth from outer space to hatch and take over the world. The only thing that stood between the giant spiders and world domination was the US Air Force, and the audience cheered the spiders on to victory which, however, was not in the end theirs, though it very nearly was.

Dieter put the giant spider on his bald head, wiping it afterwards because, said Uschi, the hairs of the spider, with irritant chemicals in them, might otherwise get in his eyes. And then came the snakes, in ascending order of dramatic quality, starting with corn and coral snakes, ascending through a boa constrictor and ending in a reticulated python, the species that grows to the greatest length known of any snake, though the anaconda can weigh more, up to 400 pounds in fact, and Colonel Fawcett, the bestselling South American explorer who disappeared in the jungle in mysterious circumstances, spent many years searching for the Dormidera, the legendary or mythical 80 feet long anaconda that was believed in inhabit the swamps of the Chaco. This particular python had more than ten feet to grow to equal the record, but it was only twelve years old and still it was, in its own way, a splendid beast. It wrapped itself round Dieter's leg not from affection but, so Uschi told us, to steady itself while Dieter held its pea-brained head aloft. One of the smaller snakes, Uschi also informed us, always sought cover and shade, and Dieter proceeded to demonstrate this. Standing in the middle of the floor, he released the snake on the floor, and it at once found the dark gap between the sole of his boots and the high heels.

For a small fee, Dieter and Uschi allowed the children to be photographed with the boa, much smaller than the python, which could easily have swallowed some of the smaller children. As such constrictors go, the boa was a small one, but even to touch it—as Dieter encouraged us all to do—was to feel the formidable strength of its musculature. Of course all the children wanted to be photographed with it, and from this natural desire Dieter and Uschi derived a considerable part of their income.

The show ended with the exhibition of a caiman, a crocodilian only a yard long, but nevertheless when seen up this close a formidable beast. Uschi told us that the caiman was intelligent, though added that this was only by comparison with snakes. Dieter allowed the caiman to walk in our direction, pulling it back when it was almost within lunging distance of those tasty morsels, our legs.

The show over, Uschi went round with a hat, asking for voluntary contributions in addition to the entrance fee if the performance had pleased us (we gave generously). She described her and Dieter's itinerary in the days to come, to other small villages, that is if the councils would agree to let the village hall to them, and asked us to recommend the show to anyone we knew, again if it had pleased us. Dieter and Uschi's existence was clearly a hand-to-mouth one.

During the show, Dieter had fixed his face in a smile, or a rictus rather; but he gave the impression of being a kind and gentle man, and he was very good with children. A man who can persuade six or seven year olds to wrap snakes round their necks that are as large as they must inspire confidence, after all, and, for all his beaten-up look, Dieter obviously knew what he was about. The posters that had appeared in St Paul le Jeune proclaimed that one of the purposes of the show was to reduce the unreasoning fear that reptiles inspired, and to replace it by love and appreciation. How much more educative this show was than another night of television!

There were many questions that I should much have liked to ask Dieter and Uschi after the show. How did they embark upon this strange life, how long had they kept it up, and did they now do it because they liked and enjoyed it still, or were they trapped into continuing it because they could do, like Luther, no other? Did it bore them to repeat the same performance over and again in out of the way places, before small audiences of utter provincials? (Uschi gave no hint of boredom, quite the reverse, but I suppose a professional can hide or disguise his or her boredom.) I did not approach them to ask, being too shy.

Whatever the answers would have been to my questions had I asked them, I warmed to Dieter and Uschi, a warmth not untinged by admiration, for they were undoubtedly courageous in following their own path. Oddly enough I found their performance reassuring, in that they were still free to take it wherever their desire—and no doubt their linguistic abilities allowed them. It could not have been an easy life, but it was a free life, and contrary to what I might previously have thought regulation had not yet made it completely impossible. I began to see why Dickens (to say nothing of Hamlet) had such an admiration and affection for strollers.

Dieter and Uschi were fine people, despite their probable membership of a subculture that I do not in other circumstances much admire, for they brought to the faces of the children expressions of happy wonderment in a world in which premature disenchantment is so often taken as evidence of maturity and sophistication. If only there were more Dieters and Uschis! The world would not be tidier, but it would be more enchanting.

6
A New Squirearchy

I t is likely—and here I speak from personal experience—that most journalists, who know full well that what they write will be forgotten even before the reader has finished reading it, harbour the hope of some kind or measure of immortality, in other words that at least something of what they have written will continue to be read after their death. And so it is not at all comforting for them to have to remember that by no means all good books survive, except in the sense of mouldering on remote shelves in the ever-fewer second-hand bookshops of the world; mere merit is no guarantee of other forms of survival.

There is a small compensating pleasure, however, in this melancholy thought: that all around us are books that are worthy to be read but that nobody does read; and that once we have found such a book, we can hug to ourselves the knowledge that we have been clever and perceptive enough to have found it. We are then in an exclusive club of one.

Recently I had the pleasure of finding and reading *Essays at Large* by Solomon Eagle. I would be surprised if you had heard of Solomon Eagle, even under his real name, J C Squire, though he was famous enough in his time. The book was published in November 1922 and reprinted a month later (I possess this recondite knowledge because the verso of the dedication page tells me so). Nobody who likes the English language could fail to enjoy it.

The book consists of thirty-nine short essays that are literary but also rooted in everyday life, making precisely the kind of connection between life and literature that I think it is one of the purposes of literary criticism to make. The essays continually bring to mind—at least to my mind—experiences not dissimilar from those of the author himself, who is often so funny that I am afraid I laughed out loud in the quiet coach of the train in which I happened to be reading his book. As the public announcement at the beginning of the journey had asked passengers to be wary of suspicious behaviour and to report it, my outbursts of mirth—we are in the middle of the worst economic crisis in eighty years, for God's sake, even those of us in the quiet coach—caused people to eye me oddly. I wanted to read them passages of Solomon Eagle to prove to my fellow passengers that, really, I was quite normal, and they would have laughed too if they had been reading Solomon Eagle, but I decided in the end that discretion was probably better than full disclosure, and no one reported me.

Let me take as an example Eagle's, or Squires', reflections on Railroadiana, that is to say an auction catalogue he had received from an American auction house which contained a collection of items having to do with the history of rail, including books but also ephemera such as time-tables. At first Squires appears rather sniffy at this, but gradually leads the reader to see that actually it is a worthy and useful goal to preserve these things.

As it happens, I had just flown from Amsterdam to London when I read this essay. On the plane next to me was an Englishman to whom I smiled when he sat down, but who did not return my friendliness. I think I soon found out why. Around his neck were some binoculars, and I assumed he was a birdwatcher (I assume there are birds in the Netherlands other than in factory farms, but I don't recall seeing any). But I was wrong. From out his pocket he took a moleskin notebook and opened it. I quickly saw what he had been doing: he had been collecting the registration numbers of airliners, and of course Schipol Airport is a rather good place to do that. People who collect aircraft registration numbers as a hobby are strange.

I was in the window seat and he peered across me trying to get yet more numbers as we taxied out. He managed to note a few more numbers before we were airborne.

When we arrived at Heathrow (presumably another aircraft number-collector's paradise) I noticed that, on the way to baggage collection he picked up all the little leaflets on offer: concerning, I think, everything from the precautions taken by customs to prevent the importation of the Colorado beetle into Britain to cheap British Airways holiday breaks in mid-November. I have little doubt, judging by the kind of man that he was, that he would preserve these leaflets in pristine condition to the day he died (he was much younger than I).

Needless to say, I felt infinitely superior to this man, I really looked down on him: that is, until I read Solomon Eagle. He says in his elegant prose style:

> I doubt if a man who is willing to take really long views and can trust his children to obey the terms of his will, could do better [from the point of handing down valuables to his descendants] than to lay down in dry, warm bins, not to be disturbed for two centuries, a complete file of *Bradshaw's Railway Guide*.

For, as he has said earlier in the essay, 'The more ordinary and common the literature was in its own time the more likely it is, as a rule, to be scarce; yet it is from this kind of thing that we are likeliest to get a peep into the minds of our ancestors or a notion of their day-to-day lives.'

I began to feel – too late – less contempt for the man who had sat next to me on the plane, less pride in my own superiority; for the whirligig of time certainly does bring in its revenges.

Another of Eagle's essays on this theme is the one about literary relics. He writes hilariously of Henry Festing Jones' collection of the relics of Samuel Butler, the nineteenth century rationalist writer, which he gave for display to St John's College, Cambridge (Butler's college). Jones, who was also Butler's companion, wrote a biography of Butler that makes Boswell's Life of Johnson seem like a mere preliminary sketch. The collection includes the menu of a dinner given to Henry Festing Jones on completion of his Memoir [of Butler]. 'Here,' says Eagle, 'we are distinctly coming down to details.' He then lists a few of the items on display: a sandwich case, a pocket magnifying glass, an address book, two pen trays, a bag for pennies, two small Dutch dolls, a matchbox that his brother gave him. I cannot forbear from quoting to demonstrate Eagle's humour, wisdom and humanity—as well as literary skill in providing an extremely powerful last line:

> It [the collection] is pretty thorough. I missed Butler's pyjamas, which are totally unrepresented; and no collection of the kind can be deemed quite complete without some sample nail-clippings, some boots, a piece of toast incised by the

hero's teeth, and some few [collar] studs. There is not even a lock of Butler's hair here. Nevertheless, as I said, it is as varied a collection of its kind as exists. And it is strange that these relics should have been brought together, placed in a Cambridge college, and dedicated to the memory of one who spent his whole life attempting to reason people out of what he considered their absurd sentimentality. On Butler's own principles his relics should have been buried with him. But disciples will be disciples, and his disciples were wiser than he.

There could hardy be a more devastating criticism of a man's work than this, and all done with good humour and without insult.

Squire was a brilliant parodist. In an essay on *The New Style of Memoir*, Squire protested against what was then a new phenomenon, that of relaying tittle-tattle about living persons in books. He was a gentleman; he thought that the abuse confidences and the reporting of private conversations were shameful, and this was so even if they were interesting.

But he was not therefore in favour of eternal blandness; he would not have wanted malicious gossip never to have found its way into print, and certainly did not believe in the rather fatuous injunction, *de mortuis nil nisi bonum*. If this were adhered to, he wrote, biographies would go something like this:

> So Henry VIII died, as he had lived, in the odour of sanctity, beloved by his wife (Catherine of Aragon) who was his first and only romance, and revered by his people. His spare features and sympathetic deep-sunken eyes, so vividly preserved for us on the canvases of Holbein, attest the unworldly character of the man and the austerity of his life.

Or:

> Napoleon, Emperor of the French, a man distinguished for the sacredness which he attached to human life and the implicit trust which he put in human nature, died at St. Helena in 1821. He had abdicated in 1815 owing to failing health, and chose that sunny island on the advice of his doctors, finding a great solace during his last years in the congenial

conversation of an Englishman, Sir Hudson Lowe, who exiled himself in order to be near his invalid friend.

His essay, then, is an implicit plea for decent respect for the exigencies of civilised social intercourse while maintaining realism about life as it is actually lived: and the balance requires judgment and the exercise of virtuous restraint.

His essay on Christmas card poetry is hilarious:

It is amazing that every publisher of Christmas cards should have 'on tap' a bard so skilful that he can turn out hundreds of these poems without ever introducing a touch of individuality or novelty. For somebody must write them, even if it is only the chairman of the manufacturing company or the compositor who does the type-setting. Who are these mysterious people? Are they scattered amateurs everywhere? Or is it here that we find the explanation of how our professional and justly celebrated poets earn their living? Or is this one of those industries which are the hereditary monopoly of a few families like flint-knapping, violin-making and gold-beating?

Then Squire thinks of another solution to the problem he has set himself:

Our enlightened capitalists are always said to be exploring new methods of eliminating waste. May it not be that it long ago occurred to one of them that a sufficient accumulation of Christmas verses was now in existence, that there was no difference between old ones and new ones, that nobody could ever remember if he had seen one of them before, and that it was criminally extravagant to go on employing labour in the fabrication of new goods before the old were worn out? Surely if these truths were not grasped by keen business minds in the old days of fat and plenty [before the First World War] they must have occurred to somebody during the war when every ounce of effort had to be put into war-work, and he was who mis-employed labour was helping the Germans. If not, are we to understand that the composers of Christmas verses, after five years' inactivity, have actually been set to work again at their own trade – or (awful thought) that some of those extraordinary tribunals [that decided who need not go into the armed forces] exempted them as indispensable?

There is in this a love of absurdity, which is almost a sufficient condition for a love of life, and also for a civilised outlook. My copy of *Essays at Large* has a small ink inscription, To Gwen from Mary Eccles, written in a hand, that I think is contemporary with the book, that does not suggest intellectuality, which in turn suggests a generally literate culture (for only a literate person would think of offering such a book as a gift, and only to another literate person). In the book I found a bookmark, with a little picture of a pixie-like figure in a jester' costume, holding in his elfin hand a glass of champagne, beneath which are the words LONG LIVE FRIENDSHIP. Above it are the words From Mary to Gwen.

And long live J C Squire, a man who had in many ways a rather tragic life. He was, by the way, the first poet of the Great War to publish anti-war poems, though he believed in the justice of the Allied cause.

7
Ancient and/or Modern

To believe or trust in the wisdom of crowds just because crowds are composed of many people and two heads are better than one seems to me absurd; but equally it is wrong to reject an opinion merely because it is held by a crowd. We are condemned, or privileged, or both, constantly to have to make up our own minds about things: to be *nonjudgmental*, as the cant word has it, means not to participate fully in or of human life. And what most people probably mean when they describe themselves (almost always in a self-congratulatory way) as being *nonjudgmental* is that they are uncensorious—other than about people who are censorious, of course. An inadequate vocabulary can be pregnant with consequences.

An article in the French leftish-liberal newspaper, *Le Monde*, for 15 September, drew attention with evident unease or even mild disapproval to the results of a poll conducted in France by the fine arts magazine, *Beaux Arts*. To the question of whether it is more important to safeguard the treasures of the past or to promote creativity, the respondents replied by a very large majority that the former is the more important. The article implied that, *pace* the advertisement, forty million Frenchman can be wrong.

Of course, France is in a slightly unusual position by comparison with many other countries. It is by far the most visited country in the world, with 70 million tourists annually; more than twice as many Frenchmen now live by tourism as by agriculture. And it isn't French modernity that people come to see: it is the French past (together, of

45

course, with the pleasures, comforts and conveniences of the present, in which the country is by no means deficient).

But I doubt very much that those who answered the poll were thinking of their pocketbooks or economic interests as they answered. They were thinking of their country; and if I had been asked I would have answered in the same way.

The unease or disapproval of the writer in *Le Monde* derived from more than one consideration. The rapid increase in the number of buildings (or even landscapes) deemed to be part of the national patrimony, and the difficulty or impossibility of withdrawing them from it once they are inscribed as such, means that France is at risk, at least in the estimation of the writer, of becoming a vast museum or theme park. Moreover, by declaring this or that building to be part of the national patrimony, the state takes on more and more financial obligations, for upkeep does not come cheap. Many of the buildings or sites of the patrimony do not pay for themselves by means of tourist receipts; and these are not times propitious for yet more government expenditure.

But I think the main concern of the author of the article is what might be called that of cultural psychology. For the author, the poll (the actual figures of which she does not give) indicates that the French are now a backward looking people, with no confidence in the future and not much ability to create one either. They are living the dream of a past than cannot be recaptured.

I will leave aside the question of whether, if one is concerned to conserve the past, one is destined to be uncreative: in other words, whether the dichotomy between preservation and creativity is a genuine one. Personally, I do not think that it is; attachment to what exists does not inhibit creative effort and in my opinion might ever spur it. The fact that so many classic books have been written has not, so far as I am aware, inhibited anyone from putting pen to paper or finger to keyboard in the hope of adding another.

But the article itself gives us a clue to the reason why the French who were polled by *Beaux Arts* magazine (who are almost certainly not a cross section of the general population, perhaps we should remember) voted the way they did. On the second page of the article is a photograph of *la cité de l'Etoile*, a housing project in Bobigny on the outskirts of Paris designed by the architect Georges Candilis and built in 1962.

These ugly, soulless, prefabricated concrete blocks have been declared by the authorities to be part of the 'patrimony of the Twentieth Century,' and therefore as being too culturally important to demolish or replace. The people who have been trapped into living in these concrete ant-heaps have protested vigorously at the designation: they know in their own persons what it is to live out the social-cum-futuristic fantasies of nth-rate French architects like Candilis, and they are demanding demolition. The only thing to do with such architecture, as far as they are concerned, is to grind it into the dust and try to forget that it ever existed.

Actually, I believe one or two such buildings ought to be deliberately preserved, to remind us of the aesthetic incompetence, lack of imagination or even criminality, of such as Candilis. But of course there is a question that haunts me: if *le cité de l'Etoile* were pulled down as it deserves, would it be replaced by anything better?

If what is built nowadays (that is to say half a century later) is anything to go by, the answer must be equivocal. I don't think anything quite as bad would be built, but almost certainly it would not be *much* better; almost certainly it would look gimcrack and not as if anyone really intended it to last longer than thirty years. The fact is that, after hundreds of years, the French have lost altogether the knack of building something that someone in the future might look upon with pleasure. They are not the only European nation to have done so; but their architects are definitely among the worst and most incompetent in the world.

It was in this context that the magazine *Beaux Arts* took the poll. With a few notable exceptions, all that has been erected in the last ninety years in France has been ugly. It is true that the worst phase in the double-millennial history of French architecture has been passed, that office blocks that are now erected in France sometimes have the kind of glassy elegance that might be pleasing to men with the souls of insects or other cold-blooded creatures (but are not to be distinguished in the slightest from such buildings erected on the other side of the globe); but where architecture is concerned, the Mandate of Heaven has passed from France, though whether it has arrived somewhere else might be doubted.

That modernism in France was and is more than a merely aesthetic mistake, but was and is motivated by a mean-spirited, envious, ideological levelling impulse, is something that the article in Le Monde makes clear:

The classification or labelling [of buildings to be preserved], without regard to the social class protected, could be a brake on modernity... It also limits brave new forms in architecture. It promotes the process of gentrification, chasing the least well-off classes from the city centres when real estate prices rise with the growth of tourism.

It seems to me that this amounts to something like the following: I cannot, and will never be able to, afford to live in the best part of Paris, therefore I would prefer that no one should live in the best part of Paris, at least as it currently exists; I would prefer it to be the kind of place that I could afford to live in, that is to say much uglier and less desirable. For this to happen, it must be ruined by, for example, the kind of buildings erected in *la cité de l'Etoile*—a single one of which, incidentally, would be more than enough to destroy the appearance of whole quarters of Paris. (If you doubt my word, look down the rue de Rennes in the direction of la tour Montparnasse; I might, of course, say the same of any of the better parts of any of the old cities of the world.) In other words, if not everyone can live in a beautiful place then no one should be able to do so, and no one should be protected merely by his money from the corrosive effect of ugliness, because an ugliness shared is an ugliness halved. Social engineering thus trumps aesthetics; the assuaging of my resentment that others are richer, better born, more fortunate, more talented than I, is more important than the aesthetic legacy I leave to my descendants, or that I have been fortunate enough to receive myself.

The problem would not arise so acutely, perhaps, were modern French architects able to create something of worth, but they are not, and haven't been able for decades. You have only to look at the exterior of Jean Nouvel's *Musée du quai Branly*, President Chirac's equivalent of the Pyramid of Cheops, not far from the Eiffel Tower, to understand the terminal incapability of modern French architects. Indeed, I am not in favour of the guillotine except prophylactically for modern French architects. (They should, of course, be given the choice between the guillotine and the fate of the architects of St Basil's Cathedral and the Taj Mahal. The latter had their eyes put out so that they would not build anything as beautiful again. Modern French architects should have their eyes put out, but for precisely the opposite reason. They do not use them anyway.)

Just as in England you cannot bring up the question of public drunkenness without someone piping up about Gin Lane, as if nothing had happened in England between 1740 and 2010, so you cannot mention the depredations of modern French architects without someone mentioning Baron Haussmann who, at the behest of Louis Napoleon, refashioned a lot of Paris, in the process pulling down a huge number of ancient buildings, mainly so that troops could take easy pot-shots at revolutionary rabbles gathering in the new boulevards. Whether the Haussmannian reconfiguration of Paris was a good thing or not, an important, indeed vital, distinction between him and modern French architects is that he not only had taste but humanity, in the sense that he knew what a civilised urban life consisted of and required. He didn't pull down old Paris in order to build Rostov-on-Don or Pyongyang.

According to one person quoted in the article in *Le Monde*, the 'over-patrimonialisation' of France, that is to say the over-protection of buildings that already exist, is an undesirable and retrograde manifestation of the French fear of globalisation (which in other contexts, such as the preservation of *les acquis*, that is to say the social charges that render French labour so uncompetitive compared with German, it would praise as anti-neoliberal). This, it seems to me, is a fundamental misunderstanding of what it is, or what is needed, to be modern in the best sense. It is magical thinking. It is as if I decided that, in order to take advantage of high-speed internet connections, I had to pull my 300 year-old house in England down and put up a glass and steel box, and then use the internet mainly to gain access to pornography because that is what the majority of people use it for.

Again, one has only to see the vast wasteland by which Paris is surrounded to understand why the French who were polled by *Beaux Arts* magazine might come to the conclusion that it would be better to preserve what exists than to give French architects and town planners their head. Of the latters' financial corruption I will not speak (how they must be salivating at the thought of *Tours Montparnasses* equivalents overlooking the *Place de la Concorde*—think of the penthouse prices!)

They—the architects and town planners—would retire to the few unspoilt parts of the city, which would undergo not gentrification as much as super-gentrification, where only *marquis* and *ducs* of the new dispensation, not mere *barons* and *comtes*, could afford, or would have sufficient political connections, to live.

Our problem is not that we preserve the past; it is that we produce so little that is, or ever will be, worth preserving. Destroying the past will not improve our performance, only make us less aware of how deficient our performance actually is. I suppose that is a solution of a kind.

8
A Word to the Wise

R ecently I read a slim volume that makes you tremble for humanity as you read it, and this is so even if it presents only a one-sided account of its subject matter as some critics allege: for that one side is more than terrible enough to induce the said trembling.

The book is *Golden Harvest: Events at the Periphery of the Holocaust* by Jan Tomasz Gross, written with the help of his wife Irena. Gross is a professor of history at Princeton, specialising in the social history of Poland during the Nazi occupation and the Holocaust; he is no stranger to controversy, to the point of being the object of threats. His main theme is the co-operation of ordinary Poles in the extermination of the Jews in Poland, and the controversy is not whether such co-operation took place, everyone admitting that it did, but over how extensive it was.

Golden Harvest is an historical meditation on a single photograph that acts as the book's frontispiece. It is of Polish peasants, together with a few militiamen, standing behind a row of human skulls with a pair of crossbones in the middle. Two of the women have shovels or spades. The ground looks bleached, like a desert; the sun is shining brightly. The ground is bleached because the topsoil consists of human ashes. The photograph was taken at Treblinka, the extermination camp, a year after the end of the war; and, according to the author, the peasants have sifted, or are about to sift, through the ashes for items of value such as gold teeth missed by the Nazis.

Personally I think the author over-interprets the photograph. He says that the people in it stare at the camera in an unembarrassed way, as if they are just going about business as usual; but actually quite a few of the people in the photograph (which is of very bad quality, and very badly reproduced by the Oxford University Press) seem to me not to be facing the camera. Perhaps they are ashamed or frightened to show their full faces, perhaps the photographer was not very good at co-ordinating his human subjects. Perhaps the group photo was coerced rather than voluntary. It is impossible to say.

Nevertheless, no one could read this book without being, yet again, horrified by man's inhumanity to man. Indeed, the term inhumanity seems almost an odd one in the circumstances, assuming as it does that Man's default setting is to decency and kindness, whereas the evidence presented in this book is that, once legal and social restraints are removed, Man becomes an utter savage.

According to Gross, people of all social strata in Poland gladly, even joyfully, plundered their Jewish neighbours; if so, they were not unique in having done so, for it happened across Europe during Nazi occupation, while in Rwanda, in 1994, ordinary Hutus happily and without conscience appropriated the property of their erstwhile but now massacred Tutsi neighbours.

The question of what proportion of the population behaved like this is obviously an important one, for upon the answer will depend one's subsequent view of average human nature. Was the behaviour statistically normal or deviant in the circumstances, or something in between the two?

Gross's answer is uncompromising: he thinks it was statistically normal. He does not make any claims of statistical exactitude, which would clearly be impossible; but he presents evidence which, in his opinion, shows that what he says is so.

He uses a method that, in a very different context (thank goodness) I have used myself. He quotes the testimony of several survivors of those times, the very language in which it is couched being very, one might say horrifically, instructive. I quote at some length just one of the cases:

> The takeover of Jewish property was so widespread in occupied Poland that it called for the emergence of rules determining distribution. Thus when in August 1941 a certain Helena Klimaszewska went from the hamlet of GoniÄ...dz to RadziÅ,ów "to get an apartment for her husband's parents because she knew that after the liquidation of the Jews

there are empty apartments," she was told on arrival that a certain "Godlewski decides what to do with 'post-Jewish' apartments." She presented her request to him but, she later testified in court, "Godlewski replied, 'don't even think about it.' When I said that Mr Godlewski has four houses at his disposal and I don't even have one he replied 'this is none of your business, I am awaiting a brother returning from Russia where the Soviets deported him and he has to have a house.' When I insisted that I need an apartment, he replied, 'when people were needed to kill the Jews, you weren't here, and now you want an apartment,'" an argument that met with a strong rebuttal from Klimaszewska's mother-in-law: "They don't want to give an apartment, but they sent my grandson to douse the house with gasoline..." And so, we are witnessing a conversation between an older woman and other adults that is premised on the assumption that one gains a right to valuable goods by taking part in murder of their owners.

Assuming that this story is not wholly false and is substantially true (there are inconsistencies in it, for surely Klimaszewska, if she was as presented here, would have replied that the returning brother needed only one house, not four, and that therefore his return could not be a reason for not giving her one), it points to a moral attitude that could not possibly have been that of one person or a few persons alone: it must have been shared by a substantial number and proportion of the population, though it would be impossible to be dogmatic about how large that number or proportion must have been. In effect, the grossest criminal behaviour was now deemed normal, acceptable and as conferring rights on those who indulge in it. Here indeed was a transvaluation of all values.

Gross insists that such anecdotal evidence, assuming it is not made up of whole cloth, is of as of great importance as more abstract statistical evidence would be, and I too have taken this view in my own work.

Let me give an example of what I mean. I was asked by the courts to examine a young woman who, under the influence of both cannabis and alcohol, had an argument with her aged great grandmother, with whom she was living, pushed her over and broke her thigh. Fortunately the old lady survived, but the young woman was charged with causing her injury.

In the course of my interview with the young woman, I asked

whether her own mother had ever been in trouble with the police. She replied that she had, and I asked what for.

'She was on the social,' she said [being 'on the social' is local argot for receiving money from social security], 'and she was working at the same time.'

'And what happened?' I asked.

'She had to give up working.'

This was said with no hint of irony, indeed as if it were so perfectly obvious that no other answer was possible and the question was almost a foolish one.

The answer did answer a quite specific question, but it also had a hinterland of meaning. It meant that money obtained by working was not considered the natural prime source of income, but rather as a top-up of the basic source of income which was social security. Work, if any, was for pocket money. And while, from this case alone, it would have been impossible to conclude anything very much about the state of society (for the young woman might have been a totally exceptional person, though this was not likely), what she said was consonant with a revealing locution that I heard many times.

In the late 1970s, people in Britain who received money from social security would say 'I get my giro on Friday.' (The giro was in effect a cheque.) Nowadays, however, they almost always say 'I get paid on Friday.'

This new form of words is very revealing, and signifies (to adapt slightly a Gramscian formulation) the long march of dependence through the mentalities: for to get paid, in normal parlance, is to receive money in return for something that one has done for another person or entity. What is it, then, that they are paid for having done? The answer is and can only be: for having continued to exist since the receipt of the last money.

Let me add, lest I should be misunderstood, that I do not consider the position of people who are in this position of dependence to be enviable. Often not of the highest intelligence, they have been badly educated by the state and then supplied with, one might almost say contemptuously tossed, a bare material sufficiency; if they work they are scarcely better off than if they do not, for their labour is worth hardly more to any possible employer than the subventions they already receive. Their only luxury is time, oceans of it. It is not to be wondered at that they lack self-respect, that they self-destruct, that their choices are often of a fantastically unwise nature, for nothing much hangs on them except the most immediate consequences. They have seen the future, and it is more of the same.

My point, however, is that the language that they use is an important clue, or entry, into their mentality. In the 1970s, the term 'I get my giro' was a neutral description of a fact; it did not imply that the receipt of the giro was in return for anything. Thirty years later, continuing to exist, that is to say not having died, had become existentially equivalent (for people in this state of dependence) or even superior to going out to work and earning a living. Such a state of mind is not conducive to individual effort: the man who goes out to work five or six days a week and is no better off than such a person, but does so in the mere hope of bettering himself or even just to retain his self-respect, is more likely to be seen as a fool rather than a hero or someone worthy of imitation.

Perhaps it is inevitable that large-scale, de-industrialising societies will result in a class of people such as I have described, essentially paupers whose pauperisation is at a much higher standard of living than that of Victorian paupers because of the vast increase in our overall productivity and wealth; perhaps any alternative, for example a nearly complete absence of any form of subvention to the unemployed, would be worse (more than one opinion is possible on this subject, and it is almost always possible for situations to get worse as well as better).

What I think is illegitimate to doubt, however, is that there is a mentality of dependence brought about by the current system, at least in Britain; and that the things that they say—such as 'I get paid on Friday,' and I could cite other locutions—virtually proves it. Words and phrases have hinterlands.

I have heard the locutions of passivity first hand, with my own ears, and many times, not just once; I am not in a position, though, to say what proportion of the population thinks and speaks like this, but any candid person would admit that it is unlikely that the numbers are small. It is equally within my experience that many people of higher social and intellectual class are not candid, perhaps for two reasons: to admit the phenomena would threaten their worldview (and nothing is defended as tenaciously as a worldview); and second because the solution, if there is one, is not easy to devise and could not be other than painful, requiring courage to implement. Better and easier, then, just to deny the phenomena. (Incidentally, the old-style left that was more interested in economics than in cultural symbolism, as is the new-style left, and that was often culturally conservative, is much better at recognising the phenomena than many modern conservatives who prefer to believe that all is nearly for the best in our highly corporatist state. The problem with the old left was their economics rather than with their ability to see what is before their eyes; but that is a lesser sin, at least in our situation, than wilfully failing to see it or even to look.)

The problem I have described is, of course, trivial by comparison with the Holocaust. Professor Gross' evidence is not first-hand, but its veracity is not what his critics deny; it is the degree to which it is representative of the whole. But even if it were only a small part of the whole, it is enough to cause us to tremble for ourselves.

9

The Profits of Blame

Who is more to blame, asked the seventeenth century Mexican nun, Sor Juana Ines de la Cruz: he who sins for pay or he who pays for sin? It is not an easy question to answer.

One does not generally look to the *Financial Times* for answers to moral dilemmas or conundrums, but yesterday (as I write this) there was an article in it by an Argentine banker who had once also been a director of the Bank of England, that tries to answer a cognate problem. His article was about a new crisis that threatens to destabilise the world banking system further, if such a thing were possible.

As far as I understand it—which may not be very far, for I am no financial expert—Argentina issued bonds under US law upon which, early in this century, it defaulted, having been unable (or unwilling), not for the first time in its history, to meet its obligations. Most creditors accepted a loss, writing off a large part of the debt in return for partial repayment, on the great moral principle that part of something is better than the whole of nothing. But some creditors, notably two 'vulture' funds, did not accept this deal and held out for repayment in full, which hitherto Argentina has refused.

A court in New York has now ordered that the Argentine government must pay what it owes to these funds which did not accept the write-down. If it fails to comply with the order, it will have defaulted yet again; such a default might result in a new financial panic.

The writer in the *FT* argues as follows: the risk of default associated with the original Argentine bonds was written into them by the high rate of interest which they bore, and that therefore the bond-holders have no moral right to complain when the bonds were in fact defaulted upon. That, after all, was what the risk was; the bondholders took a gamble and it did not altogether pay off. It makes no more (moral) sense for the bondholders to complain than for a gambler to complain that the horse upon which he staked a lot of money did not win the race. If betting were always to win, it would not be betting.

Clearly there is something in this. If I know you to be an habitual spendthrift, a person who has repeatedly reneged on debts, but I nevertheless lend you money, whether from softheartedness or in the hope of interest payments, I shall be entitled to limited sympathy when you fail to pay up. An outsider would say, and rightly say, that I had been foolish, however dishonourable you, the borrower, had been.

The situation with sovereign debt is, of course, much more complex and morally ambiguous. There is first the difficulty of the distinction between an inability to pay and a refusal to pay. By inability is meant an inability to pay while maintaining, approximately, present levels of individual consumption of the population, for example of those who had no part in borrowing the money, may not have had a part in or any benefit from the spending of it, and may not even have voted for the government that borrowed or defaulted, or both. To insist that they, who may be very numerous, pay the debts of those who contracted them is to insist upon collective responsibility, a very doubtful form of moral reasoning.

On the other hand, many people may have benefited from the loans without either approving them or realising that they were so benefiting from them. If the result of the loans was to raise aggregate demand in such a way that they prospered, even if only relatively and for a short time, then they do bear some moral responsibility for repayment, albeit a responsibility that they did not personally contract or agree to. But it also goes almost without saying that, in a modern economy, it would not necessarily be easy to distinguish between those who benefited from the loans and those who did not; there would be every gradation between those who benefited mightily and those who did not benefit at all, or even who were actually harmed by them. Thus there is, in practice, little alternative to some version of collective responsibility.

An example exists of successful repayment of foreign loans despite what most countries would have called an inability to repay them: Romania under the late Nicolae Ceausescu. People had barely enough to eat for many years, and lived under the direst conditions, but Romania emerged foreign debt-free because Ceausescu unilaterally made this the country's economic priority. It is not a model that any minimally democratic state could follow.

The Argentinian writer in the *FT* did not appeal, as he so easily might have done, to the populist-nationalist argument heard in Argentina, that the American court was indulging in form of legal imperialism. Populist nationalism has done untold damage to Argentina since the ascent to power of Juan Domingo Perón nearly seventy years ago, damage that has proved almost impossible for the country, despite its vast potential, to repair.

Instead, the writer suggested that if the court judgment were allowed to stand the consequence would be that no restructuring of unpayable debts would ever be possible (and no one seriously expects Argentina to repay its $100 billion in full); that a few creditors could hold out successfully against the majority who were prepared for pragmatic reasons to accept writedowns; that this would mean that such pragmatic creditors would cease to exist, for no one would willingly accept lesser repayments than were their more stubborn or determined co-creditors; and that this in turn would mean that countries would be prevented by their debts from borrowing money for ever, or at least until those debts had been repaid in the very distant future. It would mean, in effect, that countries would not be able to engage in the productive activity of which they were capable, and which offered some hope of profit to future creditors. The whole world would suffer as a result; it would be as if the world had cut off its nose to spite its face.

This is a purely utilitarian argument: it is better on the whole for humanity to force creditors to accept losses than to allow those same creditors to inhibit overall economic activity, and thus the prosperity of millions, in pursuit of their right to be repaid in full. We cannot let the heavens fall so that their debts might be repaid.

I think we can all see the force of this. None of us would be prepared to undergo very much hardship for the sake of turning someone else's bad debt into a performing debt.

On the other hand—there is always another hand—it is obvious that allowing people to borrow large sums of money and then write them off is not altogether an incentive to prudence or probity. If everybody could renounce his debts the moment he found it too inconvenient to repay them, the person who repays rather than defaults comes to seem naïve or foolish rather than upright. It would become normal practice to borrow without the slightest intention ever of repaying or meeting obligations. This too would constrict credit.

The only solution is prudence on the part both of borrowers and lenders (assuming that Polonius's advice to be neither a borrower nor a lender since loan oft loses both itself and friend is the counsel of an impossible perfection, and therefore not of a perfection at all). Our conclusion is not very exciting but, as Bertrand Russell I think it was, once said, there is no reason to suppose that the truth, when found, will be interesting. And so we come back to Sor Juan's question, which of the parties to a sinful or imprudent transaction is the more responsible?

Such questions arise with ever-greater frequency these days, not because the world has become more complex but because economic conditions are such that people are more inclined now than they were a few years ago to see the economy as a zero-sum game; for where people are not confident that wealth in general will increase, they hang on to what they have all the more jealously. My crumb is snatched from your mouth, and vice versa.

While the Argentinian bond crisis was developing, Hewlett-Packard was engaged in a war of words with the software company, Autonomy. Only a short time after it bought Autonomy for $11 billion H-P had to mark down its assets by $8.8 billion because Autonomy failed to produce the results that it, H-P, had hoped for and expected.

H-P alleged that Autonomy had misled it over its sales and revenues, and there is probably an element of truth in this allegation. However, the extent of the fraud (if that is what it was) was very a small by comparison with the size of the writedown. H-P was, in effect, trying to blame others for its own bad business decision.

This is not the first time, apparently, that the company has overpaid for companies. Moreover (and here I speak as a non-businessman who has to hand over his tax form to an accountant because I could not fill it myself even if I wanted to), one might have expected, *prima facie*, that even a company as large as H-P would look pretty thoroughly into the affairs of a company before buying it for $11 billion. If deception there was, it was surely not too much to expect H-P to have uncovered it. And H-P's financial and legal advisers, one imagines, were paid not ungenerously to look into Autonomy's affairs.

Finally, I would have expected H-P to exercise even greater caution than usual in purchasing a company whose value was so clearly linked to the creative personnel who worked for it. Remove those people—and they soon removed themselves by going elsewhere—and the company would be worth little more than a carton of orange juice without the orange juice.

So even if Autonomy behaved fraudulently it is likely that H-P was grossly negligent. To pay more than double, and perhaps five times, what a company is worth, when you have had your fingers burnt before in a similar way, and to more or less the same extent, looks—again, *prima facie*—like incompetence on an almost heroic scale. As Lady Bracknell would have put it, to lose $8 billion, Mr Hewlett-Packard, may be regarded as a misfortune; to lose $8 billion twice looks like carelessness.

There is only one way of sorting out the ambiguities of responsibility in the modern world: lawyers. John Stuart Mill once defined a physical object as the permanent possibility of sensation; nowadays, a corporation is the permanent possibility of a lawsuit. How the lawyers must be rubbing their hands with glee at the H-P-Autonomy imbroglio, with so many possibilities of suits and counter-suits!

It has already begun, of course. Some shareholders in H-P are suing their own company in a class action for lack of due diligence in overestimating the value of Autonomy and for having inflated its (H-P's) financial prospects as a result of having acquired it. In effect, the litigants accuse H-P of the same kind of accounting practices as H-P accused Autonomy of having used. It matters not whether H-P was acting fraudulently or negligently, the shareholders blame it for the recent halving of its share price. Presumably the shareholders must hope for a bigger settlement than what they will lose by the further decline of the share price that will occur if their class action is successful. When real economic activity falters, rent-seeking rushes in to fill the gap.

H-P, of course, will sue Autonomy, or rather the beneficiaries of the sale of Autonomy; but those beneficiaries will almost certainly mount a vigorous defence, the founder of the company not being a man to give in easily. Indeed, it is not impossible that he, or they, will launch a counter-suit. And H-P will also be able to sue its advisers who so signally failed to detect shortcomings in Autonomy's accounts.

Once we had ethics that guided our actions in advance; now we have lawsuits to tell us what we should have done.

10
The Sock Fairy

I don't believe in ghosts, spirits, djinns, demons, witches or fairies, with one notable exception: the Sock Fairy. The Sock Fairy inhabits, or hovers around, every washing machine in which my wife or I ever put my socks. He, she or it manages somehow to turn what were six perfectly matching pairs of socks when put into the machine into (say) three pairs plus three odd socks. How this transformation is achieved, I do not know, but it is achieved with the greatest regularity and efficiency. Likewise, I do not know what benefit or pleasure the Sock Fairy derives from this; I suspect it is a malign or cynical pleasure from witnessing my exasperation and impatience as I try to rematch my socks once they are removed from the machine. The Sock Fairy, by the way, follows me wherever I go, with as much persistence as the crying baby that never seems to grow up and that has been within a row or two of my seat on every flight that I have taken in the last forty years.

The Sock Fairy has been responsible for the wastage of many hours of my life and a great deal of misery and frustration. It is extremely difficult to match socks once the Fairy has been at them; for example, it cannot be done in artificial light, but only in bright natural light. This is because many socks are very similar, in pattern and colour, but not absolutely identical. Once you have made a mistake in matching them, there is a knock-on effect: the mistake is amplified, and it becomes more and more difficult to pair the socks. In the end, I am left with a number of orphan socks that I put in a separate bag (which grows ever more stuffed with socks) in the vain hope that one day I shall be able to turn them into pairs.

While not physically heavy work, matching socks once the Sock Fairy has had his, her or its way with them is emotionally trying and even exhausting. One very soon feels wrung out by it. One's despair is almost of existential proportions as one struggles with recalcitrant socks; what is life that such a trivial pursuit should take so much time and effort? When pairing my socks, I am reminded of the man that Logan Pearsall Smith once described, who considered suicide because he could no longer face the tedium of having to tie his shoe-laces every day. Half an hour of sock-pairing leaves me not only tired, but without the sense of satisfaction that successful accomplishment gives one. After all, they are only socks, the humblest of parts of a man's attire. (If they were anything other than humble, surely one would see more advertisements for them? Armani never advertises socks, even if it sells them.)

The process of pairing my socks dents my self-confidence. I think I have found a pair of identical socks but when I look more closely I discover, or think that I discover, slight differences between them, either in colour or in pattern or in texture. I am no longer sure that I can believe my own eyes; perhaps the faint difference in colour (for example) is not intrinsic to the socks, but is the result of different experience in the washing machine—in biological or human terms, the difference between them is not genetic but environmental. Then again, I assume that the two socks of a pair are identical when bought, an assumption that may not be justified and in truth I have never bothered to check when buying a pair.

The Sock Fairy is a subtle demon, as subtle as the serpent in the Garden of Eden: for he, she or it produces dissension between me and my wife. I start off with the full intention of pairing the socks exactly, but after a short time I lose my determination and think that any pairing, provided only that it is not too grossly discordant, will do. After all, if on close examination I cannot be sure that the socks are not a pair, surely no one is going to notice that they are not (if they are not) when I wear them. Nobody examines the socks of his interlocutor that closely.

When it comes to the pairing of socks, however, my wife is deontological rather than utilitarian. Good enough is not good enough. Once you accept to wear different socks, however similar they may appear on casual inspection to be, you are on the slippery slope that leads to scruffiness, to wearing ties with soup stains, to looking like a tramp. And we are fast approaching the age at which it would be very easy to let ourselves go. We might even become smelly.

A solution to the problem might be to buy a very large number of pairs of socks of exactly the same colour and design, or at least of perhaps two or three colours (one cannot wear brown socks with grey clothes, or black socks with green or beige clothes). The problem here is that stores rarely carry a sufficient number of identical socks of the right size and colour to carry one through a week or two—assuming one changes one's socks every day. One could, of course, make do with two pairs if one were prepared to wash one's socks daily instead of accumulating them for a week, but this is a counsel of perfection that is not in accordance with human psychology.

Sock manufacturing companies (which are practically all in China these days) are clearly in league with the Sock Fairy, if not actually in his, her or its pay, because, while they produce pairs of socks that are very similar to one another, they constantly change the design by just a little, sufficient to make exact pairing very difficult or near impossible. If Heraclitus were alive today, he would not remark that you cannot step into the same river twice, but that you cannot buy the same pattern of socks twice. Whether this has quite the same metaphysical significance I am not sure.

It is many years since I first became aware of the problem created by the Sock Fairy, and so far have found no solution to it. But there is an interesting lesson about human psychology here, and it is this: how quickly one assumes that an irritation in life or an apparent problem is the result of ill will on the part of an animate being with some kind of grudge against one. Of course, when socks appear to have gone missing in the washing machine, I am perfectly aware that the appearance is unlikely to be the reality: that the rule is ten socks in, tens socks out, and so forth. It is much more likely that I mistook the number of socks that I put in the machine than that any of them disappeared in the wash. And if any of them did disappear there would be a perfectly rational, that is to say materialist, explanation of their disappearance,

But although I think this with what I might call the official part of my mind, that is to say that part of my mind that I am willing to acknowledge as being fully mine, yet (if I am honest) I cannot entirely rid myself of the suspicion that there is an animate force somewhere nearby that has worked against me when socks appear to have gone missing or become dis-paired. Naturally, the suspicion is not sufficiently strong for me to do anything about it, by (for example) trying to propitiate the Sock Fairy with some kind of sacrifice. What, apart from socks, would the Sock Fairy want or be satisfied with? It is probable that socks are not an end in themselves for this nasty being: as flies to wanton boys are we to the Sock Fairy.

Our propensity to see malign forces at work against us is quite strong, and no doubt Darwinists would attribute survival potential to it (after all, we have survived with such a propensity, haven't we?).

Here is another small and trivial example of our inherent tendency to paranoia: when I drive I quite often make small mistakes, and when I make them other drivers assume not that I have made a genuine mistake, but that I have tried to obtain an advantage for myself by my conduct at the wheel. Often when I drive in a town that I have never visited before, I find myself in the wrong lane to get to my destination, and have to change it. In the meantime I might have overtaken a long line of cars in the lane that I now belatedly want to join, and it will occur to no one that I have overtaken in that lane that I am simply unfamiliar with the town. To judge from the expressions on each of the driver's faces, he interprets my action not as mistaken but as unjust, unfair, psychopathic, an underhand attempt to save myself a bit of time at his expense. The true explanation, that I am a stranger in this town who does not know his way, occurs to no one, not even for a fraction of a second, as a possibility, as part of what doctors call a differential diagnosis. And indeed, many drivers in this mental state are prepared to act upon their supposition, seeking to exact their revenge if they are able a few hundred yards up the road. One of my friends extends his paranoid interpretation of behaviour on the road to those who seek to overtake him, which he takes as a personal affront or insult.

We are never very far from paranoia. If you go to a foreign country whose language you do not speak and whose culture you do not understand, you will be inclined to think, if you hear a group of people laughing among themselves, that they might be laughing at you. You are afraid that you appear ridiculous in their eyes, especially if you are conspicuously different from them in appearance. The more delicate or fragile your ego, the more readily you will become paranoid; but no doubt almost everyone has a threshold for becoming paranoid.

The number of pathological conditions that result in or are accompanied by paranoia is very large; one might almost say that paranoia is the most common psychological consequence of physiological disturbance (that and depressed mood). I think, then, that I am justified in saying that paranoia is never very far below the surface of human mentation.

There is another aspect of our psychological propensity to attribute bad motives to others: it is highly enjoyable. Which of us does not actively enjoy speaking ill of people? And we should rather be the object of malice than the victims of chance, for at least malice directed at us reassures us that we of some significance to someone, that we are worth harming. Very occasionally I had patients whom I would not have wished to deprive of their paranoid delusions, even if I had been able to do so. Their delusions, though uncomfortable in some ways, explained to them their situation in life in a way that flattered them; they suffered because they were at the centre of an immense conspiracy organised by the most powerful forces in the world. Therefore they were not as insignificant in their own eyes as they were in those of the world, far from it. To have deprived them of their delusions upon which they had irreparably wasted their lives, to have made them face their true situation, would have been cruel, even if at times they suffered because of them.

I wonder how many of us can do entirely without our illusions, how many of us can face reality, especially about ourselves, exactly as it is? Humankind cannot bear very much reality, said T S Eliot, and I suspect he was right. On the other hand, humankind cannot survive too much illusion either. It is a difficult balance to strike, especially for oneself.

11
As a Matter of Interest

For those of us—the great majority—who are not scholars singlemindedly pursuing a particular subject, what we read is largely a matter of chance. No doubt we select among the books we come across according to some guiding principle or other, but which we come across in the first place is in the lap of the gods. It is almost as if books sought us out as much as we seek them out.

Yesterday, for example, I was in a second-hand bookshop in a small town in England with a beautiful ancient abbey, a famous school and a good Indian restaurant. The bookshop was in a low-ceilinged mediaeval building and I sneezed as soon as I entered.

'The dust,' I said to the owner, a lady in her late forties dressed with genteel shabbiness.

'Yes,' she said. 'I moved a book on a shelf yesterday.'

She was the kind of bookseller—very common among that endangered species—who acquired books faster than she sold them, with the result that there were piles behind her, piles in front of her, piles beside her. Indeed, she was in some danger of burial by books. My eye, practiced I have to admit, alighted at once on a volume in burgundy buckram, 1920s I guessed from its style of binding and lettering. I knew that it was destined for me.

The book was *Malay Poisons and Charm Cures* by John D. Gimlette, 'formerly surgeon-magistrate, Selinsing, Pahang,' published in 1929. Oddly enough it was the third edition of this highly technical work, which I suppose implied small previous print runs rather than high demand. There was something irresistible about its opening statement: 'Malays, like other Eastern people, are skilled in the art of poisoning'; though this was later qualified as follows:

> Malays are not a timid people, and, although in India secret poisoning became one of the most prominent, if not the most prevalent, of court atrocities under Mussulman rule, the Muhammadan Malay, as a general rule, attempts vengeance by means of poison when he is bearing a grudge and brooding, and when violent or other measures appear to him to be too dangerous or too uncertain. Very often, when jealousy or malice inspires him, the intention is rather to cause annoyance or injury less serious than death.

I was taken back, mentally, to the time at school when a friend and I plotted to put phenolphthalein in the tea of a master whom we disliked. Phenolphthalein, of which there was a plentiful supply in the chemistry laboratory, is a powerful laxative. I am glad to say that the pleasure of plotting, and of imagining the outcome, was so great that it we deemed it unnecessary to proceed to action.

With books in existence such as *Malay Poisons* who can possibly be bored? It seems unfair that death should put an inevitable end to the delight of such unexpected discovery; but perhaps if there were no end to it, there would be no delight in the first place.

In addition to technical accounts of the poisons found by Malays in frogs and toads, fish, beetles, moths and caterpillars, jungle plants and cultivated vegetables (to say nothing of arsenic, the employment of which may apparently be suspected by the inhibition of the growth of maggots in the corpse), are many fascinating anecdotes in Malay Poisons:

> In April, 1896, a Malay was charged at Kuala Lipis, Pahang, with causing hurt by means of poison. He pleaded not guilty; but, although the motive of his crime was never actually discovered, he was eventually convicted of having mixed kechubong seeds in a curry, thereby stupefying a Malay constable, the constable's wife, his niece, and a girl friend, as well as two men, who all partook of the same dish. The symptoms in each case were similar, namely, attacks of giddiness, passing into unconsciousness for few hours, followed by complete

recovery. This group of cases is of interest owing to the fact that one of my colleagues, the District Surgeon, Pahang, who appeared for the prosecution, was able to give evidence of a very practical kind. A sample of seeds in powder which had been found in the handkerchief of the accused was sent to the District Surgeon for identification. I am indebted to my colleague for the following notes in a persona experiment. He says: "I took pinch doses of the sample, which consisted of the bruised seeds, and had the following experience: I felt flushed, dry about the mouth and throat, and became hoarse. When I tried to walk, I staggered about like a drunken man and got very excited. I then took an emetic of zinc, and slept for about five or six hours." He was also observed in a delirious state, rolling on the floor and uttering inarticulate cries like the mewing of a kitten.

A friend of mine, a professor of pharmacology, was recently responsible for a brilliant piece of detective work involving eastern vegetable poisons. A woman of Indian descent poisoned her husband or lover (I forget which, but probably the husband, since the husbands of poisoners usually have to go first) by putting something in his curry. Clinically, it appeared to be aconite, the poison in the common plant Aconitum napellus, but no aconitine was found in the curry on chemical analysis. My friend suggested that the poisoning might have been by pseudo-aconitine instead, clinically indistinguishable in its effects from aconitine, but chemically different, and found in the close Indian relative of Aconitum napellus, Aconitum ferox. And so, on analysis, it proved, and the poisoner was convicted.

Let me conclude this paean to Malay Poisons and Charm Cures by quoting its final paragraph:

A blinding powder, that is to say, a powder used by thieves to disconcert their pursuers, obtained in 1913 from the Ulu Kesial district in Kelantan, was found by Dr. Dent, Government Analyst, Straits Settlements, to consist of pounded glass and sand containing grains of alluvial tin ore (bijeh). Another blinding powder used by Malays for the same purpose is composed of quicklime and ground pepper.

Not many years ago, a taxi driver in Birmingham told me that he always carried cayenne pepper with him, with a dropper attached to a rubber bulb, to squirt into the eyes of his drunken and obstreperous passengers. There's technical progress for you: no poly-pharmacy, as we doctors call it, but pure cayenne, uncontaminated by ground glass, quicklime or tin ore!

At the same time as this book, I bought another: a first (and perhaps only) edition of Aldous Huxley's collection of stories, *Two or Three Graces*, published in 1926. It had been bought in July of that year, presumably new, by Ethel Godfrey, of whom I know nothing. Somehow I doubt it was she—I think it must have been some subsequent owner—who underlined some passages the principle of whose selection is visible as through a glass darkly: *You lack the courage of your instincts* and *Love, after all, is the new invention; promiscuous love geologically old-fashioned.* Did these thoughts strike the underliner as new? As true? As false? We shall never know.

The title story is very long, actually a novella rather than a mere short story, as suggested by the subtitle and Other Stories. It is not one of the author's best known works, but it is a surprisingly subtle and moving exploration of the consequences of sincerity and insincerity, and of mistaking one for the other. But as with impulsive purchase of most books, I bought it because of the first page or two, which I read standing by the shelf. In these pages, Huxley provides a typology of bores:

> The word 'bore' is of doubtful etymology. Some authorities derive it from the verb meaning to pierce. A bore is a person who drills a hole in your spirit, who tunnels relentlessly through your patience, through all the crusts of voluntary deafness, inattention, rudeness, which you vainly interpose – through and through till he pierces you to the very quick of your being. But there are other authorities, as good or even better, who would derive the word from the French bourrer, to stuff, to satiate. If this etymology be correct, a bore is one who stuffs you with his thick and suffocating discourse, who rams his suety personality, like a dumpling, down your throat. He stuffs you: and you, to use an apposite modern metaphor, are 'fed up with him.' I like to think, impossibly, that both these derivations are correct; for bores are both piercers and stuffers. But they are characterized by a further quality, which drills and dough-nuts do not possess; they

cling. That is why (though no philologist) I venture to suggest a third derivation, from 'burr.' Burr, bourrer, bore – all the sticking, stuffing, piercing qualities of boredom are implicit in those three possible etymologies. Each of the three of them deserves to be correct.

In Huxley's story two of the characters are bores, though of different types: Herbert Comfrey 'who attached himself to any one who had the misfortune to come in contact with him... and could not be shaken off,... a burr-bore, a vegetable clinger;' and John Peddley, his brother-in-law, 'an active bore, an indefatigable piercer, a relentless stuffer and crammer... with a genius for dullness that caused him unfailingly to take an interest in things which interested nobody else.'

The reason that Huxley's typology struck me so forcefully is that I am always afraid not of boredom, but of being a bore; no, it is worse than that, I often am a bore, and manage to combine all three types—of piercing, stuffing and sticking—in my own single person. Sometimes, for example, when embarked upon a subject in which I am interested but others present are not, I positively pour out statistics to prove my argument (some, but not all, genuine), and continue even after my wife has kicked me, with increasing force, under the table. At other times, when I have nothing to say, I stick to people to make up for it, despite any signals they might have given of a desire to get away. It is unfortunately not true that a bore never knows that he is being boring; he is often only too aware of it, and his persistence is actually only a vain attempt to redeem himself, to prove that he is interesting, to earn the esteem of him whom he has so far bored. But the spiral is always downward, never upward.

It is because I am aware of the agonies of being a bore that my emotions are so engaged by the memory of my wife's uncle, a man whom I never met. He was, apparently, extremely boring, in the way that I fear that I am often boring. He married at a time when arranged, or at any rate strongly-advised, marriages were still quite frequent among the French bourgeoisie; his bride was a young woman with a lively mind but no economic prospects. The man who asked for her hand was a good prospect, economically, by no means a bad character, and so her parents suggested that she accept him; and she did.

Alas, he was the kind of person, by no means infrequently encountered, whose first reaction to Versailles was to wonder how it was swept; Mozart made no impression on him at the Paris opera, but the problem of cleaning the central chandelier did. Unfortunately, he was unable, or had not enough insight, to keep his banal thoughts to himself. It was so bad that, at home, his wife turned the volume of the radio up to drown out what he was saying, though apparently he never noticed.

My wife's sympathies were with her poor aunt, but mine were with her uncle. (I suppose, in reality, the two of them were to be pitied, but it is very difficult to be equally sympathetic to both parties of an unhappy couple). I am seized by a heartfelt sorrow at the thought of the good and kind man whose departure from the world meant only that his widow could at last turn off the radio.

In company, I often feel as if everything I say must be sparklingly interesting or I must hold my tongue. This is because, in our egotistical age, we fear to be thought boring far more than we fear to be thought bad. As a result, I veer between inappropriate loquacity and compete silence. That is why I read Huxley's opening paragraph with a sense of appalled recognition.

12
Time Past

There are some people whose imagination and emotions are stirred more by the past than by the future, and I am among them. We to whom time past is more important than any time to come are not world builders, we improve nothing; on the other hand, we seldom destroy anything. We tend to pessimism rather than to optimism, or at any rate to expectations that are not extravagant; supposedly imminent solutions to life's problems, after all, seem never to arrive, and disillusion is more common than fulfilment of promise. A disappointment anticipated is a disappointment halved; pessimists are therefore happy in the long run, or happier than optimists.

When, as sometimes happens as I get older, I lie awake at night unable to sleep, my mind returns to episodes from my past. As to the future, I can seldom think further ahead than the next article I am to write. I can dwell for any length in my sleeplessness only on the past.

From time to time, for reasons that I cannot explain, an episode returns to me from when I was almost sixteen. I was hitch-hiking in Scotland with a French friend; it now seems almost incredible that two boys of such an age should have been allowed by their parents to fend for themselves in this fashion, when communications were so much more difficult. We had a tent, and camped by the side of the road wherever we were when night fell. It wasn't comfortable—tents in those days were not the suburban home from home that they are now—and many a time the rain leaked through the canvas because we had touched it on the inside, which meant that we lived in a state of chronic dampness. We thought nothing of it.

In those innocent days, it never crossed our minds that those who picked us up might harm us, or the minds of those who picked us up that we might harm them. When we arrived late one night in a northern English industrial town and could find no accommodation we went to the police station where we were allowed to stay overnight in the cells; in the morning the police brought us bread and tea. How gentle the world seemed then, when people trusted one another!

This is a reminder that wealth and its consequent increased range of consumer choice (which have increased enormously since then) are not the same as freedom *tout court*: youngsters today do not have the freedom that we had, when no one thought it was negligent of parents to allow us to do what we did. Whether the anxiety of parents that would prevent them from allowing children to do as we did is objectively justified by the condition of the world, or whether the manacles are mind-forged is beside the point: an important freedom has declined greatly.

My friend and I were in a remote part of Scotland where sheep were grazed. We had been given a lift by a newlywed couple on their honeymoon. As we drove round a corner on a hill, there was a sheep by the side of the road that had been severely injured in a collision with a previous vehicle (few and far between in these parts). The sheep's guts had spilled out of its open belly, but it was not dead; it was still kicking convulsively if feebly.

The bride let out a cry of distress; she asked her young husband whether he had seen the sheep that was still alive. He said that he had seen the sheep and that it was dead. Then he turned to me and said, 'It was dead, wasn't it Theodore?'

I too had seen that it was alive; it took me a fraction of second to realise that the husband was not making an enquiry into truth, but trying to reduce his wife's clearly mounting distress.

'Yes, it was dead,' I said.

This calmed the bride, who concluded what she wished to conclude, that she must have been mistaken. And immediately afterwards I felt a great pride: pride that the groom, clearly an educated and intelligent man, had felt sufficient confidence in my intelligence and *savoir-faire* to ask me (at my age!) his question and that I would appreciate its real significance. How mature and sophisticated I felt, how proud that I had passed the test and come up to his expectations!

I have replayed the incident in my mind many times since, perhaps because it was the high-point of my psychological acuity. But there are other reasons too. I often wonder what happened to that young couple whose path I so briefly crossed. Their love was young and tender; the groom's protectiveness towards his bride would now, perhaps, be unfashionable, but seemed to me then (and now) to spring from unselfconscious love and a plain sense of duty. They were young and just starting out in life; they would now be in their early or even their middle seventies. I remember hoping at the time that their love would survive, because my own life at the time had been so singularly lacking in tenderness, so completely loveless; and that if it did survive it would be reassurance that lovelessness was neither inevitable nor the normal state of mankind (for it is easy for young people to suppose that their experience of life is all the experience that life can afford).

This tiny episode was also important because it taught me, very vividly, that the truth, or rather telling the truth, was not always a virtue, that other considerations might trump it morally. Kant, of course, would have said that I was wrong not to tell the truth about the sheep; but this seemed to me then, as it has seemed to me since, only to show that Kant was mistaken. I had enough insight even at that age to appreciate that telling the truth in such circumstances might easily spring not from a disposition to truthfulness based on an ethical principle, but from sadism, a pleasure in causing dismay for its own sake.

It also taught me the inescapable necessity for paternalism in human relations: not, of course, on every occasion, or invariable, but sometimes, on occasion, as suggested by judgment. As a doctor I have never forgotten this, though paternalism has become almost a dirty word in medical ethics. There must, of course, be a presumption in favour of truth-telling, but like almost any other principle it much not be made into a categorical imperative or, to put it more crudely, a fetish.

I have an example in my own family history of a surgeon who acted in a way that would now be deemed ethically reprehensible, and perhaps even actionable, but which seems to me to have been in the very highest tradition of his profession. His name was Cox, and I don't know whether he is still alive: by now he would be very old. I thanked him insufficiently at the time.

I was in Africa when I telephoned my mother (by no means the easy thing to do then that it is nowadays). She was about to go to America on a visit, but she told me that she had been bleeding intestinally. I told her she must abandon her visit and see a surgeon at once, which she did.

It was cancer; she underwent an operation within the week. I returned home before the operation.

My mother said that she wanted nothing hidden from her; she wanted to be told everything, and made me promise that I would hide nothing. She exuded a kind of pride in her own rationality.

After the operation, the surgeon spoke to me. Whether he was franker with me than he would have been with a son who was not a doctor I do not know; but he told me that, while he had excised all the cancerous tissue that he could see macroscopically, histology demonstrated that my mother's prognosis was very bad. There was an eighty per cent chance of recurrence within a year.

I told the surgeon that my mother had made me promise that I would tell her everything. The surgeon said that, on his estimate of my mother's character and personality, this would not be a good idea. He advised me against this course of action; and since he was clearly a man of experience and integrity, I took his advice.

My mother asked me, when she had recovered sufficiently from the operation, what the surgeon had said. I told her that, as far as he could see, he had cut out all the cancerous tissue. This was the truth, but of course not the whole truth, and I rather dreaded further questions, to which I might have to reply with outright lies: and I might not prove to be a very convincing liar. My mother was perfectly well aware that removing all cancerous tissue to the naked eye was not the whole of the matter, but to my surprise—and relief—she enquired no further. Despite her protestations beforehand, she did not want to know everything.

In the event, she lived another nineteen years without recurrence and relatively free of anxiety about her cancer because the surgeon had 'cut it all out.'

I was very impressed by the surgeon. It seemed to me then, and seems to me still, that he had acted as the very model of a fine medical practitioner. He was technically accomplished, it goes without saying; the operation went smoothly, with no avoidable complications. But more than that, he had given consideration to my mother as a person, as a human being; and on the basis of limited acquaintance with her—at most, a few examinations in the clinic—he had come to a shrewd and, I believe, accurate assessment of what was best for her, better indeed than my assessment. Surgeons are often accused of being brash, mere technicians without human subtlety, but this was certainly not the case with him.

From the standpoint of modern medical ethics, he committed two cardinal sins: he broke medical confidentiality and he was not entirely truthful with his patient. If he had acted in accordance with modern precepts, or obsessions, he would have done neither; with the peculiar result that, if he had acted ethically, he would have acted worse.

I assume that the surgeon, who is a hero to me, acted differently according to his assessment of the clinical situation confronting him: that breaking medical confidence and untruthfulness by omission were not fixed principles with him that he applied in every case. But this is surely very unlikely.

Instead, his understanding of the requirements for human decency was much more sophisticated than that of modern medical ethics. He understood that people generally live in a social situation, not as isolated beings, and that it is sometimes right for relatives to know more about an illness than the ill person him or herself. And I am sure that he knew that truthfulness can descend into indifference to suffering or even to sadism. To try to force people to know what they do not want to know can be cruel, and often ineffective into the bargain.

I thought of the couple in Scotland again last night and what became of them. They are forever fixed in my memory because of that one episode. It is surprising how egotistical memory is: if I met the couple again I would be surprised to discover how they had aged, as if my memory of them had preserved them from all change ever since. Not long ago the distinguished actor, Marius Goring, died; I had seen him at Stratford as Angelo in *Measure for Measure* more than forty years earlier, when he was middle-aged, and I was almost outraged to discover that forty years later he was not as I remember him in his burgundy velvet tunic, but was 85 years old. My having seen him was thus not as important to him as it was to me.

But when I recall the couple in Scotland, I still feel a certain pride at my moral intuition.

13
Portuguese Men-Of-Art

Recently I stayed in a flat in Paris for a few weeks that belonged to a friend's sister who had died not long before aged seventy-six. It is a strange and slightly unsettling experience to move into the home of someone who has died not long before and many of whose effects are still present: the ordinary effects of day-to-day living (little labelled pots of tarragon and paprika, for example) as well as the records of a lifetime (holiday photos and the notes taken more than fifty years before as a student of pharmacy). There were little lists of things to do, telephone numbers, books of recipes, and a tiny box of postage stamps for letters that will now never be written. Who in such circumstances would not reflect upon his own mortality and then, with a faint sense of guilt as if to do so were to demonstrate a lack of proper feeling, get on with his own life as if nothing untoward had happened? If we are still in good health, do we not continue to feel that there will always be a tomorrow for us, even though we know intellectually that there will not? And are we not aware of a slight moral superiority over the dead, a sense of complacency, as if our continuation in life were a sign of our own cleverness or virtue rather than the mere consequence of having been born years later than the deceased?

Among her books were manuals of English, dating from the time when she was in her forties. I suspect that she had always resolved to learn our language and had made intermittent efforts to do so, but never really succeeded. Such, at any rate, is the history of my own struggles with German, among several other languages.

She had been something a traveller, and likewise among her books I found a book about Portugal that dated from 1956. It was by an author of whom I had not heard, Yves Bottineau. I assume that she had been to Portugal about then, for her books about Iceland dated from the same era as her photographs of her trip there. I leafed idly though the book about Portugal, but with growing interest. I largely ignored the text, it was the photographs that captured my imagination. They were beautiful, but they were also photographs of beauty, natural but above all man-made.

Having just said that I largely ignored the text I will nevertheless quote a sentence from the first page:

> This country, which enjoys in the eyes of the tourist the reputation of being a paradise, is in reality a very human land, that is to say nuanced...

Perhaps; but it was very difficult to take the nuanced view after looking at the photographs. Portugal looked indeed a paradise which gave joy to the eye but also a sadness to the heart, for such unspoilt beauty has now almost certainly passed from the world.

Of course, the photographer (a man or woman called Yan) pointed his camera in such a way as to exclude all that was ugly or discordant. Fifty years ago, perhaps, people did not yet suffer from the diseased feeling that the ugly is somehow more real, more authentic, than the beautiful, and therefore worthier of capture on film and in book. We now believe that to search out only the beauty to the exclusion of the ugly is in some sense a wilful derogation of duty when ugliness exists alongside the beautiful, as it almost always does in this life (let alone in the Portugal of 1956). And if one had to choose between the willing suspension of the perception of the ugly and that of the beautiful, the former would be morally worse, for it is an implicit denial of the suffering that often goes along with ugliness.

In development economics, there has long been a theory, indeed by far the most popular one to judge by the books available in most of the larger bookstores, that the wealth of some countries is bought at the expense of the poverty of others; and that it is not wealth that is in need of explanation, but poverty. Likewise in aesthetics: beauty is bought only at the expense of ugliness, the ugliness being the natural consequence of social injustice. To side with beauty is therefore a betrayal of suffering humanity, the exploitation of whose misery was and is the precondition of the creation of beauty. It would be interesting to know how many modern educated people would react to *Le Portugal* by Yves Botinneau, with photographs by Yan, by saying, 'It couldn't all have been like that.'

No doubt it couldn't; and yet I don't think a sensitive person could fail to notice the importance of aesthetics in Portuguese life—an importance that may well have been unconscious, but none the less real for that—at the time the photos were taken. For one thing, they are not just of the odd corner of life or of towns or of cities or of landscapes: many of them, including of the townscapes, are of extensive views that stretch for miles into the distance where there is literally nothing that offends the eye to be seen, no excrescence that spoils the panorama. I haven't been to Portugal for a long time, but I very much doubt that it would be possible to take such photographs, certainly not so many of them, now. Surely there would be highways or tower blocks or something to spoil the view, that does to the eye what a stone in the shoe does to the comfort of walking.

I once had a discussion with a young student of philosophy with whom I happened one day to walk into a graceful square in an English provincial town that was (for me) entirely spoiled by a single sub-Mies van der Rohe glass building of fortunately stunted proportion, that was clearly built not in spite of being out of keeping with the classicism of the rest of the square but because of it, that is to say as an act of subversion or deliberate vandalism.

The young philosopher asked me why I could not still enjoy that part of the square that still existed; after all, the rest of the buildings were the same as ever they had been. I thought of an analogy.

'Suppose,' I said, 'you are in a restaurant and the meal is delicious. Suppose also that someone at the next table to yours suddenly vomits copiously. Would it be reasonable of me to say to you, "Why do you not continue to enjoy your meal? After all, the food on your plate and the décor in the restaurant is still exactly the same as it was before the man on the next table vomited?" An aesthetic experience is more than the sum of its individual components, and in fact the bad building in the square would not have caused me such pain if the other buildings had been equally bad. It was the contrast that made it painful.

Be this all as it might, the photos of Portugal taken in 1956 or just before showed nothing ugly, not even in the smallest detail of peasant life. For it is clear from the pictures that peasant life still existed in Portugal then. There were peasant fishermen, for example, whose large wooden fishing boats—rowed, not powered by engines—were objects of great beauty and elegance. It is unlikely that, during their construction, anyone thought specifically or consciously of elegance of shape or beauty of decoration, but nevertheless the constructors achieved them, as if they could do no other. The aesthetics were woven into the tapestry of their lives.

It was obviously a time of transition, for though the women, even in the port of Lisbon, still wore peasant costume that was distinctive according to the region from which they came, the men no longer did so. Women still carried baskets of bread under their arm and large and graceful earthenware pots of water on their heads which, whatever the inconvenience or drudgery of it, did wonders for their posture, which was dignified and upright.

But it was the architecture that most struck me. Even quite humble homes in ordinary villages were elegant in a way that no modern housing, at least for the poor, is elegant. It achieved both uniformity and distinctiveness at the same time: one looks at it and immediately says to oneself 'Portugal.' It could be nowhere else.

The grander buildings, gothic, baroque and eighteenth century classicising, testify to a magnificent aesthetic sense down the ages; the taste changed, but it retained its perfection. Everything harmonises, an eleventh century castle with an eighteenth century church; nothing offends.

The other thing that astonished me was how beautifully and immaculately cared-for everything was. Nothing was out of place, everything was clean; but this orderliness gave no impression of anal retentiveness, as Switzerland does, but rather of a genuine aesthetic concern. Of course Portugal at the time was a dictatorship, that of Salazar, a near-fascist who nevertheless kept the country neutral during the Second World War. Was the country so beautifully kept because Salazar imposed his will on it by means of his secret police, or was it a spontaneous manifestation of the people's love of what they had inherited?

Portugal at the time was deemed a very poor country (it is still the poorest in Western Europe). But when one looks at the picture of Lisbon taken from the city's river, the Tagus, one has no impression of poverty but rather of a tremendous wealth that could have been accumulated only down the ages (perhaps it does not do to enquire too closely how it was accumulated). It must have been a rare privilege, though one hardly noticed as a separate datum of experience, to live among such beauty.

Yet people turned their back on this world as soon as they were able to do so. The peasants' world, where machines scarcely existed, where large boats were still dragged onshore by teams of oxen and launched into the sea by the collective strength of scores of men, where barrels were made by hand and large quantities of wine moved by non-mechanised transport, where women had to go down to the well to fetch water, where they had to wash clothes in the communal troughs, and where everyone made his own entertainment, was very picturesque but also very hard, and not one such as I, who am physically lazy and find most tasks other than reading and writing intensely boring, would wish for myself. Lisbon may have been rich but not in the modern sense: few televisions, refrigerators, washing machines, telephones, cars, etc. and all things which have proved irresistible to mankind everywhere.

One of the questions that I have never been able to answer satisfactorily is why peasants the world over lose their aesthetic sense the moment they move from the country to the town, and become aficionados of kitsch. Those who until then had an instinctive understanding of form and colour seem to care about them no longer: I have observed this in India, Africa and South America. Indeed, they not only lose their instinctive good taste but acquire instinctive bad taste to replace it. What is the explanation for this? Is it that abundance and cheapness of acquired goods means that one no longer has to look at them with the same concentration as in conditions of relative shortage? Is it that, making almost nothing any more for oneself, one loses the appreciation of form and colour? Is it that, in the new conditions, all that belongs to the past comes to seem retrograde and associated in the mind with poverty and oppression? Is it that everything from the past—the earthenware pots, for example—come to seem almost childish by comparison with the modernity of aluminium pots and pans? Is it that life loses in intensity what it gains in extension?

There is certainly no turning the clock back: you cannot make eggs from an omelette, to reverse a well-known saying. Nor should we romanticise the lives of others by preventing them from voting with their feet and their purchases. But it would also be wrong to deny that in progress there is also loss. And *Le Portugal* by Yves Bottineau reminded me just how grievous that loss can be.

14
Morality, Hawk-Eyed and Pigeon-Toed

There were scenes of ferocious violence not far from my house yesterday. They were unexpected because I live, when I am in England, in an ancient and peaceful close around a church. Next door to me but three is a charming sixteenth century timber-framed building on whose whitewashed walls are inscribed the words 'In this house lived the learned and eloquent Richard Baxter 1640–1641.' For a number of years I misread the words 'learned and eloquent,' as 'learned and elegant,' probably because I found them more interesting and—well, elegant.

Richard Baxter (1615–1691) was a Puritan divine who published 130 books in his lifetime. His productiveness was in part the result of, or at any rate his response to, the ill-health that pursued him throughout his life, for though he lived to a good age he expected from quite early on to die shortly of his many complaints, real or imagined. The fear of imminent death spurred him on in his literary endeavours:

> A Life still near to Death did me possess
> With a deep sense of Time's great Preciousness...

And:

> The frequent sight of Death's most awful face,
> Rebuk'd my sloth, and bid me mend my pace.

As might be expected, Baxter inveighed against 'Drunkards, Swear-

ers, Fornicators, Scoffers at Godliness &c;' though, as might equally well
be expected, at least from the standpoint of three and a half centuries
later, he did so with indifferent success. I regret to say that he did not
think much of my townspeople, 'a very ignorant, dead-hearted people'
full of 'obdurateness.' I daresay he was right; little has changed, probably,
except that we might be more inclined nowadays to use the word obdu-
racy than obdurateness (which, however, still does exist).

Baxter was only a moderate Puritan: he believed that God had giv-
en Man his five senses in order that such qualities as beauty might lead
him to God, so that he was by no means as opposed to elegance as one
might easily have supposed. That he was eloquent is sure; but perhaps
in a restrained way he was elegant also, certainly in his prose. Here is a
sentence taken at random:

> No man is a wicked man that is converted; and no man that
> is a converted man that is wicked; so that to be a wicked man
> and to be an unconverted man is all one; and therefore in
> opening one, we shall open both.

Of course, it must be borne in mind that truth and elegance (or
eloquence, for that matter) are most certainly not one.

But to return to the shocking scenes of violence enacted near my
house yesterday: I am glad to say that they were not enacted by humans
but by birds, sparrowhawks to be precise. These were the birds that the
Duke of Wellington advised Queen Victoria were the solution to the
problem of sparrows caught in Crystal Palace built for the Great Exhibition of 1851, though he did not say what the sparrowhawks would have
done after the elimination of the sparrows.

These birds, small raptors themselves sometimes the prey of larger
raptors, were once endangered in Britain but have now recovered fully,
possibly thanks to greater pesticide control. Yesterday, out of the blue,
they attacked the pigeons in our church close that on fine days coo us
gently awake, and took no fewer than seven of them, leaving scattered
feathers on the grass where the unsuspecting pigeons had been peacefully doing whatever it is that pigeons do. This morning the pigeons—
other pigeons, that is—were back, cooing as if nothing had happened
yesterday. I suppose this is the avian proof of the old sayings that no one
is indispensable and that life must go on.

Almost certainly the offending raptors were females, for the female of the species is much larger than the male and only the females are

large enough to take pigeons. By all accounts even they are not powerful enough to kill a pigeon at a single strike; rather they capture their victim and it dies as they pluck its largest feathers and then tear at its flesh. This is a far cry from the kind of civilised behaviour we expect in our church close, though to do the sparrowhawks justice they airlifted their prey elsewhere to conduct the most savage part of their operation.

The attacks on the pigeons were so swift that one couple, walking in the close, did not realise what was happening. They looked up and, seeing some of the finer pigeon feathers floating in the air, mistook them for snowflakes, which they found strange because it was by no means cold enough for snow.

The strange thing was that I felt morally outraged by the behaviour of the sparrowhawks. I know that this is absurd, and I know also that I have animadverted previously on the poor behaviour of pigeons in my garden, that (or is it who?) self-importantly and greedily dominate the bird table and drive away the smaller birds to take all the seed for themselves, even though they seem to me quite fat enough already. But between self-importance and greed on the one hand, and outright murder on the other, there is quite a difference, at least in the sub-lunary world. It is the difference between sin and crime.

Now of course it will be said that the sparrowhawks have to live; they cannot be expected to understand Louis XIV's famous riposte to the petitioner who said, 'But Sire, I have to live,' namely that he, Louis XIV, did not see the necessity. Sparrowhawks are not properly the object of moral condemnation for, like Luther at the Diet of Worms, they can do no other than they do. They are obligatory carnivores; you cannot expect them to commit species suicide or turn vegetarian.

Rational as it is to view their behaviour as devoid of all moral significance whatsoever, and absurd as it would be to consider those birds as morally reprehensible, I find it almost impossible entirely to clear my mind of the irrational notion that the scene had a moral significance or meaning. If, for example, I had been able by some means or other to protect the pigeons from the unprovoked attack of the sparrowhawks upon them, I should have done so, even though saving the pigeons meant harming the sparrowhawks. It seemed to me terrible that the peaceful pigeons, bullies of my bird-table as they might be (though of course I did not know that these *particular*, that is to say *individual* pigeons, had ever visited it, and one should not infer the characteristics of an individual from his membership of a group), should have been subjected to so vicious an attack, and to so gory and painful a death.

I have experienced such visceral moral outrage, or at least revulsion, at the natural behaviour of lower creatures before. For example, on my land in France (I can hardly call it a garden) I once came across a snake that was in the process of swallowing a baby rabbit which, presumably, it had killed with its poison. I was furious. Not being a farmer, or even a gardener, I am still stuck at the Peter Rabbit stage in my attitude towards these creatures, viewed as a plague by those who must wrest their living from the land, or even with merely to grow a few vegetables. Though I am in the evening (the early evening, I hope) of my life, I still see rabbits as adorable, sweet and inoffensive furry animals, an adornment to any rural or pastoral scene; *a fortiori* are baby rabbits the objects of my affection.

Besides, I still have in my mind, ineradicably as it were, the view of life that I first learnt from Arthur Mee's *The Children's Encyclopaedia*. According to this view, Man was at the apex of a pyramid, and all forms of life below him were strictly graded in their moral worth in proportion to their nearness to him. Thus mammals were morally higher than birds, birds than reptiles, reptiles than fish, fish than insects, insects (and other arthropods such as arachnids and crustaceans) than molluscs, molluscs than coelenterates, coelenterates than protozoa. And I therefore thought, or felt, that it was wrong—morally wrong, against the moral order of the universe—that a lower creature should make a prey of a creature from a higher group than itself. In other words, reptiles should not eat birds, much less mammals; and likewise, birds should not eat mammals.

There was clearly (in my mind) a gradation of wrongdoing by animals. It was wrong for any animal to eat Man, of course, morally wrong; but—to take two recent cases—it was far worse for a python to have swallowed a boy in Indonesia than for wolves to have attacked and killed a boy walking home in Siberia. That is because pythons are much lower on the evolutionary scale than wolves which are, after all, close to dogs, sharing as they do 99.6 per cent of their DNA with dogs. And so I made the snake on my land in France disgorge its baby rabbit, though this could do the dead rabbit no good, to teach it, the snake, a lesson, a moral lesson that is. I was perfectly aware, I need hardly add, that reptiles are ineducable, that they are worse in this respect than the worst of congenitally antisocial humans; but anger or righteous indignation got the better of me.

What, then, of sparrowhawks attacking pigeons? Could I object to it on the same grounds as I objected to the snake killing and eating the baby rabbit? Here my evolutionary biology is a little hazy. Are hawks more highly evolved than pigeons? As far as I can remember, Arthur Mee's *The Children's Encyclopaedia* had nothing to say on this important question, for its evolutionary tree or pyramid was rather schematic and contained not many more types of creature than did the model Noah's Arc that I had as an even smaller child (though of course they were all mammals of the larger sort, such as giraffes and hippopotamuses, rather than, say, shrews or voles, let alone centipedes or scorpions, which would have been difficult to coax up the gangplank). In a very crude way, I suspect predators to be more highly evolved than their prey; after all, the latter must have existed first for the former to have had anything to prey upon. I realise that there is something wrong with this logic, though; predators may have evolved first to prey on creatures lower on the scale than themselves, and then switched their attention to those higher.

In fact, I think there ought to be some kind of class solidarity—I mean Linnean class solidarity, not Marxian. Birds of a feather not only do but ought to stick together, and support rather than prey upon one another. This was another lesson I learnt when I was very young, when I was taught that, towards the end of the reign of the dinosaurs on earth, little mammals evolved and lived by their wits, rather than by brute force and ignorance as did the dinosaurs, who therefore not only did die out but deserved to do so for being so stupid and pea-brained. Mammals represented progress, and of course they were also the underdogs, if I may so put it, which made them morally attractive. Thus in our lessons about dinosaurs and evolution, as a mammal I cheered the mammals on to the victory that I already knew would be theirs. Like every other little boy, I loved Tyrannosaurus and Brontosaurus and Ichthyosaurus and Stegosaurus, but I knew that their disappearance from the face of the world was ultimately for the good of the world. They died that we might live.

The pigeons died, too, that the sparrowhawks might live; and there is no denying that the sparrowhawks are handsome birds. But handsome is as handsome does; and try as I might to empty my mind of the ridiculous thought, I cannot but see the conduct of the sparrowhawks in my church close yesterday as thoroughly wicked. If that is what they are prepared to do in full daylight, in front of witnesses, what must they be like in private?

15

No Cant in Immanuel

My late friend, the development economist Peter Bauer, had the most beautiful manners: so beautiful that I took them for my model. Alas, I could never equal them for, though not particularly ill-mannered, I have always to *remember* to behave well. Just as style in prose should be imperceptible, as the uniquely perfect vehicle for *what* is said and indissoluble therefrom, so manners should be unconscious, not added to conduct but intrinsic to it. They should not arise from reflection but from a habit so deeply ingrained that, however much they might once have been instilled or learned, they are now entirely natural and normal to the person who has them. And since their purpose is to ease social intercourse and make it agreeable, they should not be carried to the point of making anyone uncomfortable, turning them into mere etiquette in order to distinguish those who know how to behave from those who do not.

Peter Bauer used to say that Mrs Thatcher had two great achievements to her name (and only two): that she destroyed the power of the trade unions and that she raised him to the peerage. It was a matter of pride to him, tinged by ironical amusement, that he, the son of a Budapest bookmaker, should now sit in the British House of Lords; but the fact that he did so confirmed one of his most deeply held convictions, that a class society was not at all the same thing as a closed society. Social hierarchy is perfectly compatible with social mobility, as the maliciously misunderstood history of his adopted country amply demonstrated.

My friend was by no means an unequivocal admirer of Mrs

Thatcher, and neither am I. He used to say that she spoke too much and did too little; and her somewhat strident tone, that was capable sometimes of cutting glass, gave even her best ideas a bad reputation, as if they had actually been put into practice when in fact they had not. Thus she set back her own cause by generations and made impossible the very reforms that she vaunted so rhetorically. I would go much further in my negative assessment of her: by naively believing in management as a science in itself, that could somehow be applied in the public sector to make it more efficient, she introduced the legalised corruption that is now so characteristic of her country, a legalised corruption that was (as the Soviets used to say) *creatively developed* by her follower and disciple, Anthony Blair, and that created the *nomenklatura* class that was and is largely responsible for the country's disastrous situation. In retrospect, Mrs Thatcher was just another political figure wrestling unsuccessfully with her country's inexorable, century-long decline and slide into submediocrity. But one should not blame her too much: no one could have done better and she was, after all, the greatest reformer in Argentinian history.

To my knowledge, Peter Bauer made only one great speech in the House of Lords, remarkable for its power and brevity. A bill had been introduced to allow the prosecution of alleged war criminals who had taken up residence in Britain after the Second World War. Bauer said (and here I quote from memory, which I realise with sorrow is highly fallible):

> My Lords, I am of Jewish extraction. Some of my relatives died in Auschwitz. I am opposed to this bill because it is against the Rule of Law.

Then he sat down. There may be greater speeches of fewer than thirty words; if so, I do not know them.

But it is of Peter Bauer's manners that I speak, not of his opinions. Once my wife and I visited him in hospital after he had had open heart surgery. He was then in his mid-eighties. He liked champagne and we took him four quarter bottles as an aid to recovery as soon as he was fit to drink them. As is often the case of someone so old immediately after heart surgery, he was a little confused, though he recognised us perfectly and said nothing foolish. When we made to go he, who was in a large armchair but still connected to a plethora of tubes, struggled to his feet. His instinct to stand up when a lady left the room was stronger than his confusion or his weakness after his operation.

I thought of Peter Bauer when recently I read (for the first time) Thomas De Quincey's long essay, *The Last Days of Immanuel Kant*. As with Mrs Thatcher, I am no unequivocal admirer of De Quincey. In the past I have awarded his most famous work, *Confessions of an English Opium Eater*, the following marks: 8 out of 10 for literary quality, 1 out of 10 for veracity, and 10 out of 10 for pernicious influence on subsequent generations. But *The Last Days* struck me as one of the greatest and most humane essays that I have ever read; never mind that it is actually a translation and composite of German sources of the great philosopher's declining years.

De Quincey addresses at the outset the question of whether Kant's decline was a suitable subject for a literary work:

> Perhaps the reader will be disposed to complain, that some of the notices [of his decline] are too minute and circumstantial, so as to be at one time undignified, and at another unfeeling.

To this he replies:

> With respect to the first objection, it may be answered, that biographical gossip of this sort, and ungentlemanly scrutiny into a man's private life, though not what a man of honour would allow himself to write, may be read without blame; and, where a great man is the subject, sometimes with advantage. As to the other objection, I should hardly know how to excuse Mr Wasianski [one of De Quincey's primary sources, and Kant's close friend] for kneeling at the bedside of his dying friend, in order to record, with the accuracy of a short-hand reporter, the last flutter of Kant's pulse, and the struggles of nature labouring in extremity, except by supposing that his idealised conception of Kant, as one belonging to all ages, seemed in his mind to transcend and swallow up the ordinary restraints of human sensibility...

The first reply is curious and ambiguous, for it implies that what should never have been written may nevertheless be read with propriety. Was De Quincey himself dishonourable for having translated what no man of honour would have written, thereby having given it wider currency? If so, I can say only that I am glad there are dishonourable men sometimes willing to do such work; but in fact it is clear to me that Mr Wasianski wrote from a profound sense of love and admiration for his friend. The result is a work not of titillation or of salacity, but of piety. One is astonished to learn, incidentally, that Kant (who died in 1804) was a celebrity in Königsberg; such was the press of people who wanted to pay their respects that he laid in state for days after his death; his funeral was the largest the city had ever known. One is tempted to say that by its celebrities shall ye know a culture.

The essay is profoundly moving and all doctors who have to deal with the old, the decaying and the dying ought to be enjoined to read it. Wasianski describes the night before he died, and it is worth quoting him *in extenso*:

> Though he had passed the day in a state of insensibility, yet in the evening he made intelligible signs that he wished to have his bed put in order; he was therefore lifted out in our arms, and the bedclothes and pillows being hastily arranged, he was carried back again. He did not sleep; and a spoonful of liquid, which was sometimes put to his lips, he usually pushed aside; but about one o'clock in the night he himself made a movement towards the spoon, from which I collected that he was thirsty; and I gave him a small quantity of wine and water sweetened; but the muscles of his mouth had not strength enough to retain it; so that, to prevent its flowing back, he raised his hand to his lips, until with a rattling sound it was swallowed.

> He seemed to wish for more; and I continued to give him more, until he said in a way that I was just able to understand, "It is enough." And these were his last words. It is enough! Sufficit! Mighty and symbolic words.

And here De Quincey adds a beautiful footnote:

> "*It is enough:*" – The cup of life, the cup of suffering, is drained. For those who watch, as did the Greek and the Roman, the deep meanings that oftentimes hide themselves (without design and without consciousness on the part of the utterer) in trivial phrases, this final utterance would have

seemed intensely symbolic.

Here I must add that I had a similar experience with my own father. He had bravely decided to refuse the operation that might have prolonged his life by six months from the cancer that was killing him. He was now very weak, so weak that he could not take off his own socks before getting into his bed. I removed them for him and helped him under the bedclothes. When there, he said the last words he ever said to me, words that I had never heard him utter before: 'I'm sorry.'

What did he mean by them? That he was sorry to be a nuisance, to be so helpless? Or was he apologising for the fact that, despite his great gifts, he brought nothing but unhappiness to those around him? Was he apologising for my unhappy childhood, in which moments of happiness illuminated the landscape of misery as a flash on lightning illuminates a night-time landscape enshrouded in darkness? I will never know.

But to return to manners. Here is the passage from *The Last Days* that reminded me of Peter Bauer. It describes a visit by Kant's doctor to the dying and now almost imbecilic man:

> Nine days before his death, the following little circumstance occurred, which affected us both, by recalling forcibly to our minds the ineradicable courtesy and goodness of Kant's nature. When the physician was announced, I went up to Kant, and said to him, "Here is Dr A-." Kant rose from his chair, and, offering his hand to the doctor, murmured something in which the word "posts" was frequently repeated, but with an air as though he wished to be helped out with the rest of the sentence. Dr A-, who thought that, by posts, he meant the stations for relays of post-horses, and therefore that his mind was wandering, replied, that all the horses were engaged, and begged him to compose himself. But Kant went on, with great effort to himself, and added, "Many posts – then much goodness – then much gratitude." All this was said with apparent incoherence, but with great warmth, and increasing self-possession.

> I meantime perfectly divined what it was that Kant, under his cloud of imbecility, wished to say, and I interpreted accordingly. "What the professor wishes to say, Dr A-, is this, that, considering the many and weighty posts which you fill

in the city and in the university, it argues great goodness on your part to give up so much of your time to him" (for Dr A- would never take any fees from Kant); "and that he has the deepest sense of this goodness." –

"Right," said Kant, earnestly – "right!" But he still continued to stand, and was nearly sinking to the ground. Upon which I remarked to the physician, that Kant, as I was well convinced, would not sit down, however much he suffered from stand-ing, until he knew that his visitors were seated. The doctor seemed to doubt this; but Kant, who heard what I said, by a prodigious effort confirmed my construction of his conduct, and spoke distinctly these words – "God forbid I should have sunk so low as to forget the offices of humanity."

My father believed that manners followed or expressed a good heart; where a good heart existed, good manners were sure to become habitual. (The trouble is that he did not himself have a dependably good heart.) My mother believed the opposite, that behaving well as a matter of habit would lead to a good heart, or at least ameliorate the effects of a bad one.

Of course good manners may disguise the utmost villainy; and an unmannerly man may be good-hearted. And yet, in the cases of Im-manuel Kant and Peter Bauer, there does seem to be a connection be-tween their general goodness and their refined manners. Besides, good manners should be valued for themselves; I am inclined to adapt de Toc-queville's famous dictum about liberty, that he who seeks in manners anything other than manners themselves is destined for crudity.

16
We Are All to Blame - Or Is It the Others?

When, many years ago, I started regularly to review books for profit and pleasure (my profit and pleasure, that is), I thought it would be fun to write destructive reviews of bad books. I was beguiled into this idea by having read Macaulay's eviscerating essay-review, which I found delightful, of a three-volume biography of Lord Burleigh:

> Compared with the labour of reading through these volumes, all other labour, the labour of thieves on the treadmill, of children in factories, of negroes in sugar plantations, is an agreeable recreation. There was, it is said, a criminal in Italy, who was suffered to make his choice between Guicciardini and the galleys. He chose the history. But the war of Pisa was too much for him. He changed his mind, and went to the oar.

(Guicciardini was a contemporary of Machiavelli and wrote a history of Italy.)

I soon revised my opinion, however, because I found that I preferred to praise rather than to bury. In part this was because reading bad books was a waste of time by comparison with reading good ones. And the thought occurred to me that the authors even of bad books had devoted a lot of their lives to them, and therefore that adverse criticism would pain them. Hence I began insensibly to accentuate the positive, at least toward the end of the review, so that the author, if he ever saw what I had written, would be left with the taste of honey rather than of wormwood and gall, without my having in any way encouraged the public to go out and buy the wretched book. Only if I thought a book was bad (and bad in an important way) because of outright dishonesty did I write anything destructive. Once, for example, I read a short work by a famous man who claimed to have written it in three days, no doubt to impress us with the fecundity of his genius. The book was very bad and I said that I was surprised that it took him that long. He replied with the fury of the self-important eminent who regard criticism of others in much the same way as summer holidaymakers in the north of Scotland regard the attention of the midges, that is to say very, very annoying but not dangerous.

I make these remarks prefatory to my reflections on a book I read recently, *Give Me Everything You Have: On Being Stalked*, by James Lasdun. This book is an account of the e-mail persecution of the author by a student of creative writing whom he had briefly taught, who fell in love with him and then turned against him when it became clear to her that he was not going to transform her fantasy into reality.

Lasdun lives in Upstate New York, but grew up in England. In the course of his book, which is quite short and easily read at a single sitting, there is a moving account of his relationship with his father, moving because it is full of sincere and unforced filial piety—a quality much to be treasured at a time when it is taken almost as the *sine qua non* of sensitivity that offspring should reprehend their parents.

Lasdun's father was clearly a powerful figure, so powerful in fact that Lasdun junior, on his own admission, still has difficulty in making aesthetic judgments of his own, at least where the visual arts are concerned, a sphere on which his father had very strong opinions indeed.

Lasdun's father, Denys Lasdun, was a famous architect in his day: perhaps the most famous in Britain. He was also, in my opinion, one of the worst; indeed, I doubt whether a worse, or at any rate a much worse, has ever lived (to design uglier buildings than his would be a stimulant to the imagination worthy of a prize competition). That he had a strong and sensitive aesthetic sense makes his actual productions all the worse and to me all the more incomprehensible. He was enamoured of concrete as a material and his designs were as dehumanising as any dictator's decree. And yet his son's evident respect and love for him suggests a man of many qualities. When good men do bad things—and dehumanising cities with hideous concrete buildings is bad—one suspects a generalised or epidemic spiritual sickness, in the loose meaning of the term. Architects of Denys Lasdun's times mistook destruction for creation.

Architects are not entitled to the same indulgence as the writers of bad books because bad books are easily avoided, consigned undisturbed to the remoter shelves of libraries, whereas bad buildings obtrude on passers-by and create an obligation on future ages, either to maintain or to replace them. Bad buildings are to the eye what passively-breathed smoke is to the lungs of the non-smoker: something noxious and unwanted but inescapable. An author has a right to his badness, but not an architect.

It is true, of course, that there is no universal agreement about Denys Lasdun's buildings: but I suspect that those who claim to like them are applying extra-aesthetic considerations (such as that they were at the cutting edge in the way that Lister was at the cutting edge of the surgery of his time) and indulge also in an architectural variant of Macbeth's logic: that past architectural crimes are so heinous that one has to continue them or admit them.

Nor does Denys Lasdun's probity, testified to movingly by his son, improve matters, rather the reverse. The son says that his father was not motivated either by the desire for fame or money, rather by the desire for the perfection of the work, and that his father's example had given him as a kind of artistic conscience in his own chosen field of literature. But a man who can build the worst and most inhuman of buildings with purity of heart appals me more than one who does so for mere lucre: for while the desire for the latter is comprehensible to us all (which of us, after all, has never been tempted?), the former builds from a pure and undiluted failure of taste, ability and understanding. And since architecture is an inherently social art, requiring clients or patrons for its transformation from concept to actual building, its failure is a social or at least a collective failure. An author, by contrast, can write a bad book by his own unaided efforts.

Be this all as it may, I still find James Lasdun's filial piety (an ancient but now uncommon virtue) exemplary, and wish only that I could feel and express it myself. *Alas, I cannot.*

His memoir of being persecuted by e-mail is well worth the reading because it illustrates a modern vice as well as an ancient virtue, or at least a modern way of putting a vice into action: persecution by e-mail and internet being the dark side, or a dark side, of the so-called information age. By the end of the book one trembles: for what happened to James Lasdun could *easily* happen to any of us. Each of us is but the press of the send button away from vicious denunciation, character assassination and the destruction of our reputation. This applies almost as much to private individuals as to public figures, and it is perhaps surprising that it is not more frequent than it appears to be. Perhaps it is just that even an evil requires time to gain momentum.

Lasdun's persecutor not only altered his Wikipedia entry, but wrote calumnies about him on Amazon and other sites (admittedly a hazard faced only by those who put themselves before the public in some way). These calumnies could be and were removed in time, but e-mails to his employers accusing him of things that were both inherently unlikely and difficult to disprove were far more serious, and could have been done to anyone. Lasdun stood accused of the kind of 'crimes' which always besmirch in the modern world—racism, sexism, harassment etc.—and which he himself had previously believed ought to be extirpated by administrative regulation. He found that proving a negative, even within the confines of his own mind, was not easy.

None of us is totally immune to the idea that there is no smoke without fire and unless we assume that the world is full of people of motiveless malignity (to quote Coleridge's inapt characterisation of Iago, for Iago has one of the most common, pervasive and long-enduring motives in the whole of the human repertoire), we are inclined to believe that every denunciation or calumny must contain a grain of truth—to mix slightly the smoke and fire metaphor. Yes, there must be a grain of truth in all that smoke.

Indeed, Lasdun himself almost believed it himself, of the very calumnies that have made his life a misery for three or more years. He calls himself a man of impeccably liberal views—is it only liberals who think of their own views as impeccable?—and as such wondered to what extent his persecutor's (perhaps a neologism, persecutrix would be in order in this context) complaints against him might be justified. In fact, there is not a shadow of justification, or even plausible reason, for them if his account of his own conduct is true: they are obviously the product of a wilfully unbalanced mind, a mind that has delighted to unbalance itself. It is strange how the author's certainties about some things, namely the impeccable nature of his equally unquestionable liberal views, lead to a strange lack of confidence about his own rightness in the face of outrageous persecution.

I once suffered to a very minor degree the kind of persecution that Lasdun suffered. I had written an article displeasing to an active pressure group and soon found myself not only inundated by offensive messages but the object of efforts to have me fired from the institutions in which I worked. This persecution lasted only a few days, not years like Lasdun's, but it was very unpleasant while it lasted and I will neither mention the subject here nor return to it another time, for fear of stirring up the hornets' nest again. (Yet another metaphor, I am afraid: between smoke, fire, grains of truth and hornets' nests, it seems that we live in a hazardous world). This is not very courageous of me, no doubt, but I do not care enough about the subject to endure any suffering because of my opinions about it—which, I have to confess, might not be impeccable in the sense of being indisputably true. And unlike the persecution of Lasdun, the persecution of me was at least rational: it was obviously directed at getting me never to repeat my views in public, and it worked. I have not been persecuted since.

Perhaps the most alarming thing about Lasdun's account is his complete impotence in the face of his persecutor. The police agree that she is in breach of the law, but not to a sufficient degree to make it worthwhile to prosecute her. (Here one is inclined to ask, Worthwhile for whom? He who fails to prosecute the Dane never gets rid of the need for someone to pay the Danegeld.) No doubt Lasdun could resort to the civil rather than the criminal law, but like most citizens he has insufficient means to do so and the result in practice would probably be nil in any case. He is, in a word, defenceless, at least without resorting himself to criminal means. One feels a rising sense of outrage on his behalf as the story proceeds, and also increasing anxiety.

The question that a memoir such as this cannot possibly answer (and this is not criticism of it) is whether persecution of the kind suffered by the author is on the rise. Inclined as I am to pessimism, I suspect that it is; for as the reactions to the death of Mrs Thatcher showed, people now seem not to feel the need to control their anger in the name of decorum and decency. Indeed, I suspect that you could ask a hundred people in the street how they valued decorum, and a goodly percentage of them would not know what it is and would not value it if they did. And where there is no decorum, no holding back, why should persecution of individuals not rise when the means to persecute are so readily available?

17
Of Owls and Richard the Third: Part 1

Not long ago at a conference I was asked whether I thought that boredom was an important cause of bad, and worse than bad, behaviour. I said that I thought that it probably was, though I could not positively prove it. At any rate, those who behave badly often claim to do so because they are bored, and no one claims to behave well because he is bored.

But even if it is accepted that boredom causes, or rather explains, bad behaviour, it cannot be the final explanation: for why are people bored? Is not the world interesting enough for them? What would a world be like that they found sufficiently interesting to keep them on the straight and narrow path that leads to good behaviour? It is a terrible fate for a creature endowed with consciousness and self-consciousness to find the world uninteresting.

My problem is the opposite: I find the world too interesting. This means that I am all too easily distracted, like a child confronted with too many good things to eat. I pursue things that interest me until something else distracts me, which means that I master nothing. But at least I am not bored.

I happened the other day to walk past a charity shop (called thrift shops in America) in whose window were displayed two books, one about owls and the other a biography of Richard III. Both owls and Richard III have played a small part in my life, and I went into the shop and bought them. Together they cost less than a packet of cigarettes, the smoking of which is disproportionately encountered among the bored community—we must now call all people who share a characteristic a community.

I shall deal with my relationship with Richard III in another article; suffice it to say that I became more than normally interested in him as a result of buying the book. Here I shall deal with my relationship with owls.

Owls, I confess, play a only very small part in my life. In the little town in which I live when I am in England there is a woman who is always accompanied on her shopping expeditions by a pet owl. No one finds this astonishing or, if they do, lets their astonishment be known; this is either from a laudable desire not to intrude upon the owner or not to gratify her desire for notice. And in France a pair of tawny owls to-whit to-whoo every summer night in a tree a hundred yards or so (to judge by the sound of it) from the house. I never tire of listening them; I also never see them, and so their lives are a closed book to me. They therefore reassure me that there is mystery still in the world; for a world without mystery, in which everything were revealed and known, would be a terrible place. Knowledge is wonderful, the more of it the better, but omniscience would be a nightmare.

The first owl of my life was Owl in Winnie the Pooh. I think he had a delayed effect upon my intellectual development, or perhaps I should say upon my Weltanschauung. Owl held himself to be intellectually the superior of every other character in Pooh: in fact he was the intellectual among them, and took himself very seriously, as the embodiment of knowledge and wisdom. But he wasn't very good at spelling (he signed himself WOL) nor were his thoughts always of the most brilliant. He put a notice up outside his home in a tree asking visitors to 'PLEZ CNOKE IF AN RNSR IS NOT REQID.' Of course, I delighted as a child in the absurdity of this: why would anyone go to his door if he did not want an answer (notwithstanding the fact that I sometimes rang doorbells myself and ran away).

So Owl gave me the first intimation in my life that all are not wise who claim to be learned. And Owl was a hint also that the clever could be the most foolish of all.

But why did owls symbolise wisdom in the first place? The splendid photos in my book, succinctly titled *Owls*, suggested a reason: owls seem to have only two states, the serene calmness of sleep and the most intense alertness when awake. Try as we might not to anthropomorphise, owls look serious; they indulge in no foolish or redundant movement. This is nonsense, of course: owls are bird-brained. And one of the things that I learnt from this book, delightful to me because completely useless, is that the Owl of Minerva does not necessarily spread her wings at dusk: nearly forty per cent of the 133 extant species of owls are diurnal, not nocturnal. I bet you didn't know *that*.

Reading Owls brought back my second encounter with these birds. It was with their pellets rather than with the birds themselves. I had quite forgotten that these pellets are not faeculant but rather the product of regurgitation because owls have no crops. As I learnt from this book, owls have relatively low acidity stomachs, and tend to swallow their prey whole. They are bad at digesting bones, hair and the chitin of insects, so they dispose of them by regurgitation.

I remember (vaguely) sifting through owl pellets on a nature-study weekend when I was about fifteen. The purpose of this was to learn the diet of owls. Owls taught me (alas, nearly half a century later) how important this analysis was, for it indicated not only how owls lived but—interestingly—proved the law of unintended consequences.

Cape barn owls were introduced on to islands in the Seychelles in an attempt to control the rodents there that were destroying crops: for in their own environment, Cape barn owls feed copiously on such rodents. At about the same time of their introduction into the Seychelles, however, the indigenous and unique avian fauna of the islands began to die off. This was thought initially to be because of illegal hunting and trapping by local people; but the analysis of Cape barn owl pellets soon showed that it was the owls, not the local people, who were responsible. The owls had been introduced to reduce the rodents, but they reduced the birds instead; this was because the unsuspecting birds were the easier prey. Not only humans, but owls take the path of least resistance.

The law of unintended consequences is one of the hardest for people to learn because it is so unflattering to our conception of ourselves as rational beings, and because (if it is a law) it suggests inherent limits to our power. We shall never fail to commit errors.

Some of the hidden historical information in *Owls* was to me fascinating. Ornithologists have long studied the numbers of birds which fluctuate markedly as conditions vary. Obviously predators depend greatly upon their prey; and the numbers of their prey (in the case of owls, predominantly rodents and other small mammals) depends on the state of vegetation, which goes through regular cycles. I had not quite realised just how accurate Pharaoh's dream was, a dream that applies (allegorically) to nature as to the business cycle:

Behold, there come seven years of great plenty
throughout all the land of Egypt:
and there shall arise after them seven years of famine;
and all the plenty shall be forgotten in the land of Egypt;
and the famine shall consume the land;
and the plenty shall not be known in the land by reason
of that famine following; for it shall be very grievous.

The cycle in nature may be shorter than seven years, but the description in the Bible is not an exaggeration. Lemming populations explode in good years, as do the populations of owls that prey upon them; but then the collapse comes, just as it does when traders think the bull market will never end, and the lemmings and owls are decimated by famine.

The historical information that truly astonished me in *Owls* was that studies of bird populations in Europe by ornithologists continued even throughout the First and Second World Wars. We learn, for example, which years were good and which bad for barn owls during the German occupation of the Netherlands, even as the population was close to starvation. The authors do not point out how strange this is, but I found it very moving. Others, of course, might find it disconcerting that people could seriously concern themselves with such matters even in the midst of the cataclysm surrounding them; but to me the power of mental abstraction from the surrounding cataclysm was a proof of the human spirit. In its quiet way, the continuation of the study of bird populations was as heroic as outright resistance.

One method by which ornithologists of the past estimated fluctuations in the numbers of owls was by the numbers brought to taxidermists for stuffing. The fashion for stuffed birds in glass cases seems to have passed and so this method is no longer used; but I am glad to have learnt another such (to me) completely useless fact.

Reading *Owls* destroyed one of my fantasies: that it would be good to live as an owl (provided, of course, that one had human consciousness to go with it). I had assumed that owls had no enemies, that they sat on their trees and contemplated life when not actually hunting, living as at the peak of a pyramid; that theirs was an easy life. How wrong I was! Owls have less than a one in four chance of surviving to their first birthday (though the oldest owl recorded was 68 years old). They often starve to death. And just because owls may be grouped in the same classificatory families does not mean that they have family solidarity; indeed the larger owls often prey on the smaller. If Swift had read *Owls* he might have written:

> So nat'ralists observe, an owl
> Hath smaller owls that on him fuel;
> And these have smaller owls to bite 'em.
> And so proceeds Ad infinitum.

I also learnt in *Owls* about the superiority of the Swedish social security system to the British. The Swedes noticed that the population of eagle owls had declined in their country. Owls are relatively easy to breed in captivity, and the Swedes did so. More difficult, however, is the successful release of owls bred in captivity into the wild; having got used to being fed, they fall into a state of dependency.

The Swedes, with their typical intelligent pragmatism, devised a system of rehabilitation for their home-bred owls. They put their owls in open cages into the field. The owls would fly out; to begin with would return to the cage to be fed but as they learnt to find food for themselves they would return less and less until they did not return at all. Their high rate of attrition was no higher than that of birds bred in the wild. The Swedes used social security for owls as a means to restoring them to independence.

If the Swedish ornithologists had been British, however, they would never have let the owls into the wild but kept them in their cages and gone on feeding them. They would have wanted to keep the owls dependent for ever, not for the owls' sake, but for fear of making themselves redundant and losing their jobs.

There is thus a lot to be learnt from a book about owls, and I was pleased to see from the back cover of my copy that the book had sold more than 50,000 copies since first published in 1970. My copy was dated 1995, which means that it had sold 2000 copies a year for a quarter of a century (there were thirteen printings, evenly spaced, in that time); interest in owls, while it continues no doubt to be a minority one, is perpetual, and that those who have it are not likely to be bored.

There was another aspect of the book that pleased me. The authors were John Sparks and Tony Soper. There was no biographical information in the book about them whatsoever. This meant one of two things: either the authors and publisher thought the subject was more interesting or important than the authors, or they were so famous that readers needed no biographical information. Looking them up on the internet, I found that this might have been so, for they made nature documentaries for BBC television for many years. Not having had a television since this book was first published, people who are nationally, internationally or even world famous are to me completely unknown.

But even if there were no biographical information about the authors given in the book for the second rather than the first reason, I was reassured. For it seems to me that theirs must have been a justified fame rather than a meretricious celebrity. They were people of real accomplishment, real learning. There must have been a time when even television fame was the reward of merit.

18
Of Owls and Richard the Third: Part II

By far the most important English King for me during my childhood was Richard III; or, more accurately, Shakespeare's Richard III; or, more accurately still, Laurence Olivier playing Shakespeare's Richard III. The film captivated me when I was about 10, and I have subsequently found the malignity of evil always more fascinating, emotionally and intellectually, than the beneficence of good. Fictional or dramatic heroes have been to me ever since but pale and uninteresting shadows of villains. Heroes, in fact, tend to bore me as villains seldom do. And this is thanks to Richard III, in the special sense above.

When, therefore, I saw a biography of Richard III (*Richard III: England's Black Legend* by Desmond Seward) in the window of a charity shop near my home, together with a book about owls, I bought it. Not only did I buy it but I read it, and was somewhat surprised that, in effect, it endorsed the Shakespearian view of Richard's character. Published on the 500th anniversary of Richard's accession to or usurpation of the throne, Richard emerges as very much the unscrupulous, hypocritical, treacherous monster depicted in the play.

I believe this is no longer the orthodox view of him. The accusers are now the dissenters. And a friend of mine, who grew up in the Soviet Union and lived there until he was twenty-five, dislikes Shakespeare's play because of its crude and seemingly propagandistic encomium to Henry VII, of the type to which his upbringing in the great motherland of ubiquitous and compulsory lies had made him allergic. Henry VII himself in truth was no mean slayer of his enemies, at least the equal of

Richard III at his worst, but he was the grandfather of Queen Elizabeth, reigning monarch when Shakespeare wrote. Queen Elizabeth's title to the throne depended upon Henry VII's, and *his* depended on the right of conquest rather than on any plausible claim by royal descent. That conquest could itself be justified only if Richard III were a bloody and tyrannical usurper of a quite unparalleled type; so that my friend sees the whole play as an elaborate apologia for a current political regime.

The irony here, of course, is that the objection to the play is itself highly political. The sycophantic message at its end—assuming that it was not justified by the historical facts, and that Henry VII did not 'Enrich the time to come with smooth-fac'd peace,/ With smiling plenty and fair prosperous days!'—could hardly efface, neutralise or outweigh the poetic, dramatic and psychological brilliance of what had gone before. And it should be remembered that Shakespeare's depiction of Queen Elizabeth's father in *Henry VIII* is by no means flattering: though of course he was a mere continuator of the dynasty, not its founder, so the question of his character was perhaps less a sensitive matter despite his reign having been more recent.

There is probably no finer portrayal of the intelligent, charming, plausible, unctuous, ruthless psychopath in literature than that of Richard:

> What do I fear? myself? There's none else by:
> Richard loves Richard; that is, I am I.

At first we are told by Richard that his wickedness derives from his physical condition of hunchback:

> I that am curtail'd of this fair proportion,
> Cheated of feature by dissembling nature,
> Deform'd, unfinish'd, sent before my time
> Into this breathing word, scarce half made up,
> And that so lamely and unfashionable,
> That dogs bark at me as I halt by them;
> Why, I, in this weak piping time of peace,
> Have no delight to pass away the time,
> Unless to spy my shadow in the sun,
> And descant on mine own deformity.
> And therefore, since I cannot prove a lover,
> To entertain these fair well-spoken days,

I am determined to prove a villain…

By making him a cripple, then, fate has precluded Richard from enjoying the normal comforts and pleasures of human existence. We believe what he says because it is plausible. And yet, in the very next scene, Richard seduces Anne, widow of Edward, Henry VI's son whom Richard has himself killed, and in the presence of the corpse of Henry VI, whom Richard has also killed. Later in the play he persuades Queen Elizabeth, widow of Edward IV, whose brother he has executed and whose two sons (the Princes in the Tower) he has had killed, to act as go-between in his proposed marriage to her daughter. The notion that his deformity precluded him from being a lover and therefore pointed him in the direction of villainy is clearly false, a rationalisation and a deception.

Strangely enough, those who have tried to rehabilitate Richard have tended to deny that he was crippled. It was as if they accepted the causative link between deformity and evil character. Of course they would deny this: they would say rather that they were only trying to show that the monarch's supposed deformity was just another example of the falsehoods told about him. But here I think they are not being quite truthful with themselves. They want their Richard not only to be undeformed, but handsome.

When his skeleton was found recently buried in a car park in Leicester, the town to which his body had been carried (whether ignominiously or not is still a matter of dispute) after the Battle of Bosworth Field, it was obvious that he had a marked scoliosis rather than a kyphosis. The scoliosis was severe enough to have given him a noticeable deformity—one of his shoulders was reported in contemporary documents to have been higher than the other—but not severe enough to have made him 'the bottled spider, the bunch-backed toad' of Shakespeare's play. So were his detractors or his defenders right?

There is a kind of apostolic succession among those who have sought to restore his reputation. The first was Sir George Buck, whose history of the king's reign was published in 1646, 24 years after the author's death; then came Horace Walpole, whose *Historic Doubts on the Reign and Life of King Richard III* was published in 1768; then Sir Clements Markham's history, published in 1906; and finally Josephine Tey's popular novel, *The Daughter of Time*, published in 1951, in which her fictional detective, Alan Grant, laid up in hospital after an injury, attempts to reason out who murdered the Princes in the Tower and comes to the conclusion that it was Henry VII. (Thanks to my purchase in the charity shop I have now read all these books, and others besides). I think it fair to say that the majority of work published since Tey's novel has been on the side of rehabilitation.

What can be set against this formidable array of rehabilitation? Sir Thomas More wrote what has been described as the first masterpiece of English prose about Richard—his *History of King Richard the Third*—which more or less relays the story Shakespeare told. But in a book entitled *Richard III and his early Historians 1483 – 1535*, published in 1975, the mediaeval historian, Alison Hanham, suggests that More did not intend his work to be taken literally and that it was in fact satire, at least in part.

After More there was Shakespeare, of course, who used Holinshed's rehash of More. And the fact is that the influence of one Shakespeare is greater than that of a thousand scholars. In so far as most people know anything about Richard III, they know it from Shakespeare.

There have been attempts to steer a middle course between the two schools, but on the whole they have not been successful. James Gairdner, a nineteenth century archivist whose biography of Richard went through three editions, and the value of whose work, according to the entry in the latest edition of the *Dictionary of National Biography*, was vitiated by his conservatism, granted Richard many good qualities but still made him guilty of at least some of the crimes imputed to him. It was as if Gairdner thought that in any dispute over facts there must be truth on both sides.

After the king's skeleton was discovered, a computerised reconstruction of his face was produced by an academic department of physical anthropology. I don't know enough about the reliability of this method to say whether the face produced was really that of Richard III; but a spokeswoman for the Richard the Third Society, a band of learned and dedicated people valiantly working to rehabilitate the king's reputation, was immediately recorded as saying that the face was that of a sensitive and good man. A man with a face like that, was the implication, could not have ordered the murder of his own nephews in the Tower. This suggests that murder is written on the face; as someone who has had more to do with murderers than average, I can say that this is often the case but not always. And there is murder written on many people's faces who have never committed murder.

Again, there is a dispute over what character a contemporary portrait of Richard III—the famous one in which he is putting on or taking off a ring from his little finger—suggests. In Josephine Tey's novel there is a discussion between the characters about this, and none of them agrees. For me, it is an intelligent but not kindly face; rather obviously cruel and cynical. But I concede that that is not evidence. In my heart I want Shakespeare to be right.

The crucial question about Richard III, it seems to me, is whether he did indeed order the murder of the Princes in the Tower. If he did, he was the ruthless and unscrupulous power-seeker of popular legend; if he did not, then he has been traduced. I am not sure why, after so long a lapse, it should be so important to set the record straight about him. Clearly he is powerfully symbolic of something, because there is (as far as I am aware) no King John, King Stephen or King James II Society to set the record straight about these hated or derided monarchs.

I hesitate to be hesitant, but the evidence about the Princes in the Tower points both ways. It is of course possible that they died of natural causes and were not murdered at all: it would not have been unusual in that era for two children to die in quick succession of an infectious and communicable disease. But there is no evidence in favour of this hypothesis (or against it, for that matter).

But it is more likely that they were done away with. They were taken to the Tower while Richard was Protector (more or less Regent); they were never seen again. And the fact is that when children disappear from view and are not seen again, they are usually killed close to the time they disappeared, not several years later. And Richard clearly had an interest in having them out of the way.

When he was made Protector, he accepted that Edward IV's son was heir to the throne, to reign as Edward V. But just before the coronation, the Bishop of Bath suddenly came forward with the convenient story (convenient to Richard's ambition, that is) that he had married Edward IV to Lady Eleanor Butler, and that therefore Edward's supposed marriage to the mother of the princes was bigamous and invalid, making the Princes bastards and therefore not eligible as heirs to the throne. Richard was next in line, and it was upon the bastardy of the Princes that his claim rested.

The story of bigamy all seems suspiciously convenient to me, and rests upon the word of a man of very doubtful probity; it is not likely that everyone would accept it, and many would continue to see Edward V as the real king—which they could not if he were dead. Moreover, there were contemporary rumours, for what they are worth, that Richard had had the Princes killed.

On the other hand there is no evidence that would convict Richard in a court. Curiously, on Henry VII's accession and for years afterwards the new monarch made no reference to the murder of the Princes as one of the justifications for overthrowing Richard, as surely would have been logical if the Princes had in fact been murdered by him. Now if Richard were a usurper, and Edward V were still alive at the time of the Battle of Bosworth Field, Henry VII would not be king: Edward V would be. Therefore Henry VII would have had an interest in killing the princes if they were still alive when he seized the throne. This is the case made out by Sir Clements Markham who, incidentally, was a remarkable polymath: a writer of books about Peru, the translator of Garcilaso de la Vega Inca, founder of the world rubber industry by arranging the smuggling of rubber seeds to Asia from the Amazon Basin, promoter of Polar exploration, as well as historian of Richard III.

Though the evidence about the murder of the Princes is decisive in neither direction, almost nobody fails to take up a strong position on Richard's guilt or innocence. It is as though the figure of Richard awakens every man's inner Manichaean: either he is a parfit gentil knight or a monster of depravity. We take up a position according to our inclination. Those who defend him supply him with all the virtues: he was a wise legislator, a brave warrior, a loyal brother, an uxorious husband, a fond father, modest and beloved of the people. How his detractors portray him requires no elaboration. They hold to their positions with a strength disproportionate to the evidence.

It is only right that Shakespeare should have the last word, however, because he said almost everything that can be thought. His Richard was the first Nietzschean:

Conscience is but a word that cowards use,
Devis'd at first to keep the strong in awe;
Our strong arms be our conscience, swords our law!

19
Grave Questions

Is a taste for graveyards and cemeteries morbid? If so, I have been morbid for most of my life, since about the age of twelve when I first developed it. For me, cemeteries are like bookshops: I cannot pass them without entering, though I usually leave the latter with a purchase and the former only with my thoughts and emotions.

The Victorians, at least in Britain, knew how to make a good cemetery: many a British town's best feature is its municipal burial ground that they laid down. I am old enough to remember the time when everything Victorian was despised or mocked, and it is true that after the 1840s most of their furniture was abominable, the suet pudding of interior decoration; but in fact the Victorians were far from the clumsy philistines in all respects that we took them for because we wanted to liberate ourselves from their supposed hypocrisy and moralising (to develop hypocrisy and moralising of our own).

Victorian cemeteries usually have a granite Gothic chapel or two, lichen and moss having lent them a patina of age and dignity. The Victorians' confidence that their works would survive them is shown by the trees that they planted: yews, cypresses and oaks, which are now venerable and grateful to the eye. Victorian tombstones and memorials were varied but dignified, expressions of personal choice but yet in keeping with one another and rarely making a purely egotistical gesture (and when they do so, it is a good one). The inscriptions are dignified and appear to me sincere. The Victorians understood the aesthetic value of asymmetry and did not bury their dead in military ranks as we do now, perhaps for lack of space, as if we were all privates in the army of death, all of us provided by our families with almost identical tombstones made of the kind of shiny stone used on the surfaces of kitchen islands or the walls of public lavatories in five-star hotels. No, whether by accident or design, the Victorians used materials that would age gracefully and placed their graves with an orderly randomness and spontaneity that is, emotionally and aesthetically, incomparably superior to our own unimaginative arrangements.

A good cemetery is a consolation for our own mortality.

The inscriptions on the tombs are interesting as social and demographic history. Widows and widowers of the first person buried in the grave fall, it seems to me, into two groups: those who survived the deceased by only a short time, and those who survived him or her, usually him, by many years, never to remarry. One loses oneself in reverie: did those who died soon after the death of their spouse die of a broken heart, and did those who died long after spend the rest of their lives bitterly regretting or rejoicing to be free of him?

In all such cemeteries one finds tombstones that record the deaths of many young children, often those of the same parents. Infant mortality was so high, and the causes so ill-understood, that resignation before it was psychologically necessary; Dickens even made something of a joke of it at the beginning of *Great Expectations*, being powerless to do anything else about it.

As the infant mortality rate fell, so the death of a child came to seem correspondingly more tragic as an individual event, a violation rather than a normal manifestation of the nature of things. While in Victorian times there was no special area in the cemetery for children, in later times a kind of children's corner was established. And there I have noticed a sudden change in sensibility, in about 1990, a change that I do not much care for.

Before that date (which of course is approximate rather than definite) tombstones of children were restrained and dignified. After that date, they became vulgar and sentimental, with emotionally cheap and slushy inscriptions. Moreover, the tombs of the children were now often surrounded by toys, cakes, dolls, clothes, plastic windmills, football shirts, cards covered in cellophane and so forth, that have usually rotted by neglect in our less than clement climate. It was as if people were no longer content to grieve privately, but had to manifest their emotion to all and sundry, as if they could feel nothing unless others could see by the ornaments of a child's grave that they were grieving. Others see me feel, therefore I feel. One could even detect a form of competition between the grieving parents, to see which of them could festoon the graves with the most extravagant decorations as if this would prove that their grief was the deepest, their loss the most deeply felt. In other words, they were not just experiencing an emotion, they were experiencing themselves experiencing an emotion, deriving a pleasurable self-righteousness from it: the very soul of kitsch.

In the beautiful cemetery of a town called Yeovil—pronounced Yo-ville, but that my satellite-navigation system, not altogether without justification, pronounced You-evil—I noticed the contrast of this kitsch with more genuine emotion. A very young child died and was buried in the cemetery 1964 and I noticed two years ago that the parents (I assumed it was they) had placed a single fresh flower in a vase by the little tombstone that gave nothing but the child's name and the dates of its all too short existence on earth. I was much moved that these parents were still grieving—in a private, undemonstrative and dignified fashion—47 years later. How young and fresh and full of hope they must have been when their child was born, and now they must have been in their early seventies! Of course they had got on with their lives in the meantime, but a grief must always have been just below the surface of their daily existence and I suspect that the child who died was their only child. At any rate, I happened to go to the cemetery two years later and found another fresh flower in the vase at the grave. A grief borne for 49 years, and I imagine nobly borne.

The contrast of the single flower in the vase with the sound of the plastic windmills turning in the wind and the sight of the dirty, sodden and neglected teddy bears on the more recent graves of children could hardly have been more striking. It was as if two vastly different civilisations had met in the same place; one that valued dignity and depth, and the other shallowness and a meretricious show of emotion.

Another cemetery that I came to like was that of Llanelli in South Wales. Llanelli has always had a rather poor reputation from the purely aesthetic point of view, not surprisingly perhaps in view of its principal economic activities of the past two centuries, mining and steel-making, which do not make for beauty; but nowadays the mines and the steelworks are shut and the main industry is the administration of economic decline. It is a sad and forlorn place, but I came to like the people. They started conversations at bus-stops and when they learned I was a doctor asked my medical advice which I gave them cautiously so as not to contradict their own medical advisers. More than once I met an old coal miner, a widower in his late seventies, at the bus-stop from which both he and I took the bus into town. It is highly probable that his political ideas were very different from mine, but one feels an instinctive respect for a man who has spent his life down the pits (they closed for good just as he reached retirement age). He went every day at lunchtime down to the centre of the town, and every day he was dressed immaculately. His starched snow-white shirt was dazzling; he wore a striped tie and a smart blazer; the crease of his trouser legs was sharp and his black shoes were polished. Not for him the deliberately torn jeans of spoilt youth trying, from pseudo-sympathy with the unfortunate, to look poor; he did one good to look upon, for his smartness of dress was a triumph of the human spirit. It was not vanity, it was self-respect, and one could go a hundred miles without (alas) finding its like.

I used while I was in Llanelli to go to the cemetery on fine days and there lie on the grass between the tombstones with a book, usually poetry (a feeble gesture in the direction of Romanticism), and almost invariably fall asleep under the sun. One day I woke up from my brief nap and to my surprise saw a woman in her fifties nearby dressed in the Punjabi Moslem costume of the salwar kameez. I was doubly surprised, first because hardly anybody, apart from me, seemed to visit the cemetery, and second because the last person I should have expected to see among the tombstones was a Punjabi woman. She was carrying a bunch of flowers.

She asked me, in English that she had obviously learned too late in life to master throughly, whether I knew where the grave of Margaret Davies was. Margaret Davies is not exactly a distinctive name in Wales and besides I had not committed to memory the whereabouts of hundreds or thousands of graves. But I said I would help her try to find it.

As we searched I asked her why she wanted to find it. She said that she had come to Llanelli from Pakistan as a young woman, and had lived next door to Margaret Davies. Margaret Davies had been very good to her and had become her friend. Then she, the Punjabi woman whose name I never learned, moved away. She had come back on a visit and learned that in the meantime Margaret Davies had died and was buried in this cemetery; she wanted to leave flowers on her grave as a token of gratitude and remembrance.

I was much moved by this story, the story of two ordinary people (for such I assumed they were) using their common humanity to overcome potentially bewildering and frightening difference. It must, after all, have been almost as difficult for Margaret Davies to be suddenly confronted by a Punjabi neighbour as for the Punjabi neighbour to have been suddenly translocated from the Pakistani Punjab to Llanelli.

When one hears a story like this, one is immediately prey to a certain kind of sentimentality. Why cannot everyone be like this? Why can't we all just get on together, allowing what unites us to be more important than what divides us? Why is there not universal and perpetual peace rather than widespread conflict? Surely, left to their own devices, and uninflamed by ideologues and political entrepreneurs, people would just find a *modus vivendi*? In East Africa, I had spent three months living in the home of a Punjabi Pakistani family without the faintest hint of conflict over anything. Perhaps there was a subject or two we avoided, but there always are subjects that are best avoided when people live in close association.

To the questions above I do not think any definitive answer can be given. Unfortunately men—and it is usually men—are often seized by the idea that they know the one way to live, that is to say the answers to all the difficult problems of human existence that are consequent upon the possession of consciousness. I know this in part from the inside: I have in my life sometimes been seized by it myself. I always feel ashamed, and miserable, after I have had an attack of dogmatism, especially as I have so many times resolved never to have another.

What is possible, though by no means guaranteed, between individuals, however, often turns out to be impossible or at any rate much more difficult between groups. Perhaps the good Margaret Davies would have felt very differently if her entire street had been suddenly inhabited and taken over by large numbers of Pakistani Punjabis. Then she would have moved away and quite probably have felt embittered at the loss of the world she had known. Be all that as it may, Llanelli will remain forever associated in my mind with its cemetery, and with Margaret Davies and the Pakistani Punjabi lady who wanted to put flowers on her grave.

There was another little incident that engraved itself upon my mind in Llanelli. My wife and I used to go to an Indian, or rather Bangladeshi, restaurant there, largely *faute de mieux*. It was not well-patronised, and often we fell into conversation with a young waiter there of Bangladeshi descent (the lives of waiters have long fascinated me). He spoke with a Welsh accent, and we asked him whether he had ever been abroad and if so where to.

'I went to Bangladesh once,' he said.
'Anywhere else?' I asked.

'Yes,' he said. 'I've been to England.'

That's real integration for you: a Llanelli man, born and bred, who thinks of England as a foreign country. For a brief moment I almost felt optimistic.

20
Non-Linear B

S uch was the state of historical knowledge, or perhaps I should say ignorance, of my young patients that I was most favourably impressed whenever a young man deduced by his own unaided efforts that there must have been a First World War because there had been a Second.

However, everyone's knowledge is always finite, while everyone's ignorance is always infinite: so the comparatively learned have little cause to look down their noses on the unlearned because of their ignorance, which after all is only equal to their own. Indeed, in so far as one of the objects of learning is the attainment of wisdom as well as mere knowledge for its own sake, pride in learning is especially vulgar and reprehensible. The learned above all people should appreciate the eternal appropriateness of modesty.

Therefore I do not blush to record that I once made a deduction very similar to that of my patients who concluded from the fact that there had been a Second World War that there had been a first: namely that, if there had been a Linear B script of Minoan writing there must have been a Linear A. Of neither did I know anything.

Nevertheless, the phrase 'Linear B' that has always resonated in my mind in a way that the phrase 'Linear A' has not. Is it merely that the former is more euphonious than the latter? Or could it be a faint echo from my very early childhood, not so much a memory as a shadow of a memory, when Linear B was first deciphered and the man who did it enjoyed, or rather did not enjoy, sudden fame and prominence? Could it be that, when I was 3 years old, everyone talked about it and that it left some very faint residue in my mind?

The decipherment of Linear B was a tremendous intellectual achievement of the kind completely beyond my powers, or the powers of an almost incomparably enormous proportion of mankind. Linear B was a form of writing found on tablets at Knossos in Crete in the early part of the last century by the distinguished archaeologist Sir Arthur Evans. The writing consisted of 89 characters, spindly in form, some of which clearly resembled ideograms. They were of pre-Homeric date; what sound the characters represented, what language whose written form they were, was completely unknown. There was no Rosetta stone to assist in the decipherment of the writing; it resembled somewhat writing discovered in Cyprus, and later some very similar inscriptions were found in Greece, but otherwise there was no clue.

The man who deciphered Linear B was called Michael Ventris. The brilliance of his achievement, a combination of dogged persistence, great learning and well-informed leaps of the imagination, was recognised at once: the BBC, for example, asked him to give a talk on the radio as soon as he had deciphered Linear B (which certainly would not happen nowadays).

Ventris' story is a most interesting and indeed moving one, of triumph and tragedy intimately comingled. Personally, for reasons that I cannot fully explain, I find such stories greatly more affecting than those of men who move from triumph to triumph and who, after initial success, are the precise opposite of Lot's wife and never look back.

Ventris was born into a family in which privilege and tragedy, convention and rebellion, were in constant tension, a tension which proved in his case to be a highly creative one, though also with an ultimately tragic outcome.

Ventris's father was an army man, as was his grandfather; but his father never reached the rank (general) of his own father. Already, in that fact, one senses deep if unexpressed misery and disappointment: perhaps it is easier to be the successful son of a failed father than the successful son of a more successful father.

In any case, Ventris's father suffered from tuberculosis and went with his wife to live in Switzerland where Ventris was brought up for the first part of his life. Born in 1922, he was a brilliant linguist both by natural endowment and circumstance, and learnt French, German and Swiss German; his mother was Polish, the daughter of wealthy landowners, and Ventris learnt Polish from her. Later in his life he added languages to his repertoire as others buy appliances. He was able to correspond with Swedish academics in their own language and to write to Russian emigrés in Russian. He received a classical education at a relatively unconventional school called Stowe.

His mother moved in artistic circles, and Ventris grew up with Picassos on the walls of his home. From this he developed a taste for modernism which influenced (balefully, in my opinion) his choice of career. Of reserved and modest demeanour, even as a child, his appearance became that of an extremely refined man. Physiognomy is an inexact science, no doubt, but no one who saw him could have doubted his high intelligence and intellectual ability.

Tragedy, though, irrupted into what might otherwise have been a gilded youth. His father died of his disease in 1938, when Ventris was 16; two years later his mother committed suicide by overdose of barbiturates, depressed by the war, the destruction of her country and the loss of income from her family estates.

Ventris joined the RAF and became a navigator for bombers. This, of course, was extremely dangerous work; the death rate in Bomber Command was very high. After the war he worked in Germany as an interpreter, but he soon resumed the architectural studies that he had started on leaving school. His mathematical and logical mind led him to think of architecture in principally intellectual or abstract terms, although he was also driven by an ideologically puritan loathing of decoration, which was deeply conventional at the time though not recognised as such (it can take a number of years, even decades, for ideas that take themselves to be revolutionary to be recognised as conventional). I have seen only one of his buildings, the house that he built for himself and his family, and the fact is that Venturis was a bad architect. Intellectual brilliance is not an advantage in arts when not allied to other qualities; if Ventris had been born in another age, with other conventions, he might well have been a very good architect.

He first became interested in the problem of Linear B at the age of 14, when he heard a public lecture by Sir Arthur Evans who had discovered it. After the lecture, Ventris asked him, 'Did you say the tablets haven't been deciphered, Sir?' He was gripped for the rest of his life and worked at the problem intermittently but with great concentration, doggedness and determination. His first paper on the subject was printed when he was only 18 years old, in the premier American archaeological journal of the time.

At first Ventris thought, and hoped, that Linear B might be a form of Etruscan, a non-Indo-European language about which little was known. He hoped this was so partly because it would be one in the eye for the theory, then prevalent in much of Europe, that all that was valuable in culture was of 'Aryan' origin. The temptation to think that everything good or valuable in the world must emanate from people related in some way or other to oneself is very tempting; it might be interesting for a scholar one day to trace the history of this persistent and pernicious temptation in all its myriad or hydra-headed forms, whether religious, cultural, political, economic or artistic.

But Ventris was a man who could overthrow his own ideas, a virtuous characteristic that is by no means common. By a series of brilliant deductions and leaps of the imagination he was able to show incontrovertibly that the language of Linear B was a form of early Greek. Of course, just because something is incontrovertible does not mean that it will not be controverted; there was some fierce rearguard opposition to him by people who, perhaps, were infuriated that a mere amateur had succeeded where they, the professionals, had failed.

World renown came to Ventris very suddenly: in those days celebrity was less independent of achievement than it is now. But Ventris was not interested in fame or fortune and his end was tragic. Only four years after his great achievement, aged 34, he was killed in a motor accident. In the middle of the night, on a journey whose purpose was unknown, he drove at full speed into a truck parked at the side of a road and was killed instantly.

A man of emotional detachment—such detachment might seem a wise precaution if you lose your parents early and are sent to war with a high chance either of being killed yourself or seeing everyone around you killed—Ventris was somewhat estranged, or at any rate distant, from his wife and children. (Tragedy continued to haunt the family: his son Nikki died of a heart attack aged only forty.) He had solved the problem that he had set out to solve half his then lifetime before; Linear B inscriptions turned out not to be very interesting from the literary point of view. He had alighted on no similar project upon which to engage his great intellect, and his prospects as an architect were limited.

There has been speculation as to whether or not he committed suicide, whether his death was truly an accident. The driver of the truck insisted that his lights were illuminated and that there was no reason, therefore, why Ventris should not have seen it clearly. This does not settle the matter; accidents occur by inattention as well as by circumstances such as invisibility.

I think that Ventris did commit suicide. His mother did so and suicide runs in families. Two weeks before he died he wrote a letter to the editor of the *Architects' Journal* which is clearly that of a very depressed man. The owner of the Journal, the Architectural Association, had earlier awarded Ventris a fellowship which he still held, and Ventris wrote:

> I have had a couple of weeks abroad, and had a chance to get into perspective the hash that I've been making of your Fellowship; I've come to the conclusion that it's quite unrealistic for me to pretend to you or to myself that I'm going to be able to finish off the work in the way that it should be done… you'd be justified in writing me off in a way that will make it difficult to hold up my head in the ranks of architects again, and bring pain to my family. All I can ask you is to temper your justified anger with a little compassion.

I have rarely read so painfully melancholic a letter (it is quoted in an excellent book on Ventris by Andrew Robinson, with the title *The Man Who Deciphered Linear B*). Also quoted is another painful letter, written by Ventris' son, Nikki, only two days before he died himself:

> My father was a private person and shared few of his concerns with us. In fact he seemed rather remote and very absorbed in his work to the exclusion of family life. This is not to say that he was incapable of enjoying himself: on occasion he took his part in family outings and games with obvious pleasure and we were pleased to have his company… I did not know my father at all well, and it was only at and after his death that I realized how much I had missed in not getting to know him better.

The son was only 13 when his father was killed or killed himself. One cannot help by think of Philip Larkin's verse:

> Man hands on misery to man.
> It deepens like a coastal shelf.
> Get out as early as you can,
> And don't have any kids yourself.

But a beautiful epitaph on the life of Michael Ventris by a French archaeologist, Professor Dumézil, counters this radical despair. *Devant les siècles son oeuvre est faite*: Down the centuries his work is done.

There is no simple measure or yardstick of a life, or of life itself.

21
Destiny of Crime

Those who mark books, I have noticed, tend to do so more heavily at their beginning than at their end. It is as if their attention wandered or they grew bored as they progressed; perhaps they do not even reach the last page.

My copy of a book with the title *Crime as Destiny*, published in English in 1931, is a good example. Its laudatory foreword was written by the great geneticist (and also Marxist), J B S Haldane. An unnamed previous owner has underlined in ink so much of this foreword that you might have supposed that he was trying to commit it to memory; it is not easy otherwise to guess why he should have underlined so obvious a thought as that 'often a man who recognises his weaknesses arranges his life so as to avoid situations which he knows he cannot face.' Could this really have come as a revelation to anyone, so much so that he deemed it worthy of emphasis?

The book was by Prof. Dr. Johannes Lange, Physician-in-Chief to the Munich-Schwabing Hospital and Departmental Director of the German Experimental Station for Psychiatry at the Kaiser Wilhelm Institute. It was translated by Haldane's then wife, Charlotte, who was a feminist and socialist who subsequently became disillusioned with the Soviet Union when she was sent there in 1941 by the *Daily Herald* (the British trade union daily newspaper) as a war correspondent.

Johannes Lange was a psychiatrist, a pupil of Emil Kraepelin, the founder of modern psychiatric nosology; he died five years after the Nazi takeover of power and as far as I am aware had no political problems during that time. His career continued to flourish under Nazism.

Perhaps this was not altogether surprising, given the general drift of *Crime as Destiny*. Lange is mentioned twice in Paul Weindling's *Health, Race and German Politics between National Reunification and Nazism 1870 – 1945*, an exhaustive account of the German medical profession's intellectual propensity to compulsory euthanasia as a solution to social and psychiatric problems, real or imagined. Lange was a member of a government sterilization committee that met to consider the sterilization of psychiatric patients before Hitler's arrival in power.

Crime as Destiny attempts to show that criminality is predominantly hereditary or genetic in nature. The author compared the rates of concordance for criminality of monozygotic (identical) and dizygotic (not-identical) twins: that is to say, the percentage of pairs in which, if one had a criminal record, the other had a criminal record also. The comparison is interesting because it is supposed to tease out what is caused by heredity and what by environment.

Monozygotic twins are genetically identical, whereas dizygotic twins are no more alike genetically than any other pair of siblings. It is therefore assumed that if, having been born at the same time into the same environment, dizygotic twins differ in rates of concordance of any given feature from the rates of concordance of monozygotic twins, the difference in those rates must be accounted for by heredity and not by environment. In this case, Lange found that 10 of 13 pairs of identical twins were concordant for criminal records whereas only 2 of 17 pairs of non-identical twins were concordant. Crime is destiny (or is it that Destiny is Crime?).

I will not go into the many reasons why Lange's conclusion that criminality is determined genetically was hasty and unproven at many levels of analysis; interestingly, the geneticist Haldane does not notice them in his foreword, which he concludes as follows:

> If we desire that the fight against evil should be more successful in the future than it has been in the past, our first duty is to find out [the] causes…. No one in our generation has done more to dispel [the] darkness than Professor Lange.

It is likely also that Haldane's wife endorsed Lange's work, for she ends her own prefatory note:

> The plain facts stated… could not be improved upon by any

translator.

Early in his book Lange says something that is very startling, bearing in mind that his book was published four years before the Nazi accession to power:

> We take the most comprehensive precautions to safeguard society, we sterilise thousands of criminals, and on the other hand we claim for a number of others protection on the ground of low powers of self-control which make them a danger to society, while we cannot know at all clearly who should be sterilised and who should be protected.

In his conclusion, Lange recalls one of his pair of identical twins, the Lauterbachs, both of them high-grade swindlers who, independently of one another, started companies to raise money for bogus inventions, and managed to inveigle large sums from investors. Lange says:

> One might perhaps let them go [from prison] provided one could write their records on their foreheads for everyone to read, and if one could make it impossible for them to propagate their kind.

Lange seems to take it for granted that the son of a swindling Lauterbach will himself be a swindling Lauterbach; it is hardly surprising, then, that 'we sterilise thousands of criminals.'

(Interestingly, the famous psychologist, H J Eysenck, who was born in Germany in 1916 but left in 1934 in protest against the Nazis, wrote a book published in 1964, revised and republished in 1977, entitled *Crime and Personality*, in which he maintained, like Johannes Lange, that criminality was predominantly hereditary in nature. Eysenck quoted Lange *in extenso*, most uncritically, and said of him that he was 'the first to attack this whole problem [the heritability of criminality] in a truly scientific manner.' Not surprisingly, the blurb of the 1977 edition of Eysenck's book says:

> Professor Eysenck's emphasis [is] on the importance of heredity... He sees punishment as an irrelevant concept; instead we should try to eliminate criminal behaviour by whatever means psychological and experiment suggests.

(Such as sterilization, no doubt.)

The urge to sterilize the socially expensive or inconvenient on the grounds that they reproduce themselves is often treated as though it were a German nationalist or extreme right-wing aberration, but it is not. Eugenics was introduced into the world by the polymathic genius, Sir Francis Galton; it was quickly taken up (and acted upon) in the United States. I quote from a textbook published by Macmillan in 1918, and republished in 1924, called *Applied Eugenics*, by Paul Popenoe and Roswell Hill Johnson:

> The inmates of prisons, penitentiaries, reformatories, and similar places of detention numbered 111,609 in 1910; this does not include 25,000 juvenile delinquents… it is worth noting that the number of offenders who are feeble-minded is probably not less than one-fourth or one-third. If the number of inebriates be could be added, it would greatly increase the total; and inebriacy or chronic alcoholism is generally recognized now as indicating in a majority of cases either feeble-mindedness or some other defect of the nervous system.

> The number of criminals who are in some way neurotically tainted is placed by some psychologists at 50% or more of the total prison population… The estimate has frequently been made that the United States would be much better off eugenically if it were deprived of the future racial contributions of at least 10% of its citizens… When a criminal of this [feeble-minded] type is found, the duty of society is unquestionably to protect itself by cutting off that line of descent…

And the authors go on to list the states that have sterilization laws.

Nor is it true that eugenics as a means of dealing with social problems was particularly attractive to the authoritarian right (if statist nationalism is on the right): it was equally attractive to the authoritarian left. The intellectual progenitors of the British welfare state, Beatrice and Sydney Webb, H G Wells and Bernard Shaw were strongly in favour of eugenics, both positive and negative. And by now it is well-known that Scandinavian welfare democracies continued with their eugenic programmes into the 1970s.

Oddly enough it was G K Chesterton who was the most far-sighted of opponents of eugenics. In 1922 he published a book, mostly written before the First World War, entitled *Eugenics and Other Evils*. It begins:

> The wisest thing in the world is to cry out before you are hurt. It is no good to cry out after you are hurt. People talk about the impatience of the populace; but sound historians know that most tyrannies have been possible because men moved too late. It is often necessary to resist a tyranny before it exists. It is no answer to say, with a distant optimism, that the scheme is only in the air. A blow from a hatchet can only be parried while it is in the air.

He foresaw the horrors that eugenics might bring.

Not everything about Chesterton's book is admirable, however. It contains a certain amount of casual anti-Semitism, though mild by what was soon to come elsewhere. And I think that Chesterton misunderstood the psychology behind eugenics, to which he devoted the second half of his book (the first half he devoted to proving to his own satisfaction that eugenics was based upon fundamental, and obvious, intellectual error).

Chesterton thought that eugenics was the response of a plutocratic capitalist class to an understanding, whether a conscious one or not, that it derived its wealth from the exploitation of the labour of the poor, and that it was the beneficiary of an economic system that accorded no place whatever in the unequal scheme of things to a considerable part of the population (this, after all, is what kept wages low). Under feudalism, said Chesterton, the lord and the peasant were highly unequal, but the peasant nevertheless enjoyed minimal customary rights over the parcel of land that he was allotted, from which the lord could not evict him even though he was the lord. By contrast, continued Chesterton, those at the bottom of the scale in a plutocratic capitalist state had no rights or protections at all; the homeless in such a state, for example, had neither a right to a home nor to wander homelessly about the country in search of somewhere to rest their heads. They likewise had a right neither to a subsistence nor to ask (that is to say, to beg) others for a subsistence. The only pleasure left to them in such a society was sex and its consequent reproduction; and the plutocratic class was worried that, by means of rapid and uncontrolled reproduction, the very lowest social class would increase in size relative to all the others and thereby threaten the social order, that is to say its own security. For reasons of its own survival, therefore, it came to believe that biological inferiority inhered in the lowest social class and that this inferiority was genetic in nature; therefore it was politic to prevent it from reproducing. Eugenics was the means by which this would be achieved.

There are several problems with this theory. The first is that it takes the homeless demographically fecund tramp as representative of the lowest social class. But in reality such tramps were not very common, nor was it true that the standard of living of the lowest social class was constantly falling below that of the peasant in feudal society; the protections enjoyed by the lowest social class at the time Chesterton wrote were different from those of the feudal peasant, and were no doubt insufficient for a decent life, but they were real nonetheless.

Second, it was clear to at least some of those whom Chesterton calls plutocrats that the immiseration of the general population was not necessarily in their own economic interests, if for no other reason than that a totally impoverished population would not have the wherewithal to buy the increasingly sophisticated range of products made by the plutocrats' companies. A plutocrat like Henry Ford, for example, depended on a population rich enough to buy his mass-produced products. It is in the economic interests of plutocrats that everyone should be impoverished only if an economy is a zero-sum game; the appreciation it is not such a game, and that cheapness of labour is not the royal road to economic success, while by no means universal, was actually quite widespread. Employers wanted to keep wages down in their enterprises not to immiserate workers, but to ensure that their products were cheap enough for others to buy at a profit to themselves. They did not want a majority of the world's population to be as poor as possible.

Third, socialists were at least as keen on eugenics as plutocrats, and in fact their enthusiasm for it lasted much longer.

Eugenics, I suspect, was in reality a symptom of a growing impatience of intellectuals with the intractability of the human condition, with the fact that that Man was irredeemably imperfect. And this impatience grew because of a decline in the religious understanding of life (it was no coincidence that Chesterton, who saw so easily through the pretensions of eugenics, should have been firmly Christian, while none of his opponents was). In the 1920s sterilization of the unfit would do for humanity what psychopharmacology is now supposed to do: render it happy because perfect. No one with an understanding of Original Sin could believe such a thing – even if Original Sin is not based upon an actual historical truth.

22
Butterfly Minds

When I was a boy of about 9 or 10 the BBC used to broadcast to schools (I haven't the faintest idea whether it still does). We had to sit still in rows and listen to the broadcasts, all of which I have forgotten except one. It was about dinosaurs.

The BBC had arranged for one of its correspondents to report from the dinosaur age, as from a present-day civil war in Lebanon. It was gripping. The correspondent was in the middle of a Cretaceous forest and was watching the giant herbivores such as Brontosaurus graze as the Pterodactyls glided overhead when all of a sudden, crashing on to the scene through the tree-ferns a hundred feet tall, came that perennial favourite of all schoolboys: Tyrannosaurus rex. The correspondent, for obvious reasons, had to abandon his pastoral description of the herbivores and run for his life. Whether he escaped from the terrible beast was left open; the last we heard was that he was fleeing breathlessly in his attempt not to be torn apart and eaten.

But the sub-text of the broadcast, as a literary theorist would no doubt put it nowadays, was that the dinosaurs were doomed. They might be able to catch and eat the odd BBC correspondent, but their days were numbered. The future belonged to mammals such as we. The correspondent had described how he had seen these clever little creatures, so much more alert than the pea-brained, cold-blooded (and therefore slow-thinking) saurians, preying upon the eggs of the brutes. If size were what counted, the dinosaurs would have won hands, or at least pachyderm, down; but intelligence was more valuable and successful in the long run than brute force. It was, on reflection, a subtle way of inculcating a lesson, even if it was not strictly accurate from the palaeontological standpoint. (In those days, I think, the theory that the dinosaurs died out because a collision with a giant asteroid had altered the climate not necessarily to the advantage of the dinosaurs, as the Emperor Hirohito would have put it, had not yet been put forward, or if put forward generally accepted.)

We were promised, the following week, a report from the land of the mammoth and the sabre-toothed tiger, though I do not remember whether the correspondent was to be resuscitated like Sherlock Holmes after the events at the Reichenbach Falls.

The dinosaur broadcast was well-timed, for I was then going through the dinosaur stage that all boys seem to go through (few girls share the fascination, for reasons which a brain scanner will no doubt one day reveal, at least to the satisfaction of neuroscientists). This is interesting, because of course dinosaurs were really only discovered or made popular in the 1840s and first entered imaginative literature in the opening pages of Bleak House. Has human boyhood, then, changed since 1840, or was there an equivalent stage before dinosaurs?

At any rate, I found it oddly comforting to observe a nephew of mine, at about the same age as I at the time of the broadcast, going through his dinosaur stage. I remember him playing on the floor with his model Tyrannosaurus when he should have been doing his homework which was (if I remember rightly) learning the five pillars of Islam, which he refused to do—though I think it right to point out that he would have shown an equal resistance to learning the three components of the Trinity. From a very early stage in his young life he had displayed a strong aversion to learning anything that was enjoined or forced by others to learn; he would learn only what happened to interest him. We old wiseacres predicted a grim future for him, since we were of opinion that no one could succeed unless he was prepared or able to learn what he did not feel inclined to learn, but we were wrong; when finally the boy was allowed to pursue the course of life he had mapped out for himself, and no longer forced into the procrustean bed of academic training, he was a great success and never looked back, his adolescent combativeness ceasing at once. Well, one lives and learns: not that I would erect an invariant educational theory around this experience—or any other, for that matter.

Now my main regret about my dinosaur stage is that it did not last longer, go deeper and leave a richer residue of knowledge. I was thinking this as I went looking for fossils on the land around my house in France. Really I am very ignorant of palaeontology: when it comes to the Ammonites and the Trilobites I am a little like Disraeli's wife, who could never remember which came first, the Greeks or the Romans. I think the Trilobites came first—I conceive of them either as the wood lice of their time (though, of course, they were marine, and I vaguely remember putting wood lice into water to see how long they would survive in that medium, ostensibly to see whether they were indeed like Trilobites, but really to inflict suffering), or as a defeated tribe in the Holy Land, as in 'And the Ammonites rose up and smote the Trilobites.'

When it comes to nature, it is not that I have lacunae in my knowledge, but rather knowledge (and very little of it) in my grand Lacuna.

It is too late now to fill the grand Lacuna. Alas, the awareness that one does not have an infinitude of time before one comes too late in most people's lives to repair the damage done by laziness, insouciance, and the thousand other natural vices that flesh is heir to. I know that there are some people of whom this is not true, who have lived constructively from their earliest childhood (just as there are some people who have always used their money wisely, never having frittered a penny, and who as a consequence can face their old age without financial anxiety): but they are not many, and I am not sure a world composed only of such people would be a better one.

Still, I wish I had pursued nature study (as it was then called) with more concentration, application and determination than I did. Then perhaps I would be able to answer questions with ease such as the following, that came to me quite unbidden recently: where do the butterflies that flutter all day around the lavender bushes outside my window go at night? They disappear some time before sundown as if in response to an order. Do butterflies sleep? Do they have enough mental activity for their rest to be called sleep? Do they go to their rest as individuals or collectively, and if collectively do they roost according to their various species? How do they avoid night predation? Surely lepidopterists must know the habits of the creatures they catch and collect: they are not just, well, butterfly-collectors, who merely hope for a full set issued by Nature as philatelists hope for full sets as issued by the Post Offices of countries long ago and far away (lepidopterists of my acquaintance are obsessional). How would one go about discovering the nocturnal habits of butterflies, or would one have to rely on chance observation? Could one follow butterflies to their lairs at close of day?

These questions, not very profound and perfectly obvious, occurred to me after I had observed these creatures with delight for several years. The butterflies of Europe are not very numerous as to species (by comparison with the tropical world), nor are they dramatic in size or colour, but they are, if I may so put it, tasteful. The largest and flashiest of them, the swallowtails, are creamy coloured with black markings, and their red and blue spots are restrained: there is no iridescence in the butterflies of Europe. Most of the butterflies are pure white, white with black markings, black with white stripes, or yellow. There are a several rust-coloured types, again with black markings, that make me think of Gerard Manley Hopkins' poem (that I was taught at school two or three years after the dinosaur broadcast, an epoch in a child's development):

> Glory be to God for dappled things –
> For skies of couple-colour as a brinded cow...

The only blue butterfly is tiny, not more than half an inch in wing-span, the blue of its wings matt and pale, the underside 'all in stipple upon trout that swims,' to quote Hopkins again; a very shy butterfly this (we anthropomorphise even insects, and I even feel a little sorry for a drab and undistinguished wood-brown butterfly, so much less pretty than the others), that folds its wings modestly as soon as it lands and never stays for very long, as if it felt it had no real right to stay among its bigger brethren, of whom it cannot be afraid because they have no means of attack.

In fact there is something ungraspable about the beauty of butterflies; their season is short, but more importantly even the tardiest of them do not stay longer in one place than a heart-stopping phrase of Mozart or Schubert, that would allow us to examine and—we suppose—fully to absorb their beauty, digest it and make it part of ourselves as we digest meat and potatoes. Of course one can take photographs (infinitely better than pinning them, etherised and dead, to a board), but the living qualities of butterflies, their peaceful flitting from flower to flower, their floating on the air, their rhythmic opening and closing of their wings in a breathing movement, is a large part of their beauty for us. We love them on the wing, but in the very moment of our appreciation there is decay, and thus melancholy. Everything is transient and fleeting; the wish that joy could last for ever is impossible of fulfilment. Another of Hopkins' poems begins:

> Margaret, are you grieving

Over Goldengrove unleaving?

And ends:

> It is the blight man was born for,
> It is Margaret that you mourn for.

Why, when I had spent many hours happily (though idly, from the point of view of cost-benefit analysis) looking at the butterflies on my lavender bushes, did the question of where they went after dark never occur to me before? It is not that I had not noticed that they disappeared within a short space of time more or less together, like unionised workers walking off the job when a strike is called.

The reason is that I simply took the way things were for granted, without thinking why they were as they were. Of course we have to do this for most of our lives: we cannot be paralysed by curiosity. And yet the opposite extreme, the habit of taking everything for granted, never wondering about anything, is one of the worst fates that can befall a man (if taking everything for granted can be called a fate rather than a decision). To walk in a world devoid of mystery is to embark on a voyage that is as tedious as it will appear long.

It seemed to me, from talking to many of my patients, that that was the kind of journey upon which they were embarked. They had been relieved of the requirement to take an interest in their surroundings that the often painful necessity to wrest a subsistence from them conferred, for their subsistence was assured; on the other hand, they had not been encouraged to develop or had not attained the mental attitudes to find the world of inexhaustible interest. The result was a kind of ontological boredom: they were bored with being, with existence itself. To this boredom there were two possible responses (other than to revise their attitude to the world, of course): the first was a listlessness, conducive to the grossest overeating and chronic hypnosis by television, and the second was an attempt to overcome boredom by the introduction of drama, no matter how destructive, into life, which was thereby turned into a soap opera. Better pain and misery than waking anaesthesia.

Pasteur said that fortune favoured the mind prepared; but minds, except perhaps for very rare exceptions, do not prepare themselves but have to be prepared. Do we do our best? Do we even try?

23
Gossamer Wings

There are moods and times of day when one wants to read something intelligent but undemanding, and for this purpose there is nothing better than the literary essays and biographies of Sir Edmund Gosse. Once regarded as a colossus of literature, or at least of literary criticism and scholarship, he is now almost forgotten except for his memoir of his relationship with his father, *Father and Son*, which is indeed one of the most touching evocations of a highly unusual childhood known to me.

In a mood recently to read intelligently yet without undue effort, I picked up one of Gosse's many books of essays, *Critical Kit-Kats* (a Kit-Kat, Gosse informs us in his preface, is a 'modest form of portraiture, which emphasises the head, yet does not quite exclude the hand of the sitter'). And indeed, the essays in the book are modest portraits of various writers, in which sketches of the life are interspersed with critical judgments of their achievements.

The first of the essays is about Elizabeth Barrett Browning, and in particular her *Sonnets from the Portuguese*. In this essay, Gosse made himself party to the fraud carried out by his friend Thomas J. Wise, whose career the first line of the *Dictionary of National Biography* summarises as having been that of a 'book-collector, bibliographer, editor, and forger.' Wise made a speciality of producing spurious first editions, privately-printed in very small numbers to raise their desirability and hence their price among bibliomaniacs, using his renown as a bibliographer to authenticate them. His most successful forgery was a supposed early and privately-printed edition of the *Sonnets from the Portuguese*, which ironically would now command a very high price indeed. (There is no doubt, alas, that the two words 'and forger' in the *DNB*'s description of him add immeasurably to his interest as a man. Who would not rather read about a book-collector, bibliographer, editor, *and forger* than about a mere book-collector, bibliographer, and editor? One begins to see that the sociologist, Durkheim, was not entirely wrong in believing what at first seems to be counter-intuitive, namely that societies need criminals, who do indeed serve an important social function. Whether we need quite as many criminals as we actually have is, of course, another matter entirely.)

Anyway, in his essay about Elizabeth Barrett Browning, Gosse relays a false story about the origin of the supposed early private printing of the sonnets, which was actually produced by Wise about forty years after the date inscribed on the title page. Gosse calls it 'a very pretty episode of literary history,' though in fact it is more like an amusing episode in the history of fraud. Gosse says that Elizabeth's husband, Robert Browning, told a friend the story that he, Gosse, is about to relay to the world for the first time, with the injunction that it should not be published before his, Robert's, death. The friend to whom Browning vouchsafed the story was almost certainly none other than Thomas J. Wise, who was not a friend of Browning at all but rather a very slight acquaintance of his. Even this degree of intimacy was the result of Wise's pushiness rather than any desire on Browning's part for contact with him; but by the time Wise told Gosse the story, there was no one still alive who could contradict him. The editor of Wise's letters to John Henry Wrann, the Chicago businessman to whom Wise sold most of his forgeries at very high prices, believes that Gosse was Wise's accomplice rather than his dupe; but this is most unlikely. Gosse, I think, would simply not have thought it possible that Wise, a learned and respectable man of business, was lying to him or making use of him.

Be this as it may, when Gosse turns from spurious biographical detail to literary criticism, he begins, somewhat ironically in the circumstances, by saying:

> Sincerity, indeed, is the first gift in literature, and perhaps the most uncommon.

By one of those strange associations of ideas that to me is delightful (I cannot speak for other people) I was taken back more than quarter of a century to a conversation I had in Guatemala, around which I was driving at the time in a white pick-up truck. I gave a lift to an American hitch-hiker who told me that he had just been visiting an artist friend of his in Guatemala whose work, he said, was great because it was so sincere.

In those days I was somewhat more combative in conversation than I am now, and to illustrate the point that while sincerity might be a necessary condition of great art it was certainly not a sufficient condition, I replied (or in words to this effect), 'There are many sincere artists, but there is only one Mozart.'

The proper part of sincerity in life, and perhaps in art, is a complex one; hard and fast rules are easy to come by but difficult to justify. Certain kinds of brutes believe that sincerity is always saying what they truly think; but if this is sincerity, then clearly it is not always a desirable quality (at least if the contents of my thoughts are anything to go by). When we disguise from someone a truth that can only be painful and not at all useful to him, we may sincerely wish him well, but still our words are not sincere; while to tell him that truth on the grounds that sincerity is a virtue is merely a manifestation of sadism.

I suppose by insincerity, then, we mean the quality of saying or doing something that corresponds at no level of analysis to one's true beliefs, feelings or desires. But then the problem arises as to what are a person's *true* beliefs, feelings or desires. Not only may people (including, dare I say it, ourselves) harbour contradictory beliefs, feelings and desires, but there is no decisive test as to what constitutes *true* or *real* in this context. If you say that you want to give up smoking and I point out that you never make the slightest effort in that direction, you can perfectly well retort, 'Yes, but I still want to.' Actual conduct is not an infallible guide to inner states of mind—one might add *Thank goodness*, for if it were such an infallible guide human intercourse would lose all possible interest and mystery.

If the sincerity of others and even of ourselves in the ordinary business of life is not easy to assess or to prove, then, *a fortiori*, it is even more difficult to assess the sincerity of art. And yet we do so regularly, relying largely on our instinct to do so. Who, for example, could believe that Jeff Koons is sincere in anything except a desire for fame and fortune? We should suspect those themselves of insincerity who claimed to believe him to be sincere. (The very verbiage of so much art criticism causes us to suspect that it is writing by frauds of frauds for frauds.)

In his essay Gosse makes the point clearly that while sincerity is the first quality in literature, it is certainly not the last:

> It is not granted to more than a few to express in precise and direct language their most powerful emotional experiences.

He continues:

> The attempt to render passion by artistic speech is commonly void of success to a pathetic degree. Those who have desired, enjoyed, and suffered to the very edge of human capacity, put the musical instrument to their lips to try and tell us what they felt, and the result is all discord and falsetto.

Sincerity, then, is no guarantee of accomplishment; nor is failure a sign of insincerity, for with true humanity Gosse insists that:

> There is no question that many of the coldest and most affected verses, such as we are apt to scorn for their tasteless weakness, must hide underneath the white ash of their linguistic poverty a core of red hot passion.

This is so not only in poetry, but in all fields of artistic and even of intellectual endeavour, particularly of a philosophical nature. Many of us must have been blinded by what we considered or hoped was an original insight, only to discover later that someone had thought precisely the same in 395 BC or AD 17. Our belief in our own originality, then, which was sincere at the time, turns out to have been a manifestation of our ignorance of all that has been said and thought before us, and the cause of initial exhilaration more properly a cause of lamentation and regret.

There is nothing of the sneer in what Gosse writes, however; rather of humane understanding. And this is only appropriate, because his own volumes of verses, *On Viol and Flute, Firdani in Exile, and other Poems, King Erik* and *In Russet and Silver*, are now as forgotten as any in the language. When he praises the work of others, though, I think there is no mistaking (as likewise there is no proving) his sincerity. Of EBB's sonnets he says:

> Many of the thoughts that enrich mankind and many of the purest flowers of the imagination had their roots, if the se-

crets of experience were made known, in actions, in desires, which could not bear the light of day... But this cycle of admirable sonnets, one of the acknowledged glories of our literature, is built patiently and unquestionable on the union in stainless harmony of two of the most distinguished spirits which our century has produced.

In the subsequent essay in *Critical Kit-Kats* Gosse praises Keats in a similarly sincere way. The essay is actually a speech he made in 1894 at the dedication of a monument to Keats donated by American admirers of the poet.

[His reputation] rests upon no privilege of birth, no "stake in the country," as we say; it is fostered by no alliance of powerful friends, or wide circle of influences; no one living today has seen Keats, or preserves his memory for any private purpose. In all but verse his name was, as he said, "writ in water." He is identified with no progression of ideas, no religious, or political, or social propaganda... We honour, in the lad who passed so long unobserved..., a poet, and nothing but a poet, but one of the very greatest poets that the modern world has seen... Shall I say what will startle you if I confess that I sometimes fancy that we lost in the author of the five great odes the most masterful capacity for poetic expression which the world has ever seen?

This is fulsome but not ridiculous in view the now obvious greatness of Keats as a poet (it was not always obvious, of course, as Gosse points out); what Gosse says is simultaneously heartfelt and restrained, restrained by the preamble 'Shall I say what will startle you if I confess that I sometimes fancy...'

Gosse asks 'To what does he owe his [Keats'] pre-eminence... he who had ceased to sing at an age when most were still practising their prosodical scales?' Most interestingly he discounts originality:

Originality of poetic style was not, it seems to me, the predominant characteristic of Keats... There is hardly any excellent feature in the poetry of Keats which is not superficially the feature of some well-recognised master of an age precedent to his own... But, if he makes use of modes which are already familiar to us… as the modes invented by earlier masters, it is mainly because his temperament was one which imperatively led him to select the best of all possible forms of expression.

Compared with learning from the past, from taking what was best in it and using it to the greatest advantage to create the new, originality is a cheap and pointless goal:

> [Originality] has come to poets… infinitely the inferior of Keats. Those who strive after direct originality forget that to be unlike those who have preceded us, in all the forms and methods of expression, is not by any means certainly to be either felicitous or distinguished.

Is that a lesson that one could say has been marked, learned and inwardly digested, as my teachers used to demand of me, by today's artists, architects, writers and others? I hardly think so; and therefore it is a consolation that there is some value, other than the pure pleasure it gives, to reading matter that is both intelligent and undemanding.

24
Slugs Are For The Birds

Among the many publishers who have failed to make a fortune either for themselves or for me by publishing my books is one who is a keen birdwatcher. I admire him for it because it seems (or rather once seemed) to me that birdwatching, or birding as I believe birdwatchers, or birders, now prefer to be known, is a peaceful and disinterestedly contemplative activity of the kind that I am too impatient to pursue but wished that I was not.

I have always been a little curious about the psychology of birders. Are they nature mystics, scientifically minded, or more like train spotters? I once sat next to a man on a flight from the Netherlands to England who had binoculars round his neck and was dressed as for field research. I assumed that he was an ornithologist until he got out his notebook and saw that he had been collecting aircraft registration numbers at Schipol Airport, one of the world's largest and busiest. He continued to take down numbers until the last possible minute, when our aircraft took off. What on earth was he going to do with all these numbers? My heart was suddenly seized by sorrow that a man should obtain his pleasure, perhaps even his joy, in such a futile way: but then, suddenly ecumenical, I thought, well, pleasure is pleasure and joy is joy, and the man was doing no harm by what he was doing. Who in a thousand years—fifty—will say that my pleasures were more serious, important and intelligent than his?

Are birders a little like my plane spotter? Mildly interested in the question, I happened on a book in a charity shop (thrift store) titled

Birders: Tales of a Tribe by a distinguished ornithologist and author called Mark Cocker. In truth I bought the book because it cost next to nothing, and I immediately started to read it. It was fascinating, and it somewhat overturned my beliefs about birders.

Birders, at least in Britain, have a sub-culture all their own, a scale of values and a system of ethics. So important for them is seeing a new species of bird that they are quite prepared to risk their lives to do so, and the author gives several examples of birders who have lost their lives in pursuit of a sighting, including one who was mauled to death by a tiger for the sake of birds. Practically nothing, short of death, will come between a birder and the birds he wants to see, and there is one hilarious incident in the book in which young birders are driving up to Scotland in order to see a rare bird that has been reported there. They crash (and wreck) their car, and are very nearly killed, but all they can think in the hospital to which they are taken afterwards of is getting up to Scotland to see the bird. They care nothing about the car, as most young men would; neither does the pain of their injuries deter them; they care only for seeing the bird and adding it to their list of species seen. There is something magnificent in this disregard of normal everyday concerns for the sake of a non-monetary reward, and it seems that this kind of enthusiasm is by no means dead or dying; on the contrary, every generation brings forth new birders, and I find it reassuring that such eccentricity should continue in a time that I think is characterised by a horrible uniformity of taste and interest among the young. How nice it is (sometimes) to be wrong! But yet, merely to see a bird so that you can say to other birders that you have seen it—not to discover anything new about it—seems a little vainglorious, to say the least, albeit that birders genuinely love the birds they see, spot and watch.

The first little essay in the book concerns the author's search for the Satyr Trapogan, a startlingly blood-red pheasant that lives only at 8000 feet in the Nepalese Himalayas (in pursuit of which another birding friend of the author's lost his life, probably by falling in the dark). Although I know nothing of birds, certainly not by comparison with the author, there was a passage in the essay with which I rather disagreed:

> This is a creature even more lovely than its title… Those who haven't seen one shouldn't try to conjure the beast by thinking of those beautiful but stupid birds that blunder into our car windscreens.

I would once have agreed with that our pheasants are stupid, but I can no longer agree that they, or at any rate all of them, are.

I learnt how clever pheasants can be by watching them from the windows of a large country house in which some friends of mine live. It is in a rural area where one of the main economic activities is raising pheasants for businessmen, who pay an exorbitant fee for the privilege, to shoot.

Personally I have never understood the passion for shooting birds, large or small. The last thing I want to do when I see a bird, even a vulture, is to shoot it. I can understand shooting them if one is hungry—in the sense that there is no alternative source of food, not in the sense of hunger that a quick visit to the fridge, the supermarket or the corner store would soon alleviate. But there are people whom I respect—the great writer Turgenev, for example—who are or were passionate about killing birds with guns. And I also recognise that, if it were not for the desire of people to shoot them, many birds such as the pheasant would not exist, at least not in such numbers. Whether it is better (for birds) to have lived and be shot than never to have lived at all, I shall leave it to moral philosophers to decide, the question being far too difficult for me.

A small group of pheasants would come on to the lawn that stretched away from the house, led by an absurd male who was proud and pompous as only (among humans) the head of an ancient institution can be. He was cock of the walk, but how small was the walk of which he was cock! He preceded his little following by a few yards, and woe betide any of them who forgot their place and did not keep those few yards distant. Then he would turn and fly at them with righteous indignation, whereupon, without fail, they would retreat. Order having been restored among the revolting peasants, he would then resume his stately progress across the lawn.

Why was this so irresistibly funny? I think it reminded everyone who saw it of the pretentiousness of some ambitious person whom he knew, and by extension of the absurdity of all human ambition. You couldn't look at the self-important pheasant without thinking of Ecclesiastes: vanity of vanities, all is vanity. (And goodness was that pheasant vain!)

But what has this to do with intelligence, you might ask, rather than with stupidity? Nothing, I reply: I am about to come to the intelligence of pheasants.

There was another little group of pheasants, including a one-eyed female, who came right up to the house. The male of this group (he was a bigamist) somehow discovered that if he pecked sharply and rhythmically on the window the humans inside would give him and his tiny harem food. What is interesting about this is that he devised the strategy for himself: no one, as far as I knew, had taught or encouraged him to do this. He seemed to have thought of it himself. It was as if he had used his imagination and had, to use a popular phrase among psychologists these days, a theory of mind, in particular of the human mind.

It is possible, I suppose, that someone somewhere else might have taught him the trick. But even if that were so, the bird had generalised his instruction to a new situation, surely a sign of intelligence. And I don't actually think this was the explanation of his behaviour, because there was no house for miles around where he might have been taught the trick, and pheasants (like burglars) are not great travellers. Moreover, most of the pheasants around my friends' house avoided close contact with humans rather than sought them out, and I am driven to the conclusion that this was a mental giant, a genius, among pheasants. But if he was such a giant or genius, it was likely that there were other *mute, inglorious Miltons* among pheasants. And the capacities of a species surely deserve to be known by its cleverest members, not by those of its dunces, just as a writer should be judged by his best work rather than by his worse, or even by his average work. No one, after all, can write a good book by accident.

Another amusing manifestation of pheasant intelligence was the conduct of this particular pheasant if food was not immediately forthcoming. He would then, as if in outrage or indignation, peck at the window faster, louder, more aggressively, furiously in fact, until his demand was met. And I should add that he pecked at the window only if he could see humans present in the room inside. It was altogether a most impressive performance.

It is on these grounds that I take slight issue with the characterisation by the ornithological author of the British pheasant as stupid. The bird has hidden abilities or potential which it is the duty of every gamekeeper to suppress, in case the birds learn to evade their businessmen-executioners, just as it is the effect, and possibly the purpose, of modern educational methods in British state schools to ensure that pupils, especially from poor homes, remain at a low level of attainment.

I am not alone in my belief that the pheasant is not a stupid bird. In *The Parliament of the Birds* (at least in Edward Fitzgerald's version of it, the only one I know), the Thirteenth Century Persian Sufi poet, Farid ud-Din Attar, made the pheasant the sole bird that questioned the authority of the Lapwing, the bird who claimed to have been chosen by God to lead all the other birds to Paradise. The pheasant was thus the Descartes of his phylum who questioned blind faith in a self-proclaimed authority. One is tempted to see the pheasant, then, as the bird that rebelled against the opening of the second sura of the Koran: 'This is the Scripture which cannot be doubted.'

One class of one phylum of the animal kingdom whose intelligence is not in doubt—because it has none to speak of—is the gastropod mollusc (the cephalopods, squids and octopuses, among the molluscs are different in this respect, they show intelligence). And it so happens that along with the book about birders I bought a book whose blurb said that it was 'bound to remain a standard handbook for the foreseeable future—the snail-hunter's bible.'

The snail-hunter: another, even more curious fraternity (I doubt there are many female snail-hunters, it sounds to me like a predominantly male occupation) in the great mosaic we call humanity.

The book was *A Field Guide to the Land Snails of Britain and North-west Europe*, a title which delicately avoided the fact that it was also a guide to the slugs of that geographical area. I suppose that a title including the word slugs would have put the casual buyer off—I can just imagine the sales-team at the publisher objecting strongly to its inclusion, for practically no one likes a slug and in gardens they are to be feared and killed with little blue pellets spread on the soil.

Is there a culture in which slugs are not abominated as aesthetically repellent and economically destructive? If there is not (and I am not anthropologist enough to know whether there is such a culture, for example one which worships the slug as a god), does this mean that man is born with an instinctive dislike of slugs, as chimpanzees are born with a fear of snakes? Few people like sliminess, either literal or metaphorical. For as Othello says:

An honest man he is, and hates the slime
That sticks to evil deeds.

Snails at least may have pretty shells; but slugs, even when they are pink, greenish or yellowish, or handsomely brindled, repel. Nothing can redeem a slug.

But the Germans say that every little animal has its little pleasure, to which one might add with justice that it has its collector too. My field guide informs the latter how to preserve what the great majority of mankind would wish to destroy, namely slugs, though it does not really go so far as to recommend it:

> Whole animals can be kept by pickling in alcohol. Slugs can be preserved in this way, but they shrink considerably, and their colours change.

Instead, photographs are recommended as being more useful and attractive.

The book did not convert me to the fascination of snails and slugs, whose repertoire of behaviour is much less than that of, say, pheasants (though I was surprised to learn that some snails are carnivorous, and one species becomes so, but only in captivity). However, though slugs and snails have been studied less than other types of animals, which explains why, even in an area as well-worked by naturalists as Western Europe, there are new species still to be discovered, yet I was moved by the many hours of human devotion that must have gone into the careful classification of hundreds of species, often requiring dissection ('when in doubt,' says the field guide, 'dissect,' a piece of advice that would apply equally to politicians' rhetoric).

Which all goes to show that Hamlet was right when he said:

> What a piece of work is a man! How noble in reason! how infinite in faculty!

He can even make slugs his study.

25
In Praise of a Dying Trade

My love of money is so far unrequited, perhaps because I do not love it quite enough, which is to say to the exclusion of all other possible objects of adoration and devotion. Likewise I remain firm in my admiration of those who do not work exclusively or even principally for money; and among the latter must surely be English provincial sellers of second-hand books

Theirs is indeed a dying trade, and entering their shops—now, alas, fewer and fewer—one cannot help but wonder whether it ever truly lived. As long as I can remember, which is now quite a long time, they have been cold with a kind of irredeemable cold, an absence of warmth upon which no paraffin heater, no pre-war single bar electric heater (of the kind favoured by booksellers), no clement weather, can make the slightest impression. When you take a book from a shelf of one of these bookshops you get a puff of cold air in the face, as well as of dust, as if you had opened a mediaeval tomb complete with a curse against grave-robbers. One associates dust with dry heat, but this, at least where English provincial second-hand bookshops is concerned, is a mistake. They contrive to be cold, dusty and damp at the same time.

It is all the more remarkable, then, that in so materialistic an age as our own people can be found who not only spend, but want to spend, and cannot conceive of not spending, their working lives in such conditions, and all for little monetary reward. True, they are more or less protected by their avocation from the seamier and more violent side of modern society; burglars and armed robbers in even the worst areas for crime do not think to break into second-hand bookshops; and the comings and going of governments do not trouble them. Not for them, either, the shadow-boxing of modern party politics, in which one political mountebank sets himself up as the last bastion against the depredations of another, in truth not very dissimilar, mountebank. Rather they concern themselves with the eternal verities of light foxing, cocking, small tears to dust jackets, and the like. The worst that can happen to them is a gentle slide into insolvency as rents rise (all such shops are now found in the unlikeliest places because they can survive only where rents are low) and readers decline—both in number and in discrimination. For my money (of which, incidentally, they have taken a lot down the ages) they are the unsung heroes of our culture.

Their lives are precarious. For example, the other day I went into one such bookshop in the North of England, run by a husband and wife team, and bought for a sum that nowadays no one—no bourgeois that is—would hesitate to lay out for lunch, a slimmish volume published in 1857, that was in almost pristine condition. The lady was almost pathetically grateful: she said that by my single purchase I had paid half her rent for the day. I felt as if I had almost done a good deed.

The book was *Uncle Sam and His Country: Or Sketches of America in 1854-55-56* by Alfred Pairpoint. I knew nothing of either the book or its author (that is one of the delights of browsing in a real rather than in a merely virtual bookshop), and was able to discover nothing about him on the internet, other than that I bought the book for a very good price. One of the reasons that Alfred Pairpoint is not a household name even in the households of the literati is that he was not a very good writer who, moreover, displayed no propensity to interesting thoughts; but there are few books that are totally without instruction when read in the right spirit. And Pairpoint's book is interesting not so much for what it contains as for what it does not contain.

To slavery he devotes not more than six pages of his 346. There is, it is true, a chapter devoted to 'Nigger anecdotes,' but only two and a half pages long. Its general tone can be gauged by the following:

> The American negroes generally are extremely simple-minded, but very witty and amusing, apparently happy all day long, gleesome as kittens, especially when off to a fight or a fire...

When the author visits a tobacco plantation in Virginia, he expends more pages on the care and cultivation of the plants than on the condition of the slaves, though he pronounces himself against slavery on grounds of principle. But the whole question is of no greater interest to him than the lunatic asylum of the town of Taunton, for example, or of the sewing-clubs established by the rich to assist the poor: the *Peculiar Institution* is for him just one among many. There is nothing to suggest an awareness of the cataclysm that was only four years off when the book was published.

There is surely an instructive lesson here. Alfred Pairpoint, to judge by his book, was an average man except, perhaps, in his determination to see his words, very ordinary as they were, between covers. His thoughts and feelings and prejudices were those of an ordinary man, neither particularly clever nor particularly stupid, neither outstandingly observant or penetrating, nor outstandingly blind or lacking in penetration. In this respect, he resembles most of us: and he had absolutely no conception or inkling that the most destructive war since the Napoleonic era was about to break out. Such blindness to the future seems to be the permanent condition of Mankind: and those few who, like Sir Isaac Newton, have seen a little further than others (perhaps as much by luck as by judgment, for where millions guess the future some must be right), are rarely attended to or their correct prognostications taken as the basis of action. Our ignorance of the future is not only our permanent burden but also the glory of our lives, for it makes our engagement with the world permanently necessary. If we knew everything our lives as conscious beings would be intolerable.

The very ordinariness of Alfred Pairpoint and his thoughts makes his conclusions about slavery all the more poignant. He has two pages of nineteen on the slavery question in his last chapter, where he writes:

> Example, there is no doubt, goes further than precept in such a question; - and it would be as well, if those who look so piteously on slavery, and conjure up, like Mrs Harriet Beecher Stowe and others, such harrowing scenes to enlist the sympathies of their country, would themselves show a little charity towards their sable brethren, and not exclude them, like lepers, from society. The places of amusement... the tables at hotels, the public conveyances, nay, even the houses of prayer, frequented by the white American, are shut against the negroes; - nay, so inveterate is the prejudice against them, that white children will shun little curly-headed niggers in

the street, as if the very sight of them were pollution, and as for sitting down in the same school-room with them, the idea would be preposterous. Thus, in fact, the coloured population in Northern Cities, though free, are as much under a bane, as if they were labouring in the cotton-plantations of Louisiana; and, until the Abolitionists set about reforming themselves in this particular, they are only injuring the cause and the race that they are professing to serve. If the black people are to be set free, let them be treated as brethren with the same rights, capacities, and responsibilities as the white population; - to advocate abolition on any lower principle than this, is a delusion and a fraud, - an insult to the common-sense of the whole civilized world.

And here, a propos of nothing except perhaps the present economic crisis, I cannot forebear from quoting the words of Daniel Webster that Alfred Pairpoint quotes on the subject of money:

Of all the contrivances for cheating the labouring classes of mankind, none has been more effectual than that which deludes them with paper-money, - the most effectual invention that could possibly have been devised for fertilizing the rich man's field by the sweat of the poor man's brow; and light, on the nation at large, would be the oppression of despotic tyranny and excessive taxation by comparison with those of a fraudulent currency and depreciated paper.

Let us now leave Pairpoint and progress to a nearby town whose second-hand bookshop made the first I have described seem palatial by comparison. The aged owner sat at his untidy desk awaiting customers, not very hopefully it seemed to me. He sat in front of the shelves that bore his more valuable stock which he allowed me to look over, judging that I was not a likely thief. You may judge of the scale of his commercial operations when I tell you that I bought a first edition of Aldous Huxley's novel *Antic Hay* for $15, a price for which he all but apologised; and I also bought, for $1.50, a first (and as far as I know only) edition of the co-operative effort of Joseph Conrad and Ford Madox Ford, who by then had returned to his pre-Great War surname of Hueffer, anti-German feeling having subsided somewhat, published in the year of Conrad's death, 1924, and titled *The Nature of a Crime*.

It was written many years before publication, and both authors claim in the preface not to remember how it came about.

The story (which Stefan Zweig would have written better) consists of pre-suicide letters of a man to the great love of his life, a woman who, however, has married someone else, called Robert. The author of the suicide letters is a financier whose defalcations are about to be exposed. Hitherto greatly respected as an enormously rich man of great financial acumen, the source of his fortune is embezzlement of funds from a trust of which he is a trustee. He is reprieved at the last moment from the need to commit suicide when the beneficiary of the trust withdraws his demand for accounts and unwittingly gives him the chance to make good the losses.

It is difficult to tell which pages or paragraphs are by which author, and it would hardly be worth the effort to establish it. What most interested me as a doctor in the story, however, is the fact, rather abruptly introduced, that Robert, the husband of the narrator's love, is addicted to chloral hydrate, a hypnotic and sedative still in use, albeit steeply declining, when I started my career.

The passage by which I was impressed was that in which the narrator claims to be in the process of curing Robert of his addiction. This passage shows that Conrad or Hueffer (or both) had a better instinctive grasp of the nature of addiction, including its pharmacology, than most addiction doctors.

I told you… that Robert is almost cured. I would not have told you this for the sake of arrogating to myself the position of a saviour. But I imagine you would like the cure to go on and, in the case of some accident after my death, it might go all to pieces once more. Quite simply then: I have been doing two things. In the first place I have persuaded your chemists to reduce very gradually the strength of chloral, so that the bottles contain nearly half water. And Robert perceives no difference. Now of course it is very important that he shall not know of the trick that is being played so beneficently on him – so that, in case he should go away or for one reason or another, change his chemists, it must be carefully seen to that instead of pure chloral he obtains an exactly diluted mixture. In this way he may be brought gradually to drinking almost pure water.

However, the authors are aware that merely stopping the drug is not enough:

> But that alone would hardly be satisfactory: a comparatively involuntary cure is of little value in comparison with an effort of the will. You may, conceivably, expel nature with a fork, but nothing but a passion will expel a passion. The only point to be proved is whether there exists in your husband any other passion for the sake of which he might abandon his passion for the clearness of vision which he always says his chloral gives him.

In this comparatively short passage, the authors have demonstrated that they understand two things about addiction that doctors so often neglect, even if they sometimes pay lip service to them: first that the physical aspect of addiction is frequently trifling, second that it is a man's outlook on life that plays the determining role in his 'recovery' from his addiction. And neglect of these two things leads researchers in the futile alchemical quest for the philosopher's stone of addiction, the treatment that, without any desire or effort on the part of the addicted person, will 'cure' him as antibiotics cure infections.

I will continue to haunt provincial second-hand booksellers in England as long as they continue to exist.

26

Boxing Clever

Many years ago, more indeed than I care to number, I had a discussion with my fellow-students that had a permanent influence upon my views and attitude to life. It concerned, of all things, the ethics of professional boxing, a subject to which until that moment I had not given a moment's thought. But youth is an age at which it is felt necessary to have a strong opinion about everything, and mere ignorance is no bar to passionate advocacy. The same is true, of course, of journalists. There is nothing like passionate ignorance to keep one young at heart.

Needing to take sides in the discussion, for silence was not then in my nature, I found myself echoing, or rather parroting, the views of Dr Edith Summerskill. She was a Labour Member of Parliament who ran and was principally known for a campaign to outlaw professional boxing. She was, I think, a brave woman, for her campaign was not popular among her political party's supposed constituency, the proletariat, and even excited some ridicule among them; but those were the days when there were still some politicians who fought for what they thought was right rather than for what was expedient in the careerist sense.

While many sports were dangerous, I said, boxing was the only one whose object was physically to incapacitate an opponent and even injure him. It often resulted in chronic brain damage such as Parkinson's disease and *dementia pugilistica*, or punch-drunkenness, to the great economic and emotional cost of those who suffered it and those who cared for or looked after them. It exerted a brutalising effect upon

151

spectators (here I spoke from neither experience nor information). And practically no one would go in for it who was not driven to it by desperate social and economic circumstances, so that to do so was not really a free choice at all.

I recalled my assertion about the brutalising effects of boxing as a spectacle when I attended the one and only professional boxing tournament I have ever attended as a spectator. It was in an industrial town that had once had a rather grand Victorian centre, but which had been destroyed by a combination of economic decline and modern town planning. The hall in which the boxing took place was large and dismal.

The draw of the evening was a world championship fight (the champion was a local boy), but before that there were many fights to sit through between young hopefuls on the one hand and ageing no-hopers on the other. I had not appreciated until then just how boring a brutal spectacle could be. The journeymen boxers grunted their way round the ring, taking swipes at each other that rarely connected, though occasionally they did. Sometimes blood would spurt from one of their noses and spatter the spectators close to the ring. It was then that I was glad not to have bought one of the 'better', which is to say the ringside, seats.

The boxing fans waited for the world champion as fascists waited for the arrival at a rally of their leader, which is to say with mounting tension. And when the champion boxed, even I, who am no aficionado, could see that he was possessed of a completely different order of skill. He danced elegantly round the ring, and when he threw a punch it connected exactly where it was intended to; but he gave the impression of doing it more to score points than to inflict harm on his opponent. Even if I could not agree that boxing was a noble art, let alone *the* noble art, I saw that there could be great skill in it.

But what I most remembered of the evening was a spectator in front of me, a man from the look of him who was not himself much given to athletic pursuits. When one of the journeymen boxers caught another full on the face, drawing blood, the man in front of me rose excitedly to his feet and screamed 'Kill 'im! Kill 'im!' I had the impression that he meant it in no very metaphorical sense, and that he would have been quite content to see a man beaten to death before his very eyes.

Be that as it may, the question arose in my mind as to whether the coarse brutality of his sentiment was caused by the spectacle, or rather he attended the spectacle because of his coarse brutality. Probably the relationship was dialectical: appetites are not so much fluids in a closed space waiting to be released as propensities that grow with their satisfaction. My guess, or prejudice, is that attendance at coarse spectacles makes people coarse; and Lord Macaulay's famous remark, that the Puritans hated bear-baiting not because it gave pain to the bear but because it gave pleasure to the spectators is not quite as damning of the Puritans as might be supposed.

I suspect, though I cannot prove, that boxing also exerts a brutalising effect upon its practitioners, contrary to those who believe in the hydraulic theory of human aggression. I once had as a patient a young man whose girlfriend told me that until he took up kick-boxing he had been kind and considerate, but that thereafter he became aggressive, bad-tempered and violent. Other interpretations of the story than mine are possible, and stories of a decline in violence towards others are sometimes told of those unruly youths who take up boxing. The possibility remains that the same activity has different effects on different people: where the evidence is equivocal, one does not so much suspend judgment as believe what one wants.

In my discussion all those years ago, however, I did not emphasise the allegedly brutalising effect, both on spectators and practitioners, of boxing. Rather, my main argument was the supposed inability of professional boxers to choose their career rather than be chosen by it as an inevitable consequence of their social and economic circumstances.

One of my interlocutors, a young man much more mature than I (and now an eminent surgeon), granted that most—though not all—professional boxers emerged from the poorest section of society. But that, he said, was not enough to establish my point. Not only were some professional boxers not of the lowest class, but the vast majority of the lowest class were not professional boxers. To regard professional boxers as virtually inanimate products of forces acting upon them was not generous, but to deprive them of their humanity, that is to say their powers of conscious agency. True, their decisions were affected by their circumstances: but whose are not? They chose, and chose freely.

I saw at once that he was right; that my attitude was condescending and dehumanising. But of course I did not change my opinion there and then, by admitting that he was right, rather I cleaved to it all the more obstinately. Schopenhauer has many eloquent pages on the purpose or end of argument or discussion being victory rather than truth, the latter being but a weapon, for the achievement of the former. But it does not follow from this that there is no point in discussion (other than victory): for truth seeps through the mind like damp through a wall, and eventually conquers it. I lost the habit, common among those of intellectual bent, of seeing my fellow beings as objects rather than subjects.

Not many years later, it so happened, I had as a patient the widow of a former world champion boxer. She was approaching seventy and her husband's career had been mainly pre-war. By the time the war was over he was past his peak and his career, at least as a boxer, was never so glorious again.

To my surprise, his widow was an elegant, mannerly, intelligent, cultivated and articulate woman, and in her recollections of her husband (which I encouraged, as much for my own sake as for hers) she managed to convey the same qualities in him. It was clear that she had loved and even revered him; she said that he was what one might not have expected in the milieu of professional boxing, and what to her was the highest term of praise, a gentleman. I was moved by her love for him, but also saddened by it, for it was clear that her happiness consisted of living imaginatively in that past. It is a stage of life that comes to us all, and sooner than any of us thinks.

Her husband had clearly been a most remarkable man. Born into a working-class mining family, he had used boxing as a means of making his way in the world. He was adulated in the area of his birth, without such adulation in any way turning his head. In those days, there was little in the way of medical supervision of boxers: a man could fight until his brain was destroyed if he wanted to and no one stopped him. In his great book, *Organic Psychiatry*, Lishman says of the characteristic brain damage caused by boxing:

> Severe examples date mostly from boxing careers pursued before the second world war when medical control over boxing was less rigorous than at present. Fair-ground booth boxing appears to have been especially hazardous.

My patient's husband had indeed started out as fairground-booth boxer, and in his time must have had more than a thousand fights, at least four hundred of them professional in the full sense. By luck and no doubt by skill he had avoided all brain damage; he had been a man interested in literature and other quiet intellectual pursuits.

Whether because the nature of fame and celebrity had in the meantime changed, I somewhat doubted that his like would easily be found nowadays. But the unexpected story that his wife told me nevertheless affected my development. I had a stereotype in my mind of boxers as brutes; here was a boxer who had been considerably more gentlemanly than I.

I did not draw from this the conclusion that it was wrong to have stereotypes in one's mind. Not only is the effort to eliminate stereotypes futile, and likely to lead to dishonest claims of success, but any person who did actually succeed would be in grave danger, like the very rare person who is born without the capacity to feel pain.

I still believe it likely that, on average, professional boxers are unlikely to be fine gentlemen; but I learnt from this example that one ought to retain the mental flexibility to recognise when stereotypes are no longer a guide to reality: a guide which, in the first place, is never more than rough and ready. The man without stereotypes is like the man who steps out into the world stark naked; the man who sticks to his stereotypes despite evidence is like the man who dresses the same whatever the weather.

If professional boxing is, on the whole, brutal and brutalising, is there anything that can be said in its defence? I confess that I have no desire ever to attend a professional boxing match ever again; one was enough, perhaps more than enough, for me; but personal taste is not necessarily a good guide to public policy, and even the most ferocious opponent of the sport must confess that, brutal and brutalising as it might be, only an insignificant proportion of the brutality in society could possibly be attributable to it.

At the very least, boxers must be brave; and there is something stirring about the spectacle of two men, more or less evenly matched, testing one another according to rules by which, at least in principle, they abide even in the extremity of their need to break them. Moreover, however much they may have insulted each other beforehand in an attempt to stoke their own aggression, they kiss and make up, even honour each other, immediately the fight is over. This is chivalry, albeit of a coarse kind; but chivalry is always inspiring. Rational utility is not the measure of all things, and is not the only guide as to what to permit and what to prohibit.

27

Serpentine Mind

When I was young and taken to the zoo I always wanted to go straight to the reptile house. First, however, I had to see the boring old chimpanzees, lions, hippopotamuses, etc., because those were what my adult supervisors always wanted to see. (I remember the notice in the hippopotamus house, apologising for the smell but saying that we, that is to say the hippopotamuses, like it.)

I would pester the adults by asking constantly whether we could go to the reptiles soon, much as a child in a car asks 'Are we there yet?' Eventually the adults would say Yes, but reluctantly, for they did not really want to see the reptiles, in fact they wanted not to see them. They—the adults—had craftily waited until our time in the zoo was nearly up so that, frustratingly, the visit to the reptile house was no more than a quick walk through it. I was not allowed to linger as I should have liked.

Although I have had very little to do professionally with reptiles, except in the metaphorical sense, apart from the odd snakebite and injury caused by anthropophagous crocodiles, I have continued to be fascinated by them—in a desultory kind of way. And I also developed a fascination for those who are fascinated by them to the point of wanting to keep them as pets.

I had never really associated France with such an activity: the French are too warm-blooded. Rather it is in northern climes that snake-fancying is most popular, and even there a distinctly minority interest. Herpetophilia, if I may so call it, is the province of the peculiar; and I suppose, suffering from a mild form of it myself, if only at second hand, intellectual honesty compels me to admit that I must be, to an extent, peculiar myself.

Well, I happened to be driving through, or rather past, the city of Nîmes recently, principally famous for its perfectly-preserved Roman temple and magnificent amphitheatre, when I saw an advertisement for an exhibition of reptiles and amphibians to be held at the football stadium the following Saturday and Sunday, and so I returned.

There was a queue to get in. Children have to be amused on wet Sunday afternoons as this was, and I must say that the children were very eager. It is a cliché that French parents are very good with their children, but a cliché is a cliché because it is obviously true. But liberally admixed among those on a family outing were those who would have predominated among such an event in England and, I suspect, the United States, namely the shaven-headed, heavily tattooed and pierced community. France lags in such fashions, but is catching up fast: there are now tattoo parlours in practically all French towns, including those in which, a few years ago, you would never have seen a single tattooed person.

The vogue for reptiles and tattoos has developed more or less *pari passu*. Having gained entrance to the exhibition (and sale) of reptiles, my hand having been stamped in India ink with the eye of a crocodile to show that I had paid my admission ($6.70), I spoke to a stallholder whom I liked immediately. He and his wife had been breeding reptiles for 25 years, she having been a keeper of reptiles at Paris zoo for many years, and their aim was not to make a profit but to prevent the importation of species direct from the wild. Smuggling of rare species still went on, he told me, though with the increased vigilance of the customs authorities it took a different form. Importation from countries of origin was still permitted provided the animals had been bred in captivity there, so now false birth certificates were issued by alleged reptile farmers or breeding centres. In other words, the regulations had made smuggling easier, not more difficult.

The stallholder and his wife also kept their reptiles in environments that resembles their natural habitats as closely as possible; and though I came to sneer at his stand with its prominent slogans 'To breed animals so as not to take any more from Nature' and 'All the animals presented on this stand were bred by us,' I went away with respect and even, dare I say it, with affection, for it seemed to me that this couple had a passion in life and followed their own path while actually doing good. The stallholder was not a zoologist by training (he did not say what he was), but he had an air of erudition and distinction that had nothing to do with any diplomas he might or might not have had.

He told me that a show of reptiles and amphibians such as this could not have taken place in France 20 years ago: that an French reptile-fanciers would have had to go to Belgium or Germany for such an exhibition. (I believe that Germany is still the centre of the European live snake trade, and has the least restrictive regime on the keeping of venomous species.) There were aspects of snake-keeping and collecting that he could not approve of; for example, there were some collectors who sought snakes that were rare, the rarer the better, status in the small world of herpetology being associated with the possession of the rarest kinds. There was one snake on sale in the exhibition for about $3740, for example.

I found it. It was a specimen of Python regius, not a rare species in itself, but one whose price depended on the colouring and marking of the skin (and very little on the size, which surprised me). The different appearances had different names, obviously familiar to the keepers of pythons. An ordinary 'Pastel' python was only $100, but a Firefly was $600, an Ivory $1100 and an Albino pinstripe $1200. A Spinner Mojave was $1670, a Super-Enchi Butter $3200; but it was a Banana that was the one that exercised the stallholder's ire, at $3740. It was indeed a handsome beast, in a reptilian way: cream-and-butterscotch striped.

The reason I had supposed (wrongly) that a python's price would be proportionate to its size was that its size would be an indication of the investment in food the owner had put into it. But if the size had any effect at all on the price it must have been very small, and I discovered why in the section devoted to snake food. This ranged from blocks of frozen pink rat or mice embryos to cages full of live rats. These rats were busy about their business in their cages, oblivious to the fact that they owed their very existence to their future status as snake food. Unlike the snakes, the rats looked intelligent, curious, almost self-conscious; the snakes were sluggish and mostly immobile. I could not but adapt a line from Shakespeare in my mind:

As rats to wanton snakes, are we to the gods.

I have reached the age at which almost everything calls up memories, rather like the smell of Proust's famous madeleine. In this case it was the chameleons, very much the interest of a minority of the minority. There were a few of them in the show, commanding high prices; they are not easy to keep, I believe. In their cage were grasshoppers, like the rats unaware of their purpose in life.

Chameleons are among the most fascinating of creatures, with their swivelling turret eyes, their curled tails, their long swift tongues, their slow rocking movements like those of institutionalised children, their peculiar two-toed claws and, of course, their kaleidoscopic scaly skins. I can happily watch them for hours, my mind empty of everything except idle delight in their strange beauty. They themselves are never content, however; they seem always to have a disgruntled, even angry look, like old men lamenting the state of the world, and indeed they hiss when disturbed or picked up. I have never seen a happy chameleon.

I met them in the wild in East Africa. Once I was driving along a rutted laterite road through the kind of bush through which lions prowl and wild dogs, ugly beasts, hunt. Occasionally you would see a python crossing the road, but no python ever lasted long, being angrily chopped to pieces with machetes as an inveterate enemy of mankind. The vehicle in which I was driving was a somewhat rickety land rover—no vehicle could long survive undamaged the shaking given them in the dry season by those laterite roads—and, as was ever the case in Africa, it was carrying far more people than it had ever been designed to do. My passengers were soldiers: a captain and a few recruits, each with the kind of gun that was probably more useful in putting down civilian demonstrations than fighting another army, in other words weapons formidable only against the unarmed, but then very formidable.

In front of me I saw a bright green chameleon—at least it was bright green at that moment—crossing the road. It showed no road sense, of course, and indeed vehicles were very few there, so that even with high intelligence it would have had little opportunity to learn its danger. It moved very slowly, with that slight to-ing and fro-ing that psychiatrists call ambivalence, as for example when a schizophrenic puts out his hand to shake and then withdraws it.

I stopped the land rover and got out. The captain and his soldiers looked surprised. I took their surprise to be at my interest in what for them must have been an everyday sight since childhood. (We take for granted that other people will take for granted what we take for granted. Indeed, one could almost say: Tell me what you take for granted, and I will tell you where you are from.)

I approached the chameleon: it was, in my opinion, a fine specimen. I picked it up and heard a screech coming from the land rover. With the chameleon on the palm of my hand, delighted with my capture, I returned to the vehicle. To my surprise the captain and all his soldiers suddenly clambered out of it and ran helter-skelter into the bush. It was the chameleon that had terrified them, and they would not return until I had put it from me.

On their return to the vehicle, I asked them why they had been so affrighted; everyone knew, I said airily, that chameleons were not poisonous, indeed were perfectly harmless. They denied that they had been frightened, but it was obvious from their expression at the time that they had been not merely frightened but terrified. They were ashamed to admit their superstition which they knew would appear ridiculous in my eyes, but of whose truth they could not rid their minds.

Later I heard that there was a local legend about chameleons: that once they climbed into your hair they never let go and remained entangled there for the rest of your life. I doubted that this could be the whole of the reason for the extreme funk of the soldiers, but it occurred to me that one way to take over the country (if these soldiers were anything to go by) was for conspirators to arrive simultaneously at strategic posts with a number of chameleons to frighten off the defenders of those posts. The coup would be a peaceful one and the conspirators would be safe so long as they kept the chameleons with them at all times.

When we were sitting at dusk on the terrace of my house in France recently when a bat flew by. A visitor said that when she was young she heard of an aunt into whose chignon a bat had flown, and it was impossible to get it out—for how long she was unable to say.

That night, as it happened, six bats flew into my bedroom whose windows I had left wide open. I do not have enough hair left for the bats to have entangled themselves in, but in any case the bats, uninterested in my head, flew round and round in circles near the ceiling. It seemed that the room had trapped them, for even when encouraged with a broom they did not leave and gave the impression of not knowing how to do so, since they frequently bumped into walls and the ceiling. I had thought that bats were possessed of an infallible sonar system that guided them with perfect dexterity to tiny insects: surely they could find a wide-open window?

Was this a technical defect or deficiency in their sonar system? The answer depends, of course, on what they were trying to do, that is if bats can be said to be trying to do anything. If they weren't trying to leave the room, there was no such defect or deficiency. (They were all gone, incidentally, by morning.) Where behaviour has intention, more than one interpretation of it is always possible. We can never fully and finally know why people keep reptiles or tattoo themselves.

28
Sense and Sentimentality

Recently I have participated in more public debates and discussions than usual (for me, that is). I discovered what many people before me have discovered, namely that it is not logic that convinces but emotion, and that this is so even with highly educated audiences. A carefully constructed argument tends to bore rather than to impress, and even to make him who employs it look arrogant or self-satisfied in the eyes of those who attend. A joke is more effective than a statistic.

I also discovered how difficult it is to tell the truth in public, at least on certain matters. A few days ago, for example, I took part in a public discussion in a university on the question of whether prison works. This is a very loosely-framed question because there is almost nobody who supposes that we could do altogether without prisons, for example to incapacitate persistent robbers or other violent criminals. The question is rather whether we use prison wisely or foolishly.

The students were polite, attentive and lively, just what university students should be. Perhaps not all is quite lost in our civilisation, then.

On the panel of discussants was a woman, I should estimate in her late thirties, who had been in prison for ten years and since release had run a voluntary organisation to assist woman prisoners to a better life after their release. All honour to her for that, of course; even the most punitive among us do not want punishment in effect to continue for ever, beyond the term laid down by law.

So far so good, but the woman in question went further. She depicted women prisoners as pure victims of circumstances, for example of sexual or physical or psychological abuse. She cited her own case as proof. She came from a tough area of a once-industrial city where crime and disorder were endemic, where it was easy 'to go with the wrong crowd,' as she had done, and where no one bethought him or herself of a better life. She had formed a relationship with a man thirteen years her senior who had been violent and criminal to whom she had found it difficult to say no. She was not, as she put it, in the driving seat of her own life. When she was sent to prison for what she had done she was the victim of stigmatisation and ostracism by her family and the people around her. By going into prison she had lost her child, her home, everything. She appealed for a more understanding, tolerant society, where victims of circumstance were better treated, with more compassion, and were not just thrown into gaol as bad people. 'I don't believe I'm a bad person,' she said.

This is the kind of emotional pabulum which it is very difficult to answer in public. The woman, who went round the country giving this speech, was clearly a reformed character and so her belief that she was not a bad person, in the sense of being irredeemably the Devil's spawn, was perfectly true. To have pointed out the contradictions in her story would therefore have seemed like an attack on her person rather than on her argument and would have been a rhetorical mistake as far as gaining the sympathy of the audience was concerned. In any case I am not a ruthless person and would not have wanted to humiliate someone who, whatever the falsity of her argument, was almost certainly somewhat fragile but who had nevertheless made a creditable transition. It is much easier for me to write about her in anonymity than to have confronted her directly; but my scruple about confronting her directly, which I am sure I share with many others who appear in public with her, meant that she could continue unopposed to spread her fundamentally dishonest or at least sentimental gospel around the country. And what is unopposed unfortunately tends to go by default. Silence is taken for acceptance or agreement.

Let us examine the ways in which what she said was evasive. First she gave no details of what she had done, but for a woman to have served ten years in prison in England it must have been something very bad and certainly out of the ordinary: at any rate, not shoplifting.

Then (not necessarily dishonestly, we all make the same mistake from time to time) she used the old technique of citing the denominator without the numerator, that is to say she told us that a high proportion of women prisoners had been abused without telling us how many women had been abused without becoming prisoners. This technique makes an association appear all the stronger and thus also causative in a direct way, as a brick thrown at a window causes the glass to shatter. Nor did she notice that if the causation were as close as she made out—'I was abused, I could do no other'—the penological consequences would not necessarily be in the direction of leniency, tolerance and understanding. If there really were an unbreakable causative link between abuse and crime, such that consciousness and decision-making had no part to play, then those who were abused should be held in preventive detention or at least imprisoned for a very long time for the sake of public safety.

She made much of her environment where crime was endemic and easy to 'fall into,' as Newton's supposed apple fell to the ground. She also claimed that she was the victim of stigmatisation both by her family and the people around her, without realising the contradiction. The fact that she was so stigmatised suggests that crime of the kind she committed (whatever it was), and perhaps her whole way of life that led to that crime, was not the norm in her family and social milieu, and that therefore she chose her path in life rather than merely fell into it almost by accident or by inevitability. No doubt she was a victim in the sense that she had been brought up in much less than optimal conditions, there is no reason to doubt it; but by the same token she was not just a victim and nothing but a victim.

Moreover, the story of her imprisonment was not one of futile vindictiveness on the part of the authorities, and indeed proved the worth of prison at least in her case. While in prison she had obtained a university degree by external study; it was in prison that she had decided to follow a different path. This decision, as she herself said (without necessarily realising the implications of what she said), was not the work of a moment. When she first went to prison she was surrounded by women with a criminal outlook that she shared. It took years for her to change her own outlook; had she been released much earlier than ten years, or not sent to prison at all, it is unlikely that she would have changed in the way she had changed, or achieved what she had achieved.

Had she been my patient I should have felt perfectly able to point these things out to her, firmly but I hope kindly. But if I had done so in public, especially before an audience that had probably already been sensitised by years of such sentimental pabulum that increasingly is our mental diet, I should have appeared a monster of insensitivity. So I said merely what I had set out to say, such that our respective contributions were like ships passing in the night. And she was able to go her way, in effect arguing that what she had done (whatever it was) was not her fault or her responsibility, and in effect giving an excuse in advance to those who in future would behave likewise.

She also used another argument that is rhetorically very effective but of very doubtful intellectual validity, to put it mildly. She said that, until you had lived experiences such as abuse and imprisonment you could not know or understand their effects. This is an argument often used by addicts in their grand effort to excuse themselves to themselves and to others.

It is a banal truth that one cannot know the experience of others from the inside, as it were. You cannot know the sensation of skiing in this sense without having skied. But what is true of everyone cannot be made the grounds of a scepticism that is used only to excuse wrongdoing. Moreover, it cannot be true that, just because you have not had precisely the same experiences as someone else, you can form no estimate whatever of what those experiences are like. I cannot say that, because I have never been punched on the nose, I have absolutely no idea what it is like to be punched on the nose, whether it is pleasant or unpleasant, frightening or reassuring, likely or not to break my nose or make my nose bleed. Much less can I use the fact that I have not been punched on the nose, and therefore of not knowing what it is like to be so punched, as an excuse for punching someone else on the nose. In any case extenuation is not exculpation. We should make allowances, but not to the extent of denying altogether the difference between good and evil.

Finally, the woman on the panel said something that initially sounded well to the audience but on reflection was brutal, if unintentionally so. She said that everyone deserved a second chance, and there was much sage nodding in agreement. How pleasant it is to be so universally forgiving, especially of what has been done to others!

But a moment's reflection is all that is necessary to show that there are some people who should not be given a second chance. Had Himmler and Goebbels not committed suicide, would anyone have said they should be given a second chance? To take an example on a less world-historical scale, there was a jealous violent man in England not long ago who drugged his girlfriend and, while she was drugged, gouged out her eyes and rendered her permanently blind. Why should such a man be given a second chance, a scintilla of a chance? If you cannot imagine (after a recent century of such horrors as the Holocaust, Pol Pot and the Rwandan genocide) a crime so terrible that people who commit it forfeit their *right* to live as free persons in society, then your imagination has been brutalised to an astonishing degree—or you are ignorant to an equally astonishing degree.

But if I had denied in public that everyone deserved a second chance I would most probably have been taken to mean that the woman on the platform should not have been released and should still have languished in gaol. And since she was there before us, a reformed and in many ways a sympathetic character, I would have seemed like a nasty, censorious, punitive sadist: and everything else I said could therefore have been dismissed on this ground.

To say that the man who gouged out his girlfriend's eyes should never be set at liberty is not the same as saying that he should be treated with cruelty inside prison (as, in strict justice, he would deserve to be treated, a proof, if any were needed, that justice is not the only value that we hold dear). But on the contrary, to say that he should have a second chance because everyone deserves a second chance is to say that there is nothing we find intolerable, that everything is tolerable to us. A tolerant society according to this woman was a society in which nothing was beyond the pale. A society in which nothing beyond was the pale would be extraordinarily vicious.

Does everyone deserve a third chance, a fourth chance, and so on, *ad infinitum*? And who is to pay for these chances? Generosity at the expense of others, whether it be financial or moral, is not generosity, it is moral exhibitionism. Where sentimentality pervades, we cannot make the proper distinctions.

29
Something Rotten in the Art of Denmark

E ver since I first encountered it, nearly fifty years ago, I have liked Danish painting of the Nineteenth Century, particularly of the first half commonly known as Danish art's Golden Age. As artistic golden ages go, and compared with, say, Spain or Holland's, Denmark's was modest. Købke was no Velasquez and Eckersberg was no Vermeer. But in the long run accomplished modesty seems to me better than failed ambition, which is much more frequently encountered in the history of art (though not as it is generally written, of course).

Danish romanticism in painting is to me much preferable to the German variety, even though (I suppose) everyone who takes an interest in the subject would agree that Caspar David Friederich was a greater painter than any of the Danes. It is strange that there should be so marked a difference in emotional tone between the artistic productions of two nations so geographically close. I have tried to put my finger on why I find Danish romanticism innocent and charming while I find its German equivalent chilling and sinister, ever more so as the nineteenth century progresses, culminating with the accomplished but to me odious and terrifying Böcklin. I think that the answer lies in that necessary but not sufficient quality in art, sincerity: the Danes feel, warmly and spontaneously, while the Germans try, often desperately like a constipated man trying to expel impacted faeces, to feel. And in so straining they give an impression precisely the opposite to the one they wish to give, namely that of heartlessness. Their vision is clear, but with a kind of cold-blooded reptilian clarity. They are like people who have heard of emotion but have never actually experienced any.

On my last trip to Copenhagen I actually bought a painting of the Golden Age. It was a very small picture, not more than ten inches by seven, by an unknown artist of a blond, blue-eyed, very sweet little boy in a sailor costume of the early nineteenth century, sitting in a boat with the Danish flag, the oldest and most beautiful of all national flags, fluttering behind him. The painting is saved from sentimentality by the evident and quite unmistakable love with which the boy is painted; if the artist were ever traced, one would not be surprised to discover that the little boy was his son, in fact one would be rather surprised to discover that he wasn't. The picture hangs on the landing of my stairs, which I now never climb without looking at the little boy and feeling a certain pleasurable tenderness towards him, some kind of affirmation of life's goodness, though not unmixed with melancholy of the *memento mori* type: for the boy's innocence, his freshness, could not long have outlasted the painting of the picture, and life's difficulties and sorrows must soon have overtaken him. One of the reasons surely (*a* reason, note, not *the* reason) that Mankind has found it so necessary down the ages to depict the world in which he lives and moments of his life is to protect them both from the inevitable ravages of time, which is why:

> … in the very temple of delight
> Veil'd melancholy keeps her sovereign shrine.

The two reasons why I, no Maecenas, was able to buy the picture—its small size and the anonymity of its painter—were revealing of the workings of the art market. I remember the first time I had my pictures valued for insurance purposes; I was surprised and amused to see the valuer measure them with fanatical minuteness with his tape measure. So much for a square inch for such and such a painter; a different quantity per square inch for another. He might as well have been weighing out butter or bacon, or valuing real estate in a fashionable part of an expensive city. As for anonymity, one might have thought that in a market such as that for art, aesthetics counted for all, but one would be mistaken: here is a world in which a rose definitely does not smell as sweet by any other name.

When I pass my little Danish sailor boy, I think that I do not really own him; I am but his temporary guardian until I pass him on, by sale or death, to another temporary guardian. He belongs not to me but to the world.

My interest in Danish painting is what one might call intermittent and dependent on chance rather than obsessional, let alone scholarly. I take the opportunity whenever it arises to see it, rather than seek it out. So when my brother and sister-in-law told me that they were visiting their daughter in Lille, where their daughter is a student, and where there happened to be at the time an exhibition of Danish art ('Of the Golden Age?' I asked at once) at a *La Piscine*, a municipal art gallery in a converted swimming pool, I took the opportunity.

In a certain sense the exhibition was a disappointment. Having several times visited the great collections in Copenhagen—the Carlsberg Glypotek, the Statens Museum for Kunst—I was expecting a selection of their best works, but I was mistaken. Instead there were more than a hundred pictures, many of them as small as my sailor boy, from the collection of an anonymous Frenchman, comfortably off but not extremely rich, who, having become obsessed with Danish art of the Nineteenth Century, had assembled it in a matter of a few years. There were, it is true, a few minor works by the more famous names, such as Christoffer Eckersberg, Wilhelm Bendz and Jens Juel, but most of the artists represented were not famous, at least not outside Denmark, and there were even a few anonymous pictures (not by any means the least charming). Many did not rise above the level of mediocrity although, unlike the modern variety, such mediocrity was pleasant and on the side of beauty rather than offensive and on the side of ugliness. The artists might almost as well have been called artisans as artists; if they were professional, they were painting for a small and by no means rich market. The few lines of biography of one of them, Jens Erik Carl Rasmussen, who was represented by paintings of icebergs off Greenland (a Danish possession), was tantalising, one wanted to know more:

> After training as a textile merchant, he studied at Royal Academy of Copenhagen (1862–1866)... Several journeys in Europe and to Greenland. Exhibited in Denmark and abroad. Rasmussen is principally known for his sea pictures and those of Greenland.

His dates were given as Æroskøbing 1841—disappeared in the Atlantic 1893. Tragedy was thus hinted at: shipwreck, starvation, suicide?

An exhibition of paintings of generally mediocre quality is not necessarily without value or interest, for all judgment is comparative and he who knows only the best of anything does not know it well. And, as I have already intimated, the authors of these works strove towards beauty even if they sometimes missed it. They were not to be despised.

At the price of one square inch of my painting from the Golden Age, I bought the exhibition catalogue. My instinct told me that I should, and my instinct was right, for the essays that it contained, particularly by an historian of art called Jonathan Lévy, raised important questions, at least questions that are important for me.

The majority of the pictures in the exhibition were landscapes. The Danish landscape is distinctly undramatic, like the Dutch; Nature there is not red in tooth and claw but thoroughly tamed and under Man's control. Oddly enough, and for reasons that would be worth analysing, dramatic landscapes do not usually make for the best landscape paintings, which are generally of less startling views.

I had rather supposed that the peaceful landscapes of Denmark were both productive and indicative of an inner calm, so different from the German *Sturm und Drang*, but Jonathan Lévy, obviously better-acquainted with Nineteenth Century Denmark than I, suggests quite otherwise, almost the opposite in fact.

> The first half of the Nineteenth Century—its art's Golden Age—was an era of unmitigated political and economic disaster for Denmark. Agriculturally and commercially prosperous in the Eighteenth Century, Denmark suffered an uninterrupted series of catastrophes from about 1800 to 1864. First the British, fearing French domination of the country, bombarded Copenhagen and took control of its entire fleet; then Sweden, taking advantage of Denmark's weakness, waged a war and relieved it of control both of Southern Sweden and of Norway, its largest market. Then, from 1848 to the culminating war of 1864, Prussia wrested from it control of the duchies of Schleswig and Holstein. From then on, Denmark was destined to play no important role in European history—a fate sad, perhaps, only for its political class.

According to Mr Lévy, however, these accumulated disasters caused Denmark increasingly to look inwards, to reject its previously outward-looking disposition. The calm and peaceful landscapes, far from being a manifestation of inner peace, were actually one of forced introspection and nationalistic pride in all that remained to Denmark, namely those very landscapes, so full of peasant (or what the Germans would call volkisch) virtue. A virtue was made of humiliating necessity, and a nationalist ideology, one of what one might call Danitude, grew up so that the artists of Denmark turned their back on developments elsewhere (particularly France) to concentrate on undramatic Danish meadows, woods and coastline. Here I ought to add that it is easy to appreciate one pleasant landscape painting of moderate artistic value, but it is more difficult to do so for twenty in succession. The succession undermines the virtue, and produces a kind of tedium which is unfair to the artist, who never wanted or expected his work to be exhibited in this fashion.

No artistic movement every goes entirely unopposed, and according to Mr Lévy (who is in a much better position to know than I) the inward-looking school of painters were opposed by an outward-looking school, supported by the work of Denmark's greatest literary critic, Georg Brandes. Now Brandes, though Danish by birth, was of Sephardic Jewish descent, and was therefore suspect in the eyes of nationalists and xenophobes (the latter having been much stimulated by their country's recent experience with foreign countries). Danish painters were thus divided into two categories, the blonds and the browns. The former were the nationalists and the latter the internationalists; the name referred to the colour of their hair, the implication being that the more pure ethnic Danish, those who contented themselves with Danish meadows and peasant scenes, were blond-haired, whereas the foreign element were brown-haired. On this view, my little sailor boy might personally be innocent, but the reason for painting him in the first place was not, at least when viewed through the retrospectoscope of European history. On this reading, or in this perspective, even the depiction of the Danish fields and the woods, seemingly so tranquil and so redolent of quiet and unambitious contentment, takes on an unsuspectedly sinister aspect.

But is this right? Is it even reasonable? Does it tell us more about our own obsessions than about Danish painting of a century and a half ago? I open the catalogue at random and I see Frederik Niels Martin Rodhde's painting, *Landscape of the Danish countryside with a man in a boat transporting reeds, talking to a woman sitting on the bank*. Here is a rural idyll. The sky is blue but there are clouds so that it cannot be too hot. A flight of birds wings its way towards us. The land is flat, but not so flat that it bores the eye or implies a disquieting limitlessness; in the far distance, much too far to imply that this is a theocracy, is a church, so that the land is neither overcrowded nor unpeopled.

Can this really bear the weight of interpretation put upon it? Does art not have claims that are independent of the social, historical and economic circumstances in which it was created? I look at the picture again and see only a very pleasant landscape. And yet the art historian's words return to my mind, like a banal tune that won't leave one's brain however much one wants it to.

The anonymous collector wrote a chapter in the catalogue as well. He describes how he started: 'One day, I took the leap... and bought a first painting, delivered a few days later by post.' That is just how my little sailor boy arrived.

30
Give Death Its Due

Ever since I was born about half a million people a year have died in Britain alone, making more than thirty million of them in my lifetime; yet until quite recently I hardly noticed this holocaust around me. Death played no more than a very minor part in the jejune drama of my life; I lived as if exclusively among immortals, where death, if it occurred at all, seemed almost a moral judgment on the lives of the departed rather than a purely natural event in those lives. They must have done something wrong to die.

Now all that is changing; I have reached an age at which even the deaths of those I have known but slightly affect me more deeply than the deaths of those I knew well affected me, when life without death seemed to be the norm.

It is partly a matter of numbers, of course; as one grows older, so the number of one's acquaintances who die grows larger. It is hardly an original thought that age increases the reality of death in one's thoughts; it is a sad fact of human psychology that what touches one nearest touches one most. (But is it really so sad? Imagine a life in which this was not so. It would be intolerable.)

The other day I received by e-mail a note that once upon a time might have arrived on thick-wove black-edged notepaper, informing me of the death of a woman who had worked in an administrative capacity in the hospital in which I had worked until my retirement eight years ago. To say that she had not been universally loved by the staff of the hospital would be to put it kindly; most people who had dealings with her, and who were not inhibited by the decent injunction that one should not speak ill of the (recently) dead, would attest to her difficult manner and general obstructiveness. I had little to do with her personally; that little did not encourage me to seek a deeper acquaintance, but rather to avoid her wherever possible. Words such as 'bad-tempered' or 'impossible' came unbidden to practically everyone's lips when speaking of her. In short, she was a dragon.

Oddly enough I met her in another capacity after her retirement. She worked as a volunteer in the courts where I sometimes still appeared as an expert witness, shepherding witnesses in the right direction (literal, not metaphorical). She was all sweetness and light, and I learned, somewhat late in life I must admit (but better late than never), that one should not always judge a person's character by one's brief acquaintance with it at work. I suspect now that the 'dragon' was such because she had been asked to work at a level beyond her natural capacity, and she sought to disguise her feeling of inadequacy by an artificial fierceness.

The message that I received was very sad. She had been found at home dead in a chair, after her neighbour had become alarmed by the fact that she had not opened the curtains of her front room. Dragon she might once have been, but she was not the kind of paranoid person who normally left her curtains closed to prevent her persecutors from looking in. She had died in her chair, presumably the night before, probably of a heart attack, though as yet the cause of death was not known.

Her husband had died before her, as had her brother and sister. There were no children, and no other known relatives. Though no doubt her death was swift, and let us hope painless, its utter loneliness was such as to cause one pain to imagine; and a former colleague of mine pointed out that there was no one to whom we could express our condolences. After a death we need to express such condolences, and it occurred to me then that often the person we are condoling after a death is ourselves as much as those who have lost someone. We try to comfort ourselves knowing that the fate of the departed is our own ultimate fate.

Another recent death that affected me disproportionately to the depth of my acquaintance with the dead person was that of an elderly woman who worked as a volunteer in a library where I spent three months conducting some historical research. She was there about twice a week and was so self-effacing that I exchanged no more than a few polite words with her at any one time. She was helpful and devoted to the work of the library, and she induced in me a slight sense of guilt that I was by comparison with her brash and self-seeking.

I asked after her when I returned to the library a few months later to give a talk on the results of my research, to be told that she had died suddenly of a fulminant cancer. I was saddened by the news, much more deeply than my superficial contact with this person, however worthy she might have been, would normally have justified or led me to expect. I genuinely mourned her loss for her own sake, but also for the decay of the memory of a time when I had been very happy and which I had hoped to preserve in my mind uncontaminated by change.

As a result of these deaths I began to do what I had never done before, to compile a list in my mind of all the people known to me personally who had died. My paternal grandparents died before I really understood that death was not just a temporary disappearance behind a stage curtain, the dead reappearing some time later when they want or are wanted. I was not taken to see them in their last illnesses as (I suppose) deathbed scenes were not deemed suitable for so young a child. As for my maternal grandparents, they died before I was born.

The first death, then, of which I have some recollection was that of the mother of my then best friend, from whom I was inseparable, when we were about nine. She seemed very old to us then, but I suppose she could not have been much more than forty or forty-five at the most: tragically young from my present point of view. She had a cancer of the breast for which she refused to seek medical attention, having converted to Christian Science some time before; I do not know whether her failure to do so hastened her death or affected the outcome in any way. But I remember her deathbed: the room blacked out by heavy dark red plush curtains that absorbed the sound as effectively as they excluded the light. It was like a death from another age, which I suppose it was, for bourgeois propriety had not yet been quite mocked out of existence.

Then there was the death of a close friend of mine. He was a year older than I—sixteen. He suffered terribly from intractable asthma which had deformed his chest; in those days, treatment by inhaler had just come into being and he took a drug called isoprenaline which relieved the symptoms but whose dangerous toxic effects were not fully understood. He was a brilliant linguist and I have little doubt that he would have made a mark as an academic despite his inherent modesty which at that time was not yet a severe disadvantage to those pursuing a career. His mother was a widow with another son as different from my friend as possible: he was extremely handsome but something of a waster and it was easy to predict that he would come to a sticky end (unless, that is, he succeeded brilliantly, probably in some activity not entirely respectable).

I had been away for a couple of weeks and went round to my friend's house to see him. His mother opened the door. She told me that he had died a few days before of an asthma attack while waiting for an ambulance to arrive (the ambulance telephonist had made all kind of bureaucratic difficulties lasting several minutes before sending the ambulance, which arrived just as my friend died). He had said to his mother, 'I'm dying, I'm dying!' to which she had tried to reply with emollient and comforting words. His last words were, 'Don't you understand, I'm dying!'

This was terrible enough, but then my friend's mother said something that shook me even more deeply.

'Why couldn't it have been the other one?' she said, meaning her other son who would never amount to much or be a support to her.

I was too young to know what to reply to so terrible an exclamation. Did it mean that she believed that there was a providence that demanded the sacrifice of one of her sons, and that it was impossible that both should have survived? Or did it mean, even worse, that she would actually like to be rid of her elder son? Do things said in the extremity of emotion uncover what we 'really' think or wish, as psychoanalysts might say? I fled, my mind in a whirl, never to return, too cowardly to face the emotional awkwardness of another encounter. I feel guilty now that I did not go back, for I might have provided some kind of comfort, and also that I so soon got on with my life as if nothing had happened.

The next death in my life, and the only one for many years, was in my first year at medical school. One of my fellows, much more academically gifted than I, contracted acute leukaemia and died three months later, for in those days treatment was rudimentary and survival very short. I see him now in my mind's eye, before he was ill, sitting in front of me in a lecture, his straw-coloured hair a bit of a bird's nest. When he was dying we shied away from him, not knowing what to say and thoroughly embarrassed by the situation. Whether he died alone I do not know. Perhaps he would have had a brilliant career before him had he survived; but at least, like Rupert Brooke in cultural memory, he is eternally young in my memory. Not, of course, much of a compensation for dying so young.

When I think of these deaths, as I do surprisingly often though without any additional insight into their meaning or significance, I am aware of a gnawing unease. Why was it they, not I, who died aged 45, 16 and 19? Why was it granted to me to live so many years more than they, without having done anything at all to deserve it? Why do I not thank my lucky stars (if that is what they are)? Why, instead, do I complain all the time, of such matters as that the internet connection is a bit slow today? I suppose the answer is that it is because what human beings are like, and must be like if they are to live their lives.

Though death had until recently had played so little part in my life considering its prevalence, I have always had a fondness for cemeteries, and this has lasted the whole of my life. I happen to write this not more than a hundred yards from what is probably the most celebrated cemetery in the world, Père-Lachaise in Paris.

Yesterday, being Sunday, I took a walk in it. I did not search for the tombs of the famous, though I was pleased to have spotted that of Alphonse Bertillon, the inventor of the system of Bertillonage, the system of multiple anthropometric recording that enabled a person to be distinguished with almost absolute certainty from every other human being in the world, used by the police until fingerprinting made it redundant. I noted that his tomb was neglected and overgrown with moss, unlike Oscar Wilde's, which was covered in lipstick kisses.

The tomb that most moved me was that of a man born in 1933 who was 'cowardly murdered' in 1979. (He was a security guard who carried money into and out of banks.) There was a photograph of him in a ceramic medallion, and a fresh plant placed at the tomb's foot, that meant he was not forgotten. His widow had put her name under his, with her date of birth, also 1933, but with no date of death. She was waiting, thirty-six years later, to be interred beside him.

What a wealth of suffering this tomb indicated, but also what nobility!

31
Life's a Swindle

I n my career as a doctor in prison, I met a few swindlers in my time and on the whole I liked them. They had charm and intelligence, which perhaps is unsurprising. It isn't easy to imagine a charmless swindler, after all; it is almost a *sine qua non* of the trade. Whether their charm preceded their swindling or they developed it in order to practice their swindling is hard to say, though the former is more likely. Be that as it may, their charm was their stock-in-trade and human gullibility the market in which they sold their wares.

Though I am a firm partisan of law and order, I admired, albeit somewhat guiltily, the swindlers of my acquaintance, especially if they had swindled on a large scale and had defrauded not individuals but faceless organisations. I know that individual people either owned or paid for those organisations, but somehow it seems less heinous to steal a dollar from a million people than a million dollars from one person. I remember in particular a swindler who had defrauded the exchequer of more than $50 million, the whereabouts of which he refused to disclose to the authorities though to have done so would have lessened his prison sentence considerably. He had worked out what in effect amounted to his rate of pay per year served in prison and decided that it would be worth it, especially as prison conditions in Britain had eased considerably in point of comfort, and he would enjoy a long and golden retirement once released.

His scheme was so complex that I did not understand it; only a man with a firm grasp of various tax laws and a powerful imagination could have seen the opportunity and exploited it. There was an elaborate trail of falsified invoices and other paperwork that I did not understand and I had seen at once that he was an exceptional man, not what the prison guards used to call 'your typical con' [convict], when he entered my room with a volume of Wittgenstein under his arm. Suffice it to say that Wittgenstein was not the favourite reading even of those prisoners who read. Their preferred reading was generally crime novels of the goriest kind.

The Wittgensteinian prisoner was not ill. It was I who had asked to see him rather than the other way round. I needed to know whether his cellmate, the man with whom he shared a cell, a drug smuggler, was mad, as I had reason to believe. There are few places where untreated madness is more troublesome than a prison.

As one might expect from a man who read Wittgenstein for pleasure, he was highly articulate. Prisoners often say the most interesting things and their language often has a beauty of its own, but consecutive thought is not the first characteristic of their utterances. A man such as I sometimes felt starved of conversation in the prison and so I kept the swindler with me for longer than necessary just for the pleasure of hearing him speak. He did not disappoint me.

He was completely unrepentant and was more inclined to pride in his exploit than guilt about it. Who, he asked me, had suffered by it? Large numbers of people had benefited from it, even, because the swindle involved selling goods without tax so that they were cheaper for those fortunate enough to be sold them. The government was deprived of $50 million, it is true, but though this was a large sum for an individual it was small change for the government, an infinitesimal and insignificant loss to its receipts. Besides, the government would almost certainly waste the money; for example, it had spent no less than $20 billion on a unified information system for the health service without anything whatever to show for it, except, perhaps (or even certainly), many millionaire information technology consultants. It is difficult to believe that such waste could have occurred in, or such an outcome could have resulted from, a state of complete ignorance on the part of everyone, without anyone whatever having wished it or at least taken advantage of it.

Furthermore (he told me), he had used a large part of his fortune, which he refused to believe was ill-gotten, in constructing a mansion in a so-called Third World country. He had thereby stimulated the economy of that country, giving employment to poor people much more honestly than if the government which he had allegedly defrauded had spent the same sums as he in a programme of official aid. Not only would most of the money spent have gone to those administering it, but most of what remained would have stuck to the fingers of the government of the poor country through which it would inevitably have had to be channelled. In other words, his foreign aid was much more effective and less damaging than anything the government could have done.

I should add that he said all this with a lightness of spirit that was delightful, so that one felt in listening to him that had drunk a glass of champagne. Not only did I not know what to reply to him by way of refutation, but I did not even want to refute him; on the contrary, I was on his side. My slight objection, that I made more for form's sake than from conviction, that by depriving the government of $50 million he would cause it to seek that sum elsewhere to the detriment of taxpayers, sounded hollow even as I made it. I also tried the argument, without really believing it, that if everyone did as he did the government's receipts would fall dramatically, with unforeseeable but disastrous consequences.

'But everyone won't do it,' he replied.

This was the most obvious answer to return. To do as he had done would require two qualities (at least two): first the intellect necessary to understand the laws and the gaps in them, an intellect quite out of the ordinary; and second the daring to flout the law in such a fashion.

Let us suppose that the necessary intellect were to be found in one per cent of the population. Let us suppose also that the quality of necessary daring is not only independent of that of intellect, but is (as seems to me likely) even rarer than that of intellect, say one in a thousand: then not more than one in a hundred thousand people would act as he had done. And if we take into account that nine out of ten people would also scruple to act in this way, for reasons of false moral delicacy, we now find that not more than one in a million would so act. Moreover, of those with the necessary intellect, daring and lack of scruple, not more than one in ten would actually act as he had done rather than in some other way. So now we are up to one in ten million. Therefore to object to his conduct on the grounds that it would be disastrous if everybody did it would be absurd: it would be like keeping pigs locked up because they might develop wings and fly.

Yes, the arguments were all on his side and he not only had nothing to reproach himself with but was almost a benefactor of society. If his incarceration had cost society a great deal—I have never understood quite why imprisonment should be so expensive—that was society's fault, not his.

We laughed together. Perhaps his opportunity to speak to me had been as pleasurable for him as for me: I hoped so. But as he left the room I realised that I had been caught in the web of his charm. I could easily imagine how he or someone like him might ensnare me in one of his schemes, persuading me that it was not only free of risk but perfectly legal and indeed of benefit to the world. But he would sacrifice me, throw me to the lions, without a moment's hesitation if it would save his skin. As he left, therefore, I felt almost as if I had had a lucky escape.

My reminiscences of this man were provoked by reading a wonderful portrait of the swindler Stavisky by the French writer, Joseph Kessel, published shortly after Stavisky's downfall and suicide (or murder, the case has never been satisfactorily elucidated) in 1934. The case brought down the French government of the day and provoked some of the most violent Parisian riots of the century, which is saying something.

Stavisky, known to many as Monsieur Alexandre or *Le beau Sasha*, was born in the Ukraine in 1888 and moved to France with his parents when he was 12 years old. He was one of those intelligent, gifted and ingenious people who always preferred the paths of dishonesty to those of honesty, though one feels that if only he had stuck to the latter he might have made an enduring fortune. One of the things about swindlers, however, is that they not only want to make a fortune quickly and easily without all the boring and painstaking intermediary work, but they delight to fool the world to demonstrate their superiority to it. The excitement of the moth flying close to the flame is another of their pleasures, that more solid activity would never give them.

Stavisky was a swindler for most of his adult life and once sent eighteen months in prison. But his time there did not discourage him or for that matter inhibit or disadvantage him. His next scheme was his big one, though it had humble enough origins, in the municipal pawnshop of Bayonne, a smallish town in the south-west of France.

In those days municipalities in France owned pawnshops which had the right to issue bonds according to their assets. Among other schemes, Stavisky brought the Bayonne municipal pawnshop the supposedly priceless emeralds of the former Empress of Germany, which turned out to be glass. The bonds issued by the Bayonne municipal pawnbrokers backed by such assets reached many millions in today's money, with Stavisky taking fees for his invaluable services. He lived the life of a merchant prince and took care to weave a web of contacts with people in high places, whom he bribed and flattered. That his wealth was fraudulently obtained was long suspected and on one occasion he was arrested and charged, but obtained (thanks to his contacts) postponements of his trial no fewer than nineteen times. It was because of his contacts in high places, that had enabled him so easily and for so long to evade justice, that his downfall had such a political impact, leading every citizen from left to right with the impression that *ils sont tous corrompus*, they (the people in power, the system itself) are all corrupt: precisely what everyone now says in France, and where many feel that the exasperation might lead again before long to 1934-type scenes.

Kessel, who himself was of Tsarist Russian origin, emigrating to France with his parents when he was ten years old, always knew Stavisky as Monsieur Alexandre, the refined, generous, successful and charming financier who offered to back a weekly magazine to be edited by him, without demanding any editorial control whatever. In a hundred pages or so, he sketches Stavisky's appearance, manner and character in such a way that one understands why people would have been charmed by him, why they would have trusted him, why even after his frauds were exposed they retained an affection for him. He was a genuinely kindly man, anxious to do good where he could, without malice of the more obvious kind, a devoted husband and father.

When exposure became inevitable and unavoidable, Stavisky fled. It was said he was making for Venezuela, but he never got further than Chamonix. There in a villa, surrounded by police who had traced him, and who were determined to arrest him, he shot himself. Some say the police shot him so that he could not reveal the precise nature of his contacts in high places; others that he really did commit suicide. One way of reconciling the two theories is the supposition that the police surrounded the villa and waited for so long to enter to persuade him to commit suicide.

His last letter to his wife, written before his flight is touching, and is hardly that of a wicked or evil man, much harm though he might have done:

My beloved wife,

Here for the last time you will find in these lines all my soul, all my heart and all the love I have for you. You have always been the light of my life and it is for this reason that I consider it my duty to disappear. You know with what affection

I surrounded our dear children. I leave each of them a word that they will not comprehend until they have reached the age of reason. I ask them to retain all their love for you and, if circumstances permit you – human nature being what it is – to make another life, that they are understanding. It is for you, for them, that I disappear... The situation that currently awaits me will separate me from you and them for years, if not forever. It's better that you should be free, and that I should not be an obstacle to their education and lives. What I ask of you above all is to raise them in the sentiment of honour and probity; and that when they reach the difficult age of fifteen, to be careful of their social contacts, so that they are set on the right path in life and become good people.

I would have liked to leave you in a much better material situation [he was ruined], but you are courageous, you will be able to start a little business that will allow you to live and raise the children in a dignified way. When I think that I had so much money and that I leave you in so parlous a situation, it is yet another reason for me to disappear...

Stavisky's son, Claude, having passed his childhood in the suite of a luxury hotel in Paris, spent much of his early adulthood in a psychiatric hospital. Then he became a circus performer and magician before taking a job looking after the boilers in the psychiatric hospital where he had been a patient. In 1974, at the age of 48, he was ejected for disorderly behaviour from the premiere of a film about his father.

32
Coming Up Tramps

More than half a century ago (how strange it seems to me now to be able to write such a thing!), my teacher made the class learn by heart some lines by W H Davies that stay with me still and run through my mind whenever I walk past or through a field. She gave us the weekend to learn the lines and then tested us on them on Monday morning. Woe betide us if we were not able to recite them like automata. For a time poetry and fear were associated in my mind; but in the long run I gained more by the method than I lost by it.

There is no disguising the fact, however, that the method was somewhat at variance in spirit with the poem that we learnt:

What is this life if, full of care,
We have no time to stand and stare?—

No time to stand beneath the boughs,
And stare as long as sheep and cows...

No time to see, when woods we pass,
Where squirrels hide their nuts in grass...

A poor life this if, full of care,
We have no time to stand and stare.

I suppose also that the thought and feeling of this poem might seem banal and hackneyed, and yet its resonance can only have increased in the hundred years since it was written, since then the fields have receded and men are busier than ever, notwithstanding their numerous labour-saving devices. The poem expresses something akin to Pascal's *aperçu* that Man's miseries derive from his inability to sit alone in a room. In a school in a poor area of a small town in Brazil which I once visited, the teachers had tried to break the addiction of the pupils to their electronic distractions by putting pictures of the local avifauna on the walls, so that they might see that the real world was more marvellous than the virtual, which so imprisoned their minds.

We were made also to read Davies' *The Autobiography of a Super Tramp*, for in those days it was still thought important (bizarre idea!) that children should learn to write good prose: not that they would all do so, of course, but that those capable of learning would do so. The dog-in-the-manger, no-child-left-behind variety of egalitarianism had not yet come so completely to dominate pedagogical theory as it has now.

Is W H Davies forgotten? I daresay that, such being the imper-manence of literary celebrity, you could walk down a busy street in any English-speaking city without passing anyone who had ever heard of him. But Davies was once well-known enough, as much for his life sto-ry, a remarkable one, as for his work as a poet, which was nevertheless popular. D H Lawrence derided him as a poet, or at least damned him with faint praise, saying that he had but a single sweet tone: but perhaps because I am inclined to cynicism I am easily moved by emotion sim-ply-expressed, that is to say the one note that Lawrence said that Davies sang. (Or is it the ease with which I am moved that inclines me to cyni-cism?) At any rate, lines such as the following move me:

Come, let us find a cottage, love,
That's green for half a mile around;
To laugh at every grumbling bee,
Whose sweetest blossom's not yet found…

'Tis strange how men find time to hate,
When life is all too short for love…

Yes indeed: as I age I find myself ever more reluctant to quarrel both because life is too short for it and most quarrels grow out of bad faith on both sides, including my own.

Or again:

> No doubt it is a selfish thing
> To fly from human suffering;
> No doubt he is a selfish man,
> Who shuns poor creatures, sad and wan.
>
> But 'tis a wretched life to face
> Hunger in almost every place;
> Cursed with a hand that's empty, when
> The heart is full to help all men.

Hunger has declined since Davies' day, of course, to be replaced by overeating which brings a form of suffering of its own, albeit self-inflicted (but not the less suffering for that), and there is still suffering enough in the world to give point to these verses. Indeed, they have become more pointed than ever, in so far as virtue has become less a matter of behaving well, which is always difficult to do, as of expressing the right sentiments towards those who suffer, which is always easy to do. This means that Sir Toby Belch's question, 'Dost thou think, because thou art virtuous, there shall be no more cakes and ale?', is more pertinent than ever. Only yesterday, an American friend of mine told me that he once said to a neighbour 'It's a beautiful day,' to which the neighbour replied tartly, not to say sourly, 'It's not a beautiful day in Fallujah,' as if no good weather were to be enjoyed until it were good weather everywhere, without distinction. The implication of the reply was that my friend was unfeeling and insensitive, unlike his interlocutor, who so felt the sufferings of the world that he could not enjoy anything until they were assuaged: gross hypocrisy and dishonesty, it needs hardly be said, for he had almost certainly enjoyed his breakfast that morning, as he would also enjoy his lunch.

I am no scholar of W H Davies—no doubt such scholars exist, for in a world of oedematous tertiary education there are scholars of everything—and so it came as a surprise to me to find a book by him quite by chance that was published forty years after his death in 1940. It was titled *Young Emma*, and the history of its publication is a strange one.

For the first fifty years of his life, Davies had lived as a bachelor. He was born in a pub in South Wales, and his father died when he was three. He was brought up by his father's parents, publicans of the Church Inn (a strange name in South Wales, where church and pub then mixed like oil and water), and became a delinquent youth. He then ran away to America, where he lived for several years as a tramp. The pivotal point in his life occurred when, in the company of another tramp, he jumped maladroitly from a train in Ontario and his foot was crushed, whereafter his leg had to be amputated below the knee. Ever after, he sported a wooden leg.

His Autobiography and his books of poems brought him renown if not fame and fortune, and he mixed for a time in high society. But he grew tired of that life, and retired to the countryside with a new-found wife.

Young Emma is the story of how he found his wife. He wrote it in 1924 and sent it to the eminent publisher, Jonathan Cape, who asked George Bernard Shaw's advice about it. Shaw had been a champion of Davies, but advised against publishing it, not because it was a bad book, but because he feared that it would do the author's reputation no good. Davies, who had sent the manuscript and two typescripts to the publisher, asked on refusal by the publisher for the return of the manuscript, and that he destroy the two typescripts 'as soon as he liked.' This suggested ambivalence about such destruction; and in fact they survived. They surfaced again in 1940, the year of Davies' death, when a woman then working for Cape, who was later to become an eminent historian, C V Wedgwood, was asked to advise on whether it should be published. She said it could not be published while Mrs Davies (the Emma of the title, whose real name was Helen Payne) was still alive. The poet, William Plomer, gave the same advice in 1972.

Mrs Davies died in 1979, after 39 years of widowhood, and the book was published the following year. It is the story of how he came to marry Helen Payne.

When he was fifty, Davies decided that he did not want any more to live alone, so he set about finding a wife in what seems to modern sensibilities a cold-blooded and deliberate fashion:

> In searching for a wife, I found it no easy matter to get one to my liking. One woman, whom I thought would make a good wife, refused me on account of blood-relationship. Another, who had a great admiration for my work, and liked me personally, could not make up her mind to trust her life with mine...

There was an actress and a rich woman whom he could have married, but they would not suit him:

> I wanted a woman who was worth working for, and would be
> dependent in my own loving kindness.

Davies continues by describing his appearance, strangely omitting
any mention of his wooden leg. He was no apotemnophiliac in search of
an acrotomophiliac, that is too say a man with a sexual fixation on being an amputee in search a woman with sexual attraction to amputees;
he wanted merely a companion, without intellectual or literary pretensions, for the rest of his life.

To this end, he picked up women in the street and tried them out,
as it were. In post-World War I London, this posed no great problem.
After three attempts he found Helen Payne, a farmer's daughter come up
to London. He met her as she waited at a bus stop and in what seems an
astonishingly casual way they decided to live together. She was already
pregnant, though she did not tell Davies so; she had a miscarriage from
which she might easily have died. He also thought it was she from whom
he caught the gonorrhoea and syphilis from which he suffered shortly
afterwards, though he later revised his opinion and came to the conclusion that it must have been from one of his earlier encounters. Despite
her own earlier encounters, of which there must have been at least one,
Helen was an innocent abroad who knew nothing whatever about venereal disease and did not understand what Davies was talking about
when he mentioned it to her.

A casual encounter; the woman already pregnant; false accusa-
tions of infection with venereal disease: not a triad conducive to a happy
marriage, you might have supposed. But in fact Mr and Mrs Davies were
very happy; the marriage was a good one. I don't think, if you had known
the initial conditions, you would have predicted it, rather the reverse.

Yet there were positive indications as well, of a rather unromantic
kind. Davies needed companionship and probably would have been regarded as no great catch himself; his wife was facing a most uncertain
feature when she was waiting at the bus-stop and was in need of security.
Mutual interest was at least as important as passion to the success of
their marriage. But love arrived: in 1935, at the age of 64, Davies addressed a book of love poems to his wife, with titles such as *Let us lie
closer, as lover's should*, *Our love this day is ten years' old*, *When I was
old and she was young*. These are unaffected words that remind me of an
Indian friend of mine who tells the story of his betrothal under the ar-

ranged (not forced, *nota bene*) marriage system that led to a very happy marriage, among the best that I know.

It was time he married, in the opinion of his parents, and they selected six potential brides all over India for him, and he went on a long journey to see them all. The first four did not please him; the fifth, a thousand miles away from his home, pleased him quite a lot; nevertheless, he continued on to the sixth just in case. But in the end he chose the fifth, she consented, and now, nearly forty years later, they are still happily married.

If there is a lesson in the story of W H Davies and *Young Emma* it is the unpredictability of life, which is what makes life so difficult, so worth the living.

33
The Good, the Bad and the Ugly

The epidemiology, sociology and psychology of bad taste interest me because there is so much of it about. Bad taste is the
shadow-side of self-expression, as it were; indeed, it often seems as if it
is the only side of it. This is one of the reasons I so favour reticence as
a trait, at least in the modern world. Take but reticence away, and hark
what bad taste follows!

I happen lately to have been reading about a personage who strikes
me more as a specimen of the worst possible taste than as a real person,
namely the late Simon John Beverley, alias Sid Vicious. It is dangerous,
though, to allow oneself ever to think of anybody as a mere specimen,
however horrible whatever he might supposedly be a specimen of, for
that way inhumanity lies. Even the most depraved person is precisely
that, a person, and one must never permit oneself completely to forget
it.

Normally, of course, I would not read about an uninteresting person such as Sid Vicious. I have a fairly simple attitude to rock music,
of which Mr Vicious was some kind of exponent, the same in effect as
President Coolidge's to sin: I am against it. Ideally I would like to start a
Society for the Suppression of Rock Music, but I suspect it would have
approximately the same practical effect as the Society for the Suppression of Vice founded in the early Nineteenth Century, namely nil. Suffice
it to say that whenever I hear that the youth of a country is employing
rock music to rise up against dictatorship, I rally at once to the cause of
the dictator. Civilisation can survive dictatorship, but it cannot survive

rock music.

Let us, however return to the sad (and bad) case of Mr Vicious. I read about him because I intended to write an essay about a murder committed by a man who admired Mr Vicious' life and work, and it seemed to me that this was a fact of some significance in the case. How could any person of the slightest human decency or aesthetic discrimination admire such a figure as Mr Vicious? I quickly learned that it was impossible, inconceivable.

Mr Vicious, some people will remember, was accused in 1978 of having killed his girlfriend, Nancy Spungen, in Room 100 of the Chelsea Hotel in New York. Both were aged 20 at the time. A few months later, while celebrating his release from prison on bail, Mr Vicious died of an overdose of heroin. He was never brought to trial, and as a result all kinds of wild exculpatory theories have been circulated by those weakminded or bad enough to be his admirers

Poor Mr Vicious! He was early instilled by his British mother with a philosophy of life at once stupid and horrible, at least if reports are true. 'You are you,' he told him, 'you can do anything you like… You should be able to do what the f… you like.' The crudity of both the form and content of this philosophy of life, if it deserves that title rather than that of attitude to life, hardly needs emphasis. His mother's rider, that in doing what the f… he liked he should not hurt others, was about as effective as a paper tissue to shelter from a monsoon.

Unhappily, Mr Vicious, singularly lazy and untalented (such skill as he acquired on the guitar he learnt in an afternoon) but with the ambition, or daydream, to become a rock star, encountered an unscrupulous and cynical entrepreneur of ugly youth nihilism and self-pity who saw in young Mr Vicious the potential to be really nasty and uninhibitedly transgressive, and thus make a lot of money from him. Never inclined to refinement, either by upbringing or temperament, Mr Vicious (the adoption of such a name being a true indication of his proclivities) devoted himself to the promotion of ugliness both moral and aesthetic. He drank to excess, took drugs, wrote a few horrible 'songs,' dressed in black rags, exposed himself in public, cut himself up, fought with others over nothing, swore constantly, smashed hotel rooms, and in general behaved as appallingly as his somewhat limited imagination could conceive. His every gesture, his every movement, was ugly in the extreme. The worse he behaved, the better from the point of view of publicity: for in an antinomian world, notoriety and fame are one. A persona assumed for long enough, however, soon becomes indistinguishable from a real.

Mr Vicious soon lived up to his name.

Squalor became an ideology: nothing was real unless it was squalid. Here was the squalor not of the mediaeval saint indifferent to the world, its comforts and it usages, but a squalor of self-indulgence unconstrained by thought for others or even for oneself in five minutes' time. Irrespective of whether or not Mr Vicious killed his girlfriend—I think that he did—his whole life was, in a way, exemplary, a bad example being a good example when reflected upon rather than imitated. No minimally sensitive or sensible person could take it otherwise than as a perfection of evil.

It therefore came to me as something of a surprise when I read the two letters that Mr Vicious wrote to the murdered girl's mother, Mrs Deborah Spungen, after his arrest, and which were included in the latter's memoir of her daughter, *And I Don't Want to Live this Life*. This title is itself taken from a poem written after the murder by the accused:

> But now you're gone there's only pain.
> And nothing I can do.
> And I don't want to live this life
> If I can't live for you.

This is banal, no doubt, the level of poetry one might expect to find in a greetings card of some description, but it is not crude in the way that the life of Mr Vicious had always hitherto been crude.

The letters were also better written and more refined than I should have expected. They are not, of course, literary masterpieces, as very few letters are; but neither are they the sort of crude grunts reduced to semi-literate writing that one would have predicted. Here is a paragraph:

> Frank [the father of the victim] said in the paper that Nancy was born in pain and lived in pain all her life. When I first met her, and for about six months after that, I spent practically the whole time in tears. Her pain was too much to bear. Because, you see, I spent practically the whole time in tears. But she said I must be strong for her or otherwise she would have to leave me. So I became strong for her, and she began to stop having asthma attacks and seemed to be going through a lot less pain.

Irrespective of its sincerity, this letter was that of someone who knew better than the way he and the victim had chosen to live. (The sincerity, or at least the durability, of the sentiments expressed in the letter may be doubted by the fact that Mr Vicious soon found himself another girlfriend and continued, though charged with Nancy Spungen's death, to lead a drug and drink fuelled life, in precisely the same milieu as that in which he had moved before: no bethinking himself in the bowels of Christ there, then. Admittedly he was still only twenty, but a catastrophic event such as the near-disembowelment of a girlfriend in one's room might have been expected to exert a greater effect on his subsequent lifestyle.)

My point is not so much that there was a more refined or better person deep within Mr Vicious that was trying to emerge from his crude carapace, but that he knew that the way that he was living was bad: evil would not be too strong a word for it. No man does wrong knowingly, said Socrates, but he had not had the advantage (I won't say pleasure) of meeting or reading about Sid Vicious: for the latter did wrong knowingly, self-glorifyingly in fact.

The question is 'Why?' And why was he, and is he still, admired? He was no artistic genius of the type to whom licence has often been granted, rightly or wrongly, by admirers, the good of the work more than cancelling out the evil of the life. His only discernible talent, as far as I can see, was a certain ruthlessness, an uncompromising willingness to forgo self-respect. Why would anyone want to imitate or emulate this, given the appalling moral and aesthetic consequences of doing so?

I think the answer is twofold: egotism and mental laziness. The egotism provokes the desire to cut a figure in the world, no matter what it might be. 'There is,' said Oscar Wilde, with his typically frivolous perspicuity, 'only one thing worse than being talked about, and that is not being talked about.' He did not foresee a world in which everyone would want to be famous for quarter of an hour, even if, *pace* Andy Warhol, they could not be. To melt unseen or unremarked into a crowd because one did not think one was worthy of notice became, for many, the worst wound imaginable to their self-esteem, a quality that they nursed as it were a gaping and unhealing wound. Fame at all costs was better than anonymity, fame being a kind of afterlife that guaranteed a meaning to the banality of everyday life.

In the absence of talent, however, and of the willingness to work and study (the only way talent can be brought to fruition), transgression and outrage are the only way to fame. Mozart was once described as taking dictation from God, a kind of Mohammed of music, but in his famous letter to Joseph Haydn, dedicating to him his six quartets, and full of filial piety, he said that the quartets had taken him much hard and patient study. True, hard and patient study alone could not have resulted in such wonderful works (here, surely, was the source of Salieri's animus towards him, if he really had any such, for we are rarely altogether without ill-feeling towards those more talented than ourselves, especially in our chosen fields); but genius without effort would also have remained fallow.

Lust for fame, the desire at all costs not to remain anonymous (the worst of all fates for an egotist), combined with an absence of talent, results in unscrupulousness, not only in the field of music but in all fields. The effect is particularly dire in fields that have hitherto required aesthetic accomplishment, however, for aesthetic accomplishment requires discipline, study and the like to achieve, even for the most prodigiously talented. Impatience born of laziness supervenes; only ever greater transgression can assure fame or notoriety (which are the same thing in a degraded culture).

Not everyone has the courage of his degradation, however; those who do not have the courage become admirers and hangers-on, fans and pale imitators, rather than originators or further transgressors. They are to Mr Vicious as Marie Antoinette was to real shepherdesses; they are not quite willing to take the consequences of their own bad taste and ill-will towards anything better.

Nevertheless, they have an effect by sheer weight of numbers, perhaps even greater in the aggregate than that of the original transgressors. They turn what was once a transgression into a norm or a convention. Mr Vicious' mode of dress, hideous and deliberately ugly, was once so outrageous or extraordinary that he was remarked everywhere he went and even attacked for it; soon it raised no eyebrow.

By no stretch of the imagination could the way he dressed be regarded as progress, not even in the strange, technical sense of the Victorian Rational Dress Society. On the contrary. But ugliness is much easier to achieve than beauty, as destruction is easier than construction. It is true that the result of great effort is not necessarily beauty; but the result of lack of effort is always ugly. And that is why ugliness is so tempting to mankind.

34
You Cannot Fathom Russia with Your Mind

From the point of view of complete rationalists, who think that life can be lived wholly according to a rational plan, anniversaries are odd. Why should the memory of an event be more prominent in our minds at one moment or on one date rather than another? And if we are going to have anniversaries, why should the hundredth be more important than, say, the ninety-third or the eighty-seventh? Surely, if an event was historically important, it was equally important for all the time that succeeded it? The importance given to centenaries is a relic of magical thinking. Why not celebrate or confer equal importance on the dozenth or the twelve dozenth anniversary?

However, Man does not live by rationality alone, and we must sometimes take him as he is. Indeed, we must occasionally be like him ourselves; and I doubt that there are many among us who are completely unaffected or unimpressed by the hundredth anniversary of some event we consider important. Is there anyone alive who really feels, as against thinks, that a hundredth birthday has no more allure than, say, a forty-eighth?

This year, then, it is inevitable that we shall be subjected to a lot of memorialisation of the centenary of the outbreak of the Great War. There will be historiographical battles over the meaning of that most catastrophic of all wars that ushered in the age of genocide and political mass-murder. Did it have any moral purpose whatever, was it any one power's fault more than another's? Was it the war to end all wars, to make the world safe for democracy, or was it merely a sordid struggle for hegemony in Europe and in the world? Or was it a Greek tragedy?

Fashions change in attitudes as surely as in dress, perhaps in an even more fickle way. Revulsion against the pointlessness of the slaughter was by no means immediate, at least in France and Britain. On the contrary, patriotic pride in the sacrifice and victory was the predominant response; disillusionment set in only ten years or more later, and much more among the intellectuals than among the general population, which continued to attend ceremonies at war memorials as if the war had been for a sacred cause and was not a mere disaster brought about by the arrogance and incompetence of the political class of the time. The famous war, or rather anti-war, poetry was in the great minority by comparison with the versification or doggerel of thousands of patriotic poetasters.

The spread of anti-war sentiment, the feeling that all the death and destruction had been in vain, that the war (and therefore, by extension, war itself) solved no problems, was, paradoxically, one of the causes of the Second World War, for it was the soil in which support for the appeasement of Hitler grew; and appeasement made the war, when it finally came, far worse than it would have been only a few years earlier. If history teaches anything, it is not that no one learns anything from history, it is rather that people learn the wrong lessons from history.

Some historians treat the war as if it were the bursting of an abscess that had been gathering in the previous decades which were seemingly those of peace, plenty, progress and prosperity. But what is obvious in retrospect is often not obvious in prospect. Certainly no one had much idea of what kind of war it would be if war came. But many did not even suspect that war was coming, let alone what kind of war it would be.

It is instructive, then, to read books written just before the war broke out by intelligent authors with no special faculty of foresight, none greater than the ordinary or than ours would have been. To read only the far-sighted is to fail to appreciate their far-sightedness. We must read the ordinary to appreciate our own limitations.

When, therefore, I came across a handsome book written in 1913 by a man called Hugh Stewart with the title *Provincial Russia*, I bought it and read it. After all, a cataclysm of world-shaking proportions in Russia was only four years away from the publication of the book: what inkling did the author of book have of that?

The answer is 'None whatever.' This is not because the author was a stupid man, very far from it. Born in 1884, he was a classical scholar of note who had an interesting, adventurous and tragic life. Having obtained a good degree in Classics at Cambridge, he went as a teacher to Tsarist Russia, where he learned to speak Russian fluently. He then had an academic career, becoming Professor of Classics at Canterbury College in New Zealand at a very early age. He was an accomplished mountaineer. He joined up to the New Zealand Expeditionary Force at the outbreak of the Great War, was seriously wounded at Gallipoli, promoted to colonel and highly decorated. After the war he resumed his academic career, returning a few years later to England as Professor of Classics at Leeds university and then as principal of University College, Nottingham (D. H. Lawrence's alma mater). He died suddenly at sea, aged 54, on his way back from New Zealand where he had been on holiday.

His first wife died in 1920, two weeks after giving birth to their son. His second wife died in 1928, while giving birth to a stillborn son. He himself died only four years after his third marriage, having by then had a son and a daughter. Such a story reminds us how fragile was the human hold on life only a couple of generations ago.

And indeed Stewart's short but handsome book has medical details that are of interest to me as a reminder of how recently-won has been our current state of (medical) enlightenment—other forms of enlightenment being another question altogether. My grandfather came from a region, White Russia, where, twenty years after he left it, 'Illnesses are signs of the Devil's forces.' The beliefs of the locals are picturesque and in a way charming, but not very medically effective:

> The fever that haunts the dwellers is an ugly old woman who creeps up to the sleeper and kisses him, and will not part from him. But then, she may be tricked in various ways. Once a sick man expecting her visit pretended to be dead. He lay down under the ikons and bade his relatives weep for him. When the fever came and saw them weeping, she believed him dead, and went away. You may also frighten her, for instance, by firing a gun over the invalid, for she is a great coward.

However, the medical credulity of the highly-educated author was not much less than that of the White Russian peasants. This is what he has to say about the Crimea and its healing mud:

The mud consists largely of vegetable matter, whose peculiar chemical qualities make it efficacious for the treatment of such diseases as scrofula, gout, or tuberculosis. This cure was employed by the Tartars, who dug a hole in the dried bottom of the lake into which they put the invalid, covering him except for the head with the freshly exposed mud. The method followed at the present day is essentially the same. The invalid is sunk into his mud bath and left for about twenty minutes with an umbrella sheltering his head from the hot sun. Then he is washed with warm water and carried back to his room, where he sweats in pools and will drink as much as ten tumblers of thin lemon-flavoured tea.

The invalids of whom the author is talking are the cream of Russian society, highly educated and cosmopolitan. Before we laugh too loud at such pitiful ignorance even of the best-educated, perhaps we should try to imagine what remedies we should be prepared to try ourselves if we were attacked by a slow wasting disease for which there was no indubitably effective or scientifically proven treatment.

Provincial Russia is not a political book, a fact which is itself very revealing. Politics, where touched upon at all, are mentioned *en passant*, not as being the main interest or purpose of life. By contrast, no book about Russia published after 1917 could be other than political, obsessively so. Every author took a political stand, for or against. The landscape disappeared from view. The Revolution politicised existence itself.

In Stewart's book, the landscape is still important. He quotes physical descriptions of it by Gogol, Aksakov and Chekhov. The customs and beliefs of the peasantry are more important to him than their economic arrangements or the politics of the land question. The autocracy is not mentioned once. The many pictures that accompany the text are by an artist called Frédéric de Haenen (1857–1928) are folkloric, even those that depict a convoy of prisoners, not necessarily political, heading for Siberia. The hunt for an escaped prisoner is indistinguishable in spirit from the hunt for a bear, and is almost a form of sport. The peasants in the pictures are often shown dancing, but not in the way they are shown dancing once the Soviet propaganda state had been established: there is no implication here that they dance because they are so happy with the political and economic state of affairs.

There is no sense of impending doom or catastrophe in the book, no intimation that a regime is soon to be established in the country that will regularly kill more people in a day than its predecessor in a century. On the contrary, if anything the march of progress, of ever-increasing wealth, education and enlightenment is taken for granted, as being more or less inevitable and unstoppable. Little did the author guess that it would take many years for Russia once again to reach the level of production of the year of publication of his book.

I do not wish to ridicule the author when I say that in his pages appeared one of the least prescient prognostications I have ever seen in print. Here is the passage:

> Since the emancipation [of the peasants in 1861] the peasants have made immense progress. And now the rate of improvement can only accelerate with the influence of education, the breaking up of the commune, which was a heavy drag on rural enterprise, the political franchise, and the increased facilities offered by the spread of railways for disposing of surplus crops and developing the internal resources of the country. A great future assuredly lies before this remarkable people, with its physical and mental powers, it vigour, elasticity and youth. This may be a question of time, but it can scarcely be a matter for doubt.

I do not need to point out the inaccuracy of this prediction, unless being the victim of one of the greatest and most vicious political experiments in history be counted 'a great future' for a people. Yet the author is not a fool, quite the reverse; he is not a liar; he is not blind; he is not ill-intentioned; he is not blinded by ideology. By all accounts he learnt the language of the country very well, sufficiently well to be able to describe the variation of its dialects with authority; he travelled extensively within the Empire. He was well-versed in Russia's literature and history. Nor were these his only qualifications or accomplishments; as a classicist he was acquainted with historical precedent and the fate of empires.

He made the cardinal mistake of confusing a projection with a prediction. It is a mistake that I doubt many of us have altogether avoided in our lives. He thought that because immense progress had been made in the recent past in Russia it would continue indefinitely into the future, along the same line of the graph as it were. He was like the man who thinks that because he has driven safely at 150 miles an hour for a hundred miles, he can continue at that speed without danger.

The prescient man is not the man who knows most. He is like the chess-player who takes in the situation on a board at once, the result of much study and the possession of instinct. The man who has not studied is blinded by prejudice; the man who has studied, but has no instinct, is blinded by learning.

35
Of Horlicks and Heroism

When I was young there was a milky drink called Horlicks that some people took just before they went to bed to assure themselves a good night's sleep. I knew that it was disgusting even without ever having tried it—one was able in those days to know many such things without experience—and that it was consumed (at least in my opinion) mainly by middle aged, middle class insomniacs with indigestion. I believe that the drink is still sold today and is produced by a giant pharmaceutical company, one of the largest in the world.

In those days it was advertised with a slogan that stuck in my mind: 'Prevents night starvation.' I intuited from the first that this was balderdash: I didn't know much human physiology, but the concept of night starvation, of people going to bed well-fed and waking up skeletal, seemed to me intrinsically absurd. But clearly it was an effective slogan, at least in the sense of sticking in my mind if not that of selling me the product, for here I am, more than fifty years later, remembering it vividly, as pupils a century and a half ago remembered Latin tags.

At any rate, it was one of the advertising slogans that first alerted me to the fact that advertising was not intended to inform but to influence, and not necessarily to the advantage of the person influenced. I wouldn't go so far as to say that I have been completely uninfluenced by advertisements ever since—I vaguely remember reading Vance Packard's *The Hidden Persuaders* a few years later, and no man can claim to be utterly impervious to the wiles of publicists—but I think I am less influenced by them that average. No advertising campaign has caused me to buy something I would not otherwise have bought.

Actually the slogan about Horlicks was already old by the time I first heard it. It was devised (as I learned recently) in 1931 by a man called Norman Cameron. The latter was an advertising copywriter who, as it happened, was a poet, much admired by his contemporaries though he has never been accorded much popular recognition.

Cameron (1905–1953) was a distant relative of Lord Macaulay. His father was a military chaplain to a Scots regiment in India, who died at precisely the same age, 48, as his son was to do, and of precisely the same disease, hypertension leading to cerebral haemorrhage. At Oxford, where he scraped a degree, he knew Auden and others who were to become famous. For a time after graduation he went to live in Majorca, with Robert Graves and Laura Riding, whose disciple he was. On returning to England, having tired of discipleship, he found work with an advertising agency, but kept up his literary friendships and acquaintances. He was a heavy drinker and counted as Dylan Thomas' best friend, though he wrote and published a scabrous poem about him called *The Dirty Little Accuser*:

> Who invited him in? What was he doing here,
> That insolent little ruffian, that crapulous lout?
> When he quitted a sofa, he left behind him a smear.
> My wife says he even tried to paw her about.

Why, then, the dirty little accuser? The next verse makes this clear:

> What was worse, if, as often happened, we caught him out
> Stealing or pinching the maid's backside, he would leer,
> With a cigarette on his lip and a shiny snout,
> With a hint: 'You and I are all in the same galère.'

In other words, cleanliness, honesty etc. are but a veneer thinly disguising our true nature, which is similar to Thomas's.

Even if this is the metaphysical message of the poem (that after all ends with the line that 'We shall never be able to answer his accusation'), I am not sure that I should be entirely pleased if my best friend described me as leaving a smear on a sofa when I got up from it, especially if I knew that there was some truth in it. I have seen it written that Cameron's poem was affectionate, but if so I should not have cared to be the butt of his contempt.

Cameron's fame, such as it is, rests upon about seventy published poems, none of them very long. He was also a translator from the French and German, including of Hitler's table talk: but no one remembers or long honours a translator, however good. His complete poems make a slender volume, my copy of which, bought second-hand, smells ferociously of smoked tobacco: I imagine it was previously owned by a pipe-man of considerable literary culture, who read it closely, always smoking, in his book-lined study. The tobacco must have done for him in the end, for no one who would buy such a book would sell it before his death.

No one, I suppose, would claim that Cameron was a major poet: apart from anything else, his oeuvre is far too slender. But Robert Graves said that many more of his lines stuck in the mind than those of more celebrated poets: and surely part of the purpose of poetry (this is me, not Robert Graves, speaking) is to furnish the mind with allusions.

His poetry is relatively straightforward but not therefore shallow. *The Thespians at Thermopylae*, for example, raises an important question about the nature of courage, and no doubt by implication of other virtues. At the battle of Thermopylae, the Spartans, led by King Leonidas, fought a desperate rearguard action against the huge invading Persian army of Xerxes and were annihilated. The Spartans were not alone, however: they were assisted by the Thespians, not actors but citizens of the city of Thespiae. The poem begins:

> The honours that the people give always
> Pass to those use-besotted gentlemen
> Whose numskull courage is a kind of fear,
> A fear of thought and of the oafish mothers…
> … in their rear.

In other words, their bravery, if it deserves the name, is unreflecting and customary; it is habit rather than choice. The Spartans are brave because they are afraid to be anything else; it is little else but a different kind of cowardice. Only what is freely chosen can be a moral quality. The poem ends (conflating the hoplites of Thespiae with the followers of Thespis, allegedly the first actor:

> But we, actors and critics of one play,
> Of sober-witted judgment, who could see
> So many roads, and chose the Spartan way,

What has the popular report to say
Of us, the Thespians at Thermopylae?

Posterity does not always award its medals according to merit.

Cameron took part in the war in the North Africa theatre and also
lived in Vienna during the first years after it, the Vienna of *The Third
Man*. Cameron had been an anti-Nazi from an early date, travelling in
Nazi Germany, an experience that persuaded him that the German pop-
ulace knew far more about the evils of Nazism than it claimed after the
war was over. But unlike many anti-Nazis, he was not tempted by com-
munism. He was suspicious of too-great attachment to abstract causes,
which he accounted 'hysterical,' that is to say forced and false.

One of his poems was inspired by post-war Vienna in winter, when
the city was still under four-power occupation, and is called *Liberation
in Vienna*. Its first line is memorable:

Totalitarian Winter, Occupying Power!

Winter is made to stand for totalitarianism. Its effect is everywhere and
inescapable, and the poem continues:

Like savage troops in grimy battledress
His piles of dirty snow sit there and glower,
Holding the streets in terror and duress.

But winter does not last forever, of course. Luckily the seasons change:

But now the glorious legions of the sun
Assault the roof-tops – their El Alamein!
The formed platoons of Winter break and run,
Their dingy corpses tumble down the drain.

But no victory of summer over winter is final, just as no political victory
is final, no triumph over totalitarianism or other type of political pathol-
ogy complete, no better political arrangement proof against degenera-
tion back into something horrible. Cameron warns us that, celebrate the
return of summer as we might, we cannot rest assured:

Heap grapes and roses high on Summer's altar:

Winter is gone, with all his dreadful crew.
Yet still they have the words to make us falter:
'Wait, citizens, till Winter comes anew.'

By all accounts Cameron was a modest man who did not obtrude himself upon the world by self-advertisement (Horlicks he advertised, but not himself). He did not inflate the size of his corpus in order to impress it with his industry or the fecundity of his mind. When asked whether he intended his poetry to be useful to himself or others, he replied, 'Neither: I write a poem because I think it wants to be written.' It was almost as if something that existed was speaking through his mouth rather than originated with him. At any rather, this was not a boastful way to describe either his method of composition or his purposes. In this he was the polar opposite of the woman, Laura Riding, whose disciple he had once been. She thought that poetry would one day usher in the new heaven, the new earth. It is curious how sensible men may sometimes attach themselves to crazed gurus, as if immodesty were a hook to catch the modest.

Cameron was also asked what he thought distinguished him as a poet from the ordinary man. To this he replied that it was a: 'Lack of interest in ordinary human, masculine activities, such as sport, learning and making a career.' But 'in so far as I am interested in these, the less I am a poet.' In fact, Cameron was not completely uninterested in these; he liked good clothes and was not indifferent to good food, the kind of things with which only a tolerably successful worldly career could provide him. Moreover, he said that compassion was a finer quality, and more important to him, than any literary quality. I suppose that literary achievement of the highest level usually demands a certain ruthlessness, a willingness to sacrifice everything else on the altar of literary art, though the contrary examples of Shakespeare and Chekhov come to mind. So cool a character as Cameron could not, therefore, have been a major poet.

But advertising? Surely nothing could be more antithetical to poesy, or indeed compassion, than that. Nothing could be less poetical than to sell a sweetened, fattening drink to the gullible (though did any of them truly believe in night *starvation*?), a sales pitch that involved more or less persuading them to go to bed on a full stomach.

Yet there are elective affinities, perhaps, between publicity and poetry. In the first place, the copy writer must be a master of concision. He must imply, connote, as much as possible in very few words. Perhaps there is no finer training in concision than copy-writing. Hegel, for example, would never have made it in the advertising world, and that is not necessarily a compliment to him.

Advertising slogans must be rhythmical as well as concise. And no copy writer can afford to ignore euphony, as so many prose writers can or at any rate do. I remember, for example, a slogan for an analgesic called Anadin: Nothing acts faster than Anadin. (The wits among us responded, 'Take nothing, then. It's cheaper.') Rhythm and euphony: perfection of its type.

If the poet wants to furnish us with allusions, so does the advertising man. He wants his slogan to explode in our minds and then remain there, like shrapnel. I remember—and have never forgotten—an advertisement for the beer called Guinness: 'I've never tried it because I don't like it.' It is a brilliant line, worthy of a great poet.

Adverts are such stuff as dreams are made on: Come to Marlboro country, We are the world. The poet-copy-writer must at least be *au fait* with the dreams of his fellows even if, in his poetry, he does not subscribe to them, indeed punctures them.

36
The Art of Automutilation

On my way to lunch in Paris the other day I passed the Sciences Po, that is to say the *Institut d'études politiques de Paris*, France's foremost academic institution of its kind. I noticed that all the cars parked in the vicinity had been posted with a sheet of white paper, clearly not the usual type of advertisement for night clubs or other resorts of entertainment. At the head of the sheet of paper, in very large print, were the words:

L'ART EST UN MENSONGE

Here was something intellectual, so I took the sheet and read it.

It was written by Andrés Mediavilla, of whom I have been able to discover nothing except that he is Spanish; that he has attended universities in both Spain and France but without graduating because he believes that the important things are to be discovered by people rather than taught them; that he was once fined 3000 francs for distributing a tract he had written (I think with the modest title *The Earth Cannot Be Saved Except by Justice*) without *Dépôt legal*, that is to say without first registering it at the National Library of France, though he says on the internet that when he tried to do so he was told that it was not the kind of publication that required or was qualified for such registration, so that in effect he was fined for not registering what was not capable of being registered, a Kafka-esque situation if ever there was one; and that for quite a number of years he has distributed his little tracts, gratis, in the environs of the Sciences Po. Of course, it may be that their recipients, who seem to have no choice in the matter, might not want them, but if that constitutes aggression it is so minor that it hardly counts. How otherwise he keeps himself, finds food and lodging, I do not know, except that his parents supported him during his abortive university studies; but having discovered all the above about him, I cannot but feel that a world without Andrés Mediavilla would be a slightly poorer one. He is a kind of street-Nietzsche, who writes things such as 'Life is beautiful but it is in a complete mess. In fact, life is horrible.'

Art does not exist: Mr Mediavilla's latest thesis is even more radical than that art is whatever can be passed off as art, or whatever those who claim to be qualified to distinguish art from anything and everything else say is art. Our author says instead that 'That the human being can "create" nothing. In order to make something, it is necessary that it should already exist as a possibility.' He goes on to say that 'to make something come of nothing—such is the prerogative of a god. In taking himself for a "creator" a human being mistakes himself and his nature.'

This seems to me merely a play on words. If to create means to bring something into being *ex nihilo*, then of course Man cannot be a creator (and philosophers might argue about whether a god, or God, could be one either). When someone says, perfectly legitimately, that Michelangelo created his *Pietà*, he does not mean that the sculptor made the marble, but that he fashioned the marble in a quite startling way that was unique to his imagination and capacity.

Our distributor of tracts continues, with neo-pagan certainty:

> It [to believe that a man can create something] falsifies his personality and all he does (his life, his society, his world). His 'divinity' prevents him from seeing himself—from knowing himself—as a simple instrument of the planet (and therefore of the universe of which he is ignorant of everything essential).

This is surely rather odd. Man cannot create, but a universe can have a purpose or purposes that make an instrument of Man. Beliefs in impersonal teleologies, religious and secular, have often led men into the most brutal and terrifying acts of fanaticism, mistaking their own purposes for those of something much beyond themselves. Indeed, they continue to do so, and will do so as long as Men claim the universe as alibi.

'To admire, even adore, "works of art" represents the height of error and the humiliation of Man himself:' so continues the tract. 'However, present day Man still has a need of the religion of Art to make up for his impoverished life. Thus, he does not hesitate to sacrifice himself—personal dissociation, disequilibrium, with the overemployment of one capacity at the expense of others, recourse to artificial stimulants, etc.—to "create" so that he becomes a "creator", a "genius." This is absolutely immoral and what is more, inhuman. To go into raptures over, to kneel spiritually before, the sounds, colours, lines, words, bodily movements, stories, stones, etc., whatever the intelligence or other qualities that went into them, is completely ridiculous (as is to queue to get into an exhibition of painting or a museum of other "fine arts", or into a concert, as is to read a novel, or see a film, or indulge in "artistic" tourism, etc.).'

The author ends his tirade, his diatribe, against art as follows:

> It is certain that there is not, cannot be, any Art in the world. We are not, we cannot be, 'creators.' We are not, and there cannot be artists. Art is a lie. To believe in it is to be mistaken. To need it is unworthy of a 'man.' It is the pleasure of gods (and of small minds). Art is incompatible with Man in his fullness (and the negation of truth and authenticity).

This irritation with art, or rather with those who claim that art is the whole focus or purpose of their lives when we know perfectly well that the slightest practical inconvenience prostrates them with rage and frustration, is something that I understand and in part share. Nevertheless, there is looseness of thought and insincerity of its own in this little tract.

The author is a man with whom nothing that exists finds much favour, to put it no higher (or lower). For example, in previous tracts he has said that the Science Po is for him more a factory of ignorance than knowledge; and people there are taught not so much political science as politicking. He says of the Science Po:

> Those in charge do not accept their ignorance because of their personal dishonesty.

> They hand out diplomas that certify the ignorance of those who receive them; to give positions to people on the basis of these diplomas is to decompose society. To do so 'maintains the people in the most degrading ignorance (and also impotence).'

Just because he doesn't think much of the teachers at the Science Po doesn't mean that he is happy in his own skin. He says that negativity is forced upon him:

> I am for. I am not against. These people force me to show myself against.

If it were not for 'these people,' then, he would be a kind of Dale Carnegie, Norman Vincent Peale or Napoleon Hill of philosophy.

His opinion of others, quite apart from the teachers at the Sciences Po, is not very high. Here are a few of his reflections on mankind:

> The problem is the minorities and the people. It is total. People do what they can while not doing what they could. The gap is the drama of humanity.

> A change of personality is the basis of everything. The only solution.

> My contemporaries all, all have a false personality.

One suspects that he might be a little lonely:

> Man is an individual He is not a couple, a group, a crowd, even if he can pass through these stages.

The question, though, is whether his loneliness is the result of his opinions, or his opinions the result of his loneliness?

From reflection on my own past, I know how easy it is to project one's personal dissatisfactions on to the universe (or some other vast entity) and then blame the universe (or that other vast entity) for them.

Although he seems to be an outsider, the author of these little tracts—which I much enjoyed reading, incidentally—captures quite a lot of the flavour of the times. His insistence that there is no such thing as art would be grateful to the ears of all kinds of relativists. If nothing is art, everything can partake of the kudos of art once only the connotation remains after the denotation has been removed. And if there is no art, there can—I think it follows—be no good and no bad art. Everything is the same, and we neither have to try very hard at anything nor make the painful discovery that we are not geniuses, that the achievements of, say, a Mozart or a Shakespeare are further removed from our own attempts than are our bank balances from those of Bill Gates.

Oddly enough, two days before my lunch near the Sciences Po I had visited the *Mondial du Tatuage*, a world convention of tattooists, held in the old Nineteenth Century abattoir of Paris, now an exhibition centre in the midst of a wasteland of French modern architecture (among the worst in the world, the architects ever in search of ways to out-Pyongyang Pyongyang). There were hundreds of tattooists exhibiting their work and thousands of visitors, who paid $40 each for admission. If the French economy had grown as fast in the last ten years as the number of professional tattooists working in the country, it would by now be by far the richest country in the world: the number having grown by 1000 per cent in that time.

The tattooists of France are apparently divided into two opposing camps, those who think that they should be considered artisans and those who think they should be considered artists. Those in the latter camp do not base their claim on the argument that art is what you think it is or persuade other people into accepting it as being; rather they think that they are in succession to real, indisputable artists such as Velasquez or Chardin. Only the material on which they work—human skin—happens to be different.

This camp mistakes skill for art. It is undoubtedly true that tattooists often show astounding skill in, for example, indelibly dyeing someone's back with a realistic portrait of a celebrity (Elvis Presley by far the most commonly). But skill is not art, at least not in the sense meant, and skill exercised in the production of something that ought not to have been produced at all makes it the worse, indeed much worse, rather than the better. A skilled man who produces a monstrosity is worse than an incompetent one who does the same.

The French used to be relatively resistant to the vile fashion for tattoos, but they are now following it like sheep for the shearing. At one time I was sufficiently Francophile to believe that France's people were too intelligent and cultivated to follow blindly the wild Anglo-Saxons *outre-Manche* (across the Channel). Alas, I was mistaken: the vicious bad taste of the English has spread among them like smallpox. The French are now only a few years behind the British in popular stupidity.

There seems to be a dialectic between Sr. Mediavilla's opinions of art on the one hand and the vogue for tattooing on the other. If nothing is art, then everything, including tattooing, is art. Therefore people can prove either their artistic ability or their sensibility by doing and having tattoos. (Or both, of course, for most tattooists are themselves heavily tattooed. *Le patron automutile ici.*) And of course, the more people who do it, the lower the opinion of humanity that seems justified.

It is just possible, I suppose, that Sr. Mediavilla himself is tattooed. I hope not, though. I was impressed by how much food for thought he gave me on the way to lunch, and I like to think of him as a *résistant* to one of the brutalising fashions of our time.

37

Ford and Against

Until quite recently I had never read John Ford's *'Tis Pity She's a Whore* though I had always meant to do so, partly (I suspect) on account of its title. But while it is Man that proposes, it is Time that disposes; and it is one of the glories, or at least the consolations, as well as the frustrations, of our human existence that we never have time enough to achieve all our projects and purposes. Imagine what life would be after such complete achievement, how time would stretch before us featureless as oblivion but with the torment of awareness and the awareness of awareness, without any subject except itself to be aware of! No wonder people without projects or purposes go off the rails! At least self-inflicted crises give the illusion of meaning.

Enough of philosophy, as characters say in Russian novels. I finally found time recently to read the play, which was published in 1633, only nine years before the Puritan closure of the theatres. A refrain ran through my mind as I read: 'This is not Shakespeare.' Of course, such a response is absurd on two counts: first Ford wrote the play twenty years after Shakespeare retired from the stage, seventeen years after his death, and no art can stand still; and second, only Shakespeare is Shakespeare. No art can consist only of its supreme achievement, but that does not mean that all else is without value.

Far fewer biographical details are known of Ford than of Shakespeare, for example even the date and manner of his death are matters of conjecture, but no one, as far as I know, has suggested that therefore his later plays must really have been written by George Villiers, Duke of

Buckingham. True, this theory might stumble on the fact that the Duke was assassinated in 1628, but publication of the later 'Ford' plays might have been held back to protect the Duke from the social ignominy of exposure for having written for the stage; and the fact that the second Duke, born in the year of his father's death, also wrote plays, by which time such writing had increased in social prestige by as much as it had declined in quality, and that literary ambition and talent are often inherited, lends support to our theory.

The work is always more important than the biography, however. The poetry of *'Tis Pity* never rises to Shakespeare's level (Ford's verse was strong and muscular, competent rather than inspired, unmemorable even by those with a good memory for poetry) and it seems to me that the characters are marionettes, always manipulated by the puppet-master rather that acting from inner compulsion, as it were. They are mere instances of some characteristic or other rather than self-actuated human characters; the plot, in which as high a proportion of characters end up slain as in Hamlet, is creakingly contrived. The comedy is lamentable, though not apparently as bad as in his other plays. Ford, then, does not command our willing suspension of disbelief as does Shakespeare.

Of all Ford's works it is only *'Tis Pity* that is ever regularly revived, and then not often: his other works are now but fodder for scholars of Jacobean and Caroline literature, a kind of PhD mine for those intent on an academic career. It is easy to see why *'Tis Pity* is revived, though, for its theme is incestuous love, a subject that is as perennially interesting as it is taboo (indeed, it is interesting because it is taboo). And some of the discussion of the morality of sex that it contains is astonishingly modern and apposite to our times—probably to all times. Vasques, the servant to Soranzo, one of the main characters, exclaims, 'O horrible! To what a height of liberty in damnation hath the devil turned our age!' Was there ever an age when this could not justly have been exclaimed? Man's conduct always disappoints men, and it always will.

Giovanni and Annabella love each other passionately, sexually, but unfortunately are brother and sister. They consummate their love and continue to do so even as Annabella consents to wed Soranzo in order to wean her from her illicit passion. Just before the wedding feast, Giovanni slays his sister from jealousy and outrage at her 'betrayal' of him. His attitude is that of many a modern jealous murderer who kills: 'If I can't have her, no one else will.'

The play begins *in medias res*. Giovanni is confessing, and trying to justify, his passion to the friar, Bonaventura. The friar has the opening lines:

> Dispute no more in this, for know, young man,
> These are no school-points; nice philosophy
> May tolerate unlikely arguments,
> But Heaven admits no jests...

Throughout the play, intermittently, the friar and Giovanni dispute the rightness or otherwise of incest. Giovanni's argument is that the incest taboo is merely customary, a prejudice that would prevent him or cut him off from loving her whom he loves. In the first scene he says:

> Shall a peevish sound,
> A customary form, from man to man,
> Of brother and of sister, be a bar
> 'Twixt my perpetual happiness and me?

Giovanni argues that, in fact, his love is superior to that of other types because, as brother and sister,

> Are we not therefore to each other bound
> So much the more by nature? by the links
> Of blood, of reason? Nay, if you will have't,
> Even of religion, to be ever one,
> One soul, one flesh, one love, one heart, on all?

This is Giovanni's intellectualisation of his frustration at society's prohibition of his love which he thinks denies him what we would now, no doubt, call his fundamental human right to love and be loved. 'Must I not do what all men else may, love?' he exclaims, in tones of the most genuine and most universal of all emotions, self-pity.

Giovanni is able to intellectualise his desire because he is a student at Bologna University, and a brilliant one at that (the friar has been his tutor there). The friar says, with all the pain of the teacher disappointed in his prize pupil:

> O, Giovanni, hast thou left the schools
> Of knowledge to converse with lust and death?

Another of Giovanni's arguments, enunciated later in the play, is the neo-Platonist one, a version of which Keats later summarised and that (taken more seriously or literally than Keats can really have intended) is deeply evil:

> "Beauty is truth, truth beauty," – that is all
> Ye know on earth, and all ye need to know.

Giovanni turns Bonaventura's teaching back on himself, for he later says to him:

> What I have done I'll prove both fit and good.
> It is a principle (which you have taught
> When I was yet your scholar), that the frame
> And composition of the mind doth follow
> The frame and composition of the body:
> So where the body's furniture is beauty,
> The mind's must needs be virtue; which allowed,
> Virtue itself is reason but refined,
> And love the quintessence of that.

To this Bonaventura can only reply:

> O ignorance in knowledge.

In other words, Giovanni's ratiocinations are an instance, a confirmation, of F. H. Bradley's famous (and brilliant) dictum three and a half centuries later, that 'Metaphysics is the finding of bad reasons for what we believe upon instinct;' though he added 'but to find these reasons is no less an instinct.' In this case, however, it is not so much what Giovanni wants to believe on instinct, but what he wants to do on instinct: and I doubt that any of us has never used an abstract argument in this dishonest way.

What does Bonaventura reply to Giovanni, other than expressions of grief? His arguments would cut little ice today, being all from authority: and authority (except our own) is precisely what we are disinclined to obey. In his very first speech, Bonaventura says:

> ... wits that presumed
> On wit too much, by striving how to prove
> There was no God, with foolish grounds of art,

Discovered the nearest way to hell...

Better, then, just to accept things as they are:

> Such questions, youth, are fond; for better 'tis
> To bless the sun than reason why it shines...

As to incest, it is forbidden because it is forbidden by God:

> Indeed, if we were sure there is no deity,
> Nor Heaven nor hell, then to be led alone
> By nature's light (as were philosophers
> Of elder times), might instance some defence.
> But 'tis not so; then, madman, thou wilt find
> That nature is in Heaven's positions blind.

Here is an early exposition of Dostoevsky's view that if God does not exist, everything, including incest, is permitted.

That incest is against God's law is the only argument that Bonaventura offers; he does not venture, as he could not possibly have done at the time, into genetics, arguing that the offspring of consanguineous unions (and Annabella in the play does become pregnant by her brother) are much more likely than others to have birth defects—to which argument, in any case, a modern Giovanni might return that the risk is much reduced with modern methods of contraception and ante-natal diagnosis, so that if there is any sin in incest it is that of neglecting precautions either before or after conception.

In his essay about Ford published in 1932, T. S. Eliot asks whether, in his use of brother-sister incest as a theme, Ford was able 'to give universal significance to a perversion of nature which, unlike some other aberrations, is defended by no one.' And he adds that 'The fact that it is defended by no one might, indeed, lend some colour of inoffensiveness to its dramatic use.' Here, it seems to me, Eliot shows his limitations as a social commentator (limitations we all have) for, like J. S. Mill in his *Essay on Liberty*, he shows himself incapable of envisaging a moral sensibility very different from the one regnant at the time of writing. Mill couldn't imagine a sensibility very different from his of a respectable Victorian bourgeois, and Eliot did not foresee the changes that were soon to come. The introduction to my edition of *'Tis Pity*—a cheap one, obviously for the use of university students of English literature, written in 1968 by the Professor of English Literature at the University of Sheffield, ends with these words: 'it [the play] raises poignant social questions for our age, and it may help us to exorcize them with truth.' In other words, in a space of 36 years only, the permissibility of what was 'a perversion of nature… defended by no one' had become a real question. And the most obvious explanation of why this should have been so is the vast increase in tertiary education that had happened in the intervening period, and a corresponding increase in the means of disseminating a questioning attitude to everything.

It is no coincidence that Giovanni should have been a student at Bologna University—one of the most celebrated of the time—and that there he should have learned the kind of sophistry that turns a man into his own moral authority, who accepts nothing that he cannot prove to and then finds that there is nothing that he cannot prove, so that desire becomes truth.

In the play Annabella has a 'tut'ress' who plays more or less the part of the Nurse in *Romeo and Juliet*, whose name (Ford sometimes lacked subtlety) is Putana. When Annabella, who loves or lusts after her brother in a fully reciprocal fashion, dithers about whether it was morally permissible to have consummated her love, Putana, earthy and without intellectualisation, says that desire is its own justification:

> Your brother's a man, I hope, and I say still, if a young wench
> feel the fit upon her, let her take anybody, father or brother,
> all is one.

It takes education, however, to turn this attitude into a matter of doctrine, and to believe that every principle that one has inherited and not derived from one's own supposedly unaided thinking is but 'a peevish sound, a customary form.'

38
Fifty Shades of Gray

Few are the people who love dogs and cats equally, and there are those who love neither. I am a doggish person and I frequently stop in the street to admire, and often to speak to, dogs (they always reply, I find, with the greatest good sense). The strange thing is that their owners who have them on leads are always pleased and proud that their dogs should be so addressed by a complete stranger, though they would shrink away from such a stranger, as from a dangerous lunatic, if he addressed them, the owners, directly. Dogs are the greatest diplomats, or at least aids to diplomacy.

To cats I am indifferent. I don't object to them, except when they have a screeching fight below my bedroom window, and I recognise their elegance, but I find their aloofness faintly disturbing, unalloyed as it is to the kind of intelligence that dogs display. Cats incarnate the sin of pride. But I would rather have a cat in the house than no animal at all.

Recently I stayed with friends in Dublin who had a cat called Selim. Selim is completely black and has green eyes; he is very old and spends most of the day sleeping on the window sill. For some reason he has incurred the deep enmity of the neighbouring cat, a large tabby, who is much younger and more vigorous than Selim, and who at night comes to the window, scratching it with his claws, and making threatening noises that frighten Selim who would be in no condition to defend himself if his enemy were to effect entrance. I suppose it is all about territorial dominance or some such triviality; but we humans are not in a position to look down on feline territorial disputes as absurd or trivial. What else is human history, stripped to its essentials, than this, up to and including the current spat over the Ukraine and the Crimea? Indeed, the struggle between Selim and the tabby (whose name I do not know) is quite a good metaphor for recent events.

Now I happened one day to walk into a Dublin bookshop where I found a rather splendid edition of six of Thomas Gray's poems (not that he wrote very many more). Published in 1753, while Gray was still alive, it was the kind of luxurious though slender volume that people with more money than needs must once have bought to tickle their jaded desires. It was provided with grand, not to say grandiloquent, engraved illustrations by Richard Bentley. Apparently it was no sooner published than it sold out.

One of the poems in the volume is *Ode on the Death of a Favourite Cat Drowned in a Tub of Gold Fishes*: Horace Walpole's cat, to be exact, whose name was Selima (I had read the poem several times before, but had quite forgotten the cat's name). This coincidence, surely, was a signal from the gods that I should buy the book, and so I did.

Doctor Johnson, in his *Life of Gray*, has some rather severe things to say about the Ode. Selima (who was a tabby rather than black, though she had Selim's 'emerald eyes') climbed on to the edge of a bowl with goldfish in it and fell into the water in trying to grab the fish, and drowned after eight attempts to climb out:

> The hapless Nymph with wonder saw:
> A whisker first and then a claw,
>   With many an ardent wish,
> She stretch'd in vain to reach the prize.
> What female heart can gold despise?
>   What Cat's averse to fish?

Dr Johnson says of the Ode that 'The poem on the Cat was doubt-less by its author considered as a trifle, but it is not a happy trifle... Selima, the Cat, is called a nymph, with some violence both to language and sense...' This, surely, is to aim a howitzer at a sandcastle; it is like complaining that there is no excitement in a railway timetable. Railway timetables are not for excitement and humorous poetic trifles not for 'correct' mythological metaphors. Indeed, correctness would be an er-ror.

But one is never more than a few lines in Doctor Johnson from good sense, for his writing abounds, as he says that Gray's *Elegy* abounds, 'with images which find a mirrour in every mind, and with sentiments to which every bosom returns an echo… I have never seen the notions in any other place; yet he that reads them here, persuades himself that he has always felt them.' This is the effect also of so many of Johnson's own reflections, which are simultaneously obvious and revelatory. Referring to Gray's various travels, both in Britain and in Europe, Dr Johnson says that 'it is by studying at home that we must obtain the ability of travelling with intelligence and improvement.' This is precisely so: travel should be a philosophical activity and not merely a manifestation of restlessness or boredom, though it may be those things as well. 'Chance favours only the mind prepared,' said Pasteur of scientific experiment; he might have said the same of travel.

The curious thing about Gray is that he wrote one immortal poem, and one only. Two other lines are also immortal, if immortality consists of coining a phrase that becomes a cliché wherever English is spoken (but it was not a cliché when he coined it, so it reflects no ill on him). In his *Ode on a Distant Prospect of Eton College* Gray sees children playing happily and is filled with melancholy:

> Alas, regardless of their doom.
> The little victims play!
> No sense they have of ills to come,
> No care beyond to-day;
> Yet see how all round 'em wait
> The Ministers of human fate,
> And black misfortune's baleful train!

The last stanza reads:

> To each his suff'rings: all are men,
> Condemn'd alike to groan,
> The tender for another's pain;
> Th'unfeeling for his own.
> Yet ah! why should they know their fate?
> Since sorrow never comes too late,
> And happiness too swiftly flies.
> Thought would destroy their paradise.
> No more; where ignorance is bliss,
> 'Tis folly to be wise.

Needless to say, the last lines would not meet with the approval of contemporary medical ethicists, those latterday Savonarolas of personal autonomy; but I doubt there is anyone living who has never found occasion to quote Gray's words as an excuse for his own lack of frankness.

Few are the people also who would deny that Gray's *Elegy In a Country Churchyard* is one of the great poems in English: it has that quality which marks out masterpieces from other works, namely that its impact never lessens however many times it is read. General Wolfe was reputed to have said, the night before the successful British assault on Quebec, when he read the *Elegy*, that he would rather have written these lines than take the city the following day: a remark, if he really did make it, that does him credit, at least in my opinion, for it implies that he valued literature above the profession of arms. I was about to say a correct valuation, but perhaps I should merely say one that coincides with my own. And Doctor Johnson relaxed his strictures on Gray's poetry by concluding his *Life*:

> In the character of his *Elegy* I rejoice to concur with the common reader; for by the common sense of readers uncorrupted with literary prejudices, after all the refinements of subtilty and the dogmatism of learning, must be finally decided all claim to poetical honours... Had Gray written often thus it had been vain to blame, and useless to praise him.

The theme of the *Elegy* is the vanity of human pride, whether it be in temporal power, or learning, or riches, or accomplishment, or in anything else; The *Elegy* suggests an equality far beyond the political variety, namely an existential kind, for:

> The boast of heraldry, the pomp of power,
> And all that beauty, all that wealth e'er gave,
> Awaits alike the inevitable hour.
> The paths of glory lead but to the grave.

This is not an original thought, of course, but that is no real criticism as Pope knew, for:

> True Wit is Nature to Advantage drest,
> What oft was Thought, but ne'er so well Exprest,
> Something, whose Truth convinc'd at Sight we find,

That gives us back the Image of our Mind…

That Johnson was sympathetic to the Elegy is not surprising, for his own greatest poem was *The Vanity of Human Wishes*, which expressed thought not dissimilar:

Yet hope not Life from Grief or Danger free,
Nor think the Doom of Man revers'd for thee:
Deign on the passing World to turn thine Eyes,
And pause awhile from Learning to be wise…

(I once read, I forget now where, a very severe Johnsonian-style attack on the first lines of this poem, *Let Observation, with extensive View/ Survey Mankind, from China to Peru*: for, said the critic, 'with extensive view' added nothing to 'observation' and was so much mere pompous afflatus. But then Johnson might himself reply with Pope:

A perfect Judge will read each Work of Wit
With the same Spirit that its Author writ,
Survey the Whole, nor seek slight Faults to find,
Where Nature moves, and Rapture warms the Mind…

and this is so because

Whoever thinks a faultless Piece to see,
Thinks what ne'er was, nor is, nor e'er shall be.)

Thoughts about vanity were long on Gray's mind, for in his earliest published poem, *Ode on the Spring*, he says:

Where'er the oak's thick branches stretch
    A broader, browner shade;
Where'er the rude and moss-grown beech
    O'er-canopies the glade,
Beside some water's rushy brink
With me the Muse shall sit, and think
    (At ease reclin'd in rustic state)
How vain the ardour of the Crowd,
How low, how little are the Proud,
    How indigent the Great!

Given the transience of human life, and that the paths of glory lead but to the grave, it is not surprising that Gray warns us that we should, in looking at the graves who left no great name behind them:

> Let not ambition mock their useful toil,
> Their homely joys, and destiny obscure;
> Nor Grandeur hear with a disdainful smile,
> The short and simple annals of the poor.

Again, this was a sentiment in favour of humility with which Doctor Johnson would have sympathised. In my favourite poem of Johnson's, he movingly extols the humble labours of a poor and obscure surgeon, Robert Levet, to whom he had long given shelter:

> CONDEMN'D to Hope's delusive mine,
> As on we toil from day to day,
> By sudden blasts or slow decline
> Our social comforts drop away.
>
> Well tried through many a varying year,
> See LEVET to the grave descend;
> Officious, innocent, sincere,
> Of ev'ry friendless name the friend.
>
> Yet still he fills affection's eye,
> Obscurely wise, and coarsely kind;
> Nor, letter'd arrogance, deny
> Thy praise to merit unrefin'd...
>
> His virtues walk'd their narrow round,
> Nor made a pause, nor left a void;
> And sure th' Eternal Master found
> The single talent well employ'd.

This, I think, is deeply felt, as are Gray's sentiments, though critics often level the accusation at eighteenth century poetry that its forms are better suited to the expression of witticisms than to that of deep feeling, thus necessitating and indeed provoking a Romantic revolution. For all that, however, Gray's lines never cease to move (me, at least); and when I move among a human crowd which seems to me unattractive I try always to remember the generous lines:

> But knowledge to their eyes her ample page
> Rich with the spoils of time did ne'er unroll;
> Chill Penury repress'd their noble rage,
> And froze the genial current of the soul.
>
> Full many a gem of purest ray serene,
> The dark unfathom'd caves of ocean bear:
> Full many a flower is born to blush unseen,
> And waste its sweetness on the desert air.

I am moved; but then unbidden into my mind come the lines:

> I wish I loved the Human Race;
> I wish I loved its silly face;
> I wish I liked the way it walks;
> I wish I liked the way it talks;
> And when I'm introduced to one,
> I wish I thought "What Jolly Fun!"

And I console myself with the thought that Gray and Johnson did not always heed themselves their warning against the blandishments of the senior partner of the seven deadly sins, Pride, and I likewise recall La Rochefoucauld's wise remark, that it is easier to give good advice than to take it. This is why we return to the *Elegy* over and over, for its lesson is never learned.

Lightning Source UK Ltd.
Milton Keynes UK
UKOW03f0248041014

239560UK00002B/62/P